Spirits of Place

Edited by John Reppion

Daily Grail Publishing

CONTENTS

INTRODUCTION

John Reppion

When I was a child I had a vision of fourth dimensional time; of paths trod by my own ghosts, past and future. My parents and my grandparents lived six houses apart on the same suburban South Liverpool street. In front of my parents' house (where they still reside) is a square of turf for kids to play on which we call "the grass patch". A journey from one house to the other could be made one of three ways: diagonally across the grass patch; via the strip of pavement which runs round its front closest to the road; or on the pavement round its back, past the front fences of numbers 50, 48, 46, and 44, and then at a right-angle up the far side, past the garage at number 42. I was on my way home from Gran's at the age of perhaps seven or eight when I was suddenly struck by the thought that I must already have made the journey a hundred times, and that I would make it thousands more. I crossed over on to the opposite side of the road so I could get a better look at that strip of land where, I realised with a weird dizzy feeling, I had already spent a good chunk of my young life. I saw – imagined, I suppose, but with absolute clarity – at first just a handful, but gradually a crowd. The diagonal route across the grass was the most heavily populated, in spite of all those warnings about muddy shoes. There I was at the age of three, four, five, and as I stared longer, there I was at ten, at seventeen, at twenty, at thirty; infant, child, adolescent, and adult overlaid in a blur of bodies, limbs and faces. An entire lifetime of journeys between those two fixed points in a single image – an image I can still recall perfectly to this day. My younger selves dominate the picture, not because of nostalgia, but because I would walk the walk five or six or more times a day when I was a child, the frequency growing less and less beyond the age of ten. Gran died in 2010, Grandad followed her the next year, and their house – the house my mum was born in – was sold soon after. I couldn't have known that then, yet still there were (and are) very few, if any, versions of myself in that strange multi-exposure vision much past the age of thirty. For a long, long time after that mid-80s day, every time I made the journey I *knew* I was walking among, and with, and through all those other versions of myself. Versions which remain frozen there to this day – not just in my head, but in some very real sense. I've never discussed any of this with anyone – never even thought about it in any terms other than those which my younger self *knew* to be true – and in fact, I had all but forgotten about it up until just a few days ago.

How can I best define the concept of "Spirits of Place"? It sounds good, but what do I even mean by the phrase? These are some of the questions I was asking myself last week. You might well think I should already have answered them quite a while ago; before commissioning the twelve pieces for this book, or indeed organising the conference/ritual mash-up thing which led to its creation. But no. At least, not exactly. It's easy enough to give people a rough idea of what you mean about something, especially if you're trying to give them just enough to spin their own ideas out of it. So, let's backtrack a little here. Not as far back as the 1980s, but to the first quarter of this year.

Spirits of Place was the name I chose for a one day event I organised and put on here in Liverpool in April, 2016. The idea came about when I saw that there was a conference space available for hire in the former Manor House in Calderstones Park; a park which I've been visiting on a regular basis for most of my life. There you'll find a playground, the duck and goose crowded mini-lake, a café, an ice-cream parlour, ornamental gardens, a miniature railway, and the remains of a Neolithic chambered tomb.

The tomb stood just outside the boundaries of the park between 3000 BCE (give or take a few centuries) and 1804 CE, when it was pulled apart to make way for a house being built. All that survived of the tomb were six stones, each covered with curious spirals, circles, and other ancient engravings. These Calderstones – the origin of the name long lost now – were re-arranged into a rough stone circle under orders of lead shot manufacturer Joseph Need Walker in 1845. Standing at the South East entrance to Walker's estate – mere metres from the tomb's original position – the stones soon drew the interest of several 19th century antiquarians believing it to be their original "Druidic" location and configuration. There they remained until 1954 when they were removed under orders of Liverpool Corporation. Covered with more than a century's worth of moss and soot, the stones were cleaned and latex impressions taken, revealing details of carving which had previously been all but invisible to the naked eye. The first thorough survey of the stones was made based on these (now lost) moulds by J. L. Forde-Johnson and the results were published in his 1957 paper "Megalithic Art in the North West of Britain, The Calderstones, Liverpool". In 1964 the stones were relocated inside the park which by now bore their name. There in a hexagonal glass house (known as "the vestibule") which served as an entranceway to the Greenhill Greenhouses where a huge botanical collection was kept, the ancient, fragile Calderstones were set into grey slabs of quick drying concrete. The Greenhill Greenhouses were bulldozed in the 1980s following a strike by Liverpool council parks and gardens workers. The vestibule survived, standing alone; the Calderstones visible only to those who knew where to look, peering through the ivy and graffiti covered glass to see the sextet of standing stones holding their silent communion.

The first time I ever got to see the Calderstones up close was in 2007 on a Halloween tour of the park. The vestibule was warm and damp – electric heaters working against the foggy October air in an effort to shield the megaliths from winter's chill. Fine spider's webs, spun across the pitted surfaces of the menhirs, were frosted with moisture, glistening in the glow of the heater elements. The engravings shimmered fierily as if each stone had a core of liquid magma beneath its brittle sandy surface. Our guide hurried through a truncated history of the stones and, for a precious few moments, the assembled crowd stared at them in absolute wonder. But, all too soon, the spell was broken. The park ranger had no eerie tale directly connected to the stones to tell. By the time we left the vestibule, his latest off the peg ghost story had all but erased the circle of crumbling stones' brief, vague history from most people's minds. With each step away from the dilapidated greenhouse, the illusionary fire within the ancient sigils seemed to dim. My own interest did not, however.

I became more fascinated than ever with the Calderstones and their history. How these man-made objects had been a permanent feature of the local landscape since mammoths walked the earth. Key elements of a tomb built before the Egyptian pyramids, marked with symbols which pre-date written language in this part of the world; their original meanings and purpose lost in the mists of time. In December 2014 I had one of these magical marks – a thumbprint-like spiral pattern from the Calderstone that Forde-Johnson designated as Stone E – tattooed in black ink on my right forearm. Although I have no way of knowing what it meant when it was carved, I know what it represents now. It is a connection between myself and the landscape; between the people who lived and died and left the mark here five millennia ago, and the life myself and my family live here now. A five-thousand year 4D snapshot of that crucial not-quite-a-mile of South Liverpool parkland would show the Calderstones as the only constant feature – the spiral patterns graven upon their surfaces an almost perfect map of their glacial, stop-motion meanderings around its narrow environs. The Calderstones physically anchor Calderstones Park to England's ancient past. They are the proverbial heavy ball-bearing on the rubber-sheet of Time; creating a pocket of deep history into which stories, and spirits, are drawn in ever-decreasing orbits. And that is why I decided that putting on an event in the park would be a good idea. An attempt at harnessing that energy, and raising those spirits; the Spirits of Place.

The core concept of the symposium became that of this book: stories are embedded in the world around us – in metal, in brick, in concrete, and in wood. In the very earth beneath our feet. Our history surrounds us and the tales we tell, true or otherwise, are always rooted in what has gone before. The event was structured like a spiral: the Calderstones as its centre, with nine incredible speakers spinning their talks out of that single point in ever broadening arcs. I wanted to make it almost like a kind of happening, or a ritual, crossed with a regular conference; a magical experience in a very real sense. And, it worked. Perhaps too well.

My own opening talk that day was entitled "Invoking the Spirits of Place" and served not just as a preamble, but as an explicit calling. My closing paragraph read as follows:

Today we call upon the spirits of this place; the spirits of those pre-English ancestors who moved and marked stones and mounded earth with their bare hands, not just to honour their dead, but so that we might know something of what they believed and knew. Upon the hidden race of fairies and elves which they they later became in popular folklore and imagination. Vertumnos – god of growth and fruit and seasons, Ceres – goddess of agriculture, grain, fertility and motherhood, Hercules – strong and powerful man-god protector of this parkland's gateway. The kodarna, the canoti, the wood sprites, boggarts, goblins, and pooka. We call upon the Lady of the Forest, upon the spirit of the ancient Allerton Oak. All of these spirits we invoke, and we ask them to show us, to teach us. To share with us their knowledge of this place – this small suburban green-space which is all green-space, which is everything. A slice of the natural world which we kid ourselves we have altered and mastered and tamed but which, in reality, is merely a fraction, a sliver of the true order of things. A tiny piece of the ancient green-land which waits impatiently for the moment when it might reclaim what is rightfully its. All across South Liverpool centuries-old roots ripple through tarmac, absorb railings and bow walls. Stop-motion brambles wind cunningly around fallen sandstone slabs, spider-walk through skull-socket knotholes, cascade over weather-worn fence-panel and post in a prickled, black-fruit foamed spray. The thin veneer of civilisation can be seen, almost heard, crumbling one driveway-fracturing dandelion at a time. This place does not belong to us alone, here our ancestors, our history, our folklore are all alive and waiting to be rediscovered. To reclaim and re-enchant this earthly realm.

So, I bid you welcome. Welcome to South Liverpool, to Calderstones Park, and to Spirits of Place.

On that day, standing there in Joseph Need Walker's Manor House in the heart of the park, speaking those words felt truly powerful, truly magical. A spell was cast, and though I had intended as much, I hadn't anticipated it to work in such a literal sense. If I had expected it, I would surely have thought to lay the ghosts – to release the spirits – at the end of the day. But I didn't. There was no dismissal, no formal farewell to the host of ancestors, thought-forms, and deities myself, guests, and attendees had spent six or so hours talking and thinking, remembering and imagining into life.

I'd made an attempt at recording the day's talks and that evening managed a very quick listen through to check the quality. It wasn't great, which I had pretty much expected. I only had two mics set up and most people were moving around a lot giving their talks. It was no big thing; it would have been nice if it worked out but didn't really matter that it hadn't. The only part that sounded okay was the last talk of the day which had been a sit down interview with Ramsey Campbell about his use of Merseyside, Liverpool, and even Calderstones Park itself in his fiction. I cringed, as many people do, at the sound of my own voice asking the questions, but otherwise it was fine. Exhausted then, I passed up the kind offer of speakers Cat Vincent, David Southwell, and Gary Budden to join them for a pint or three, and instead opted for a rare early night.

In my dream that night I was wearing my headphones, listening to my own voice on the recorder. It wasn't the interview with Ramsey this time though, it was my own opening invocation. The quality was better than I'd thought. Only, now I didn't recognise the words. I couldn't remember saying any of this. And then, as one does in dreams, I knew that it wasn't me I could hear; it was something else using my recorded voice to speak. I asked out loud who it was, and my voice answered with an electric hiss "the spirits in the wires". It was the kind of nightmare that doesn't really make sense if you try to explain it, but those whispered words had me wide awake, heart pounding, drenched in sweat that night.

Night terrors notwithstanding, Spirits of Place was a success. Out of that success came the entirely unexpected offer from Daily Grail Publishing to put together a book based on the same idea. Almost immediately though, I realised a book would need to be handled very differently. The event was about being in that specific physical place on that specific day – about shared experience rooted, one way or another, in that landscape. The book needed to tap into more universal themes and ideas about the relationships between landscape, history, story, art, magic, and humanity. Once I realised this, I knew I had to look further afield than the U.K., and beyond those who might be thought of as "the usual suspects" when it came to this kind of writing. Well okay, maybe *some* of those usual suspects are here, but you may note that London and Northampton are barely mentioned, let alone visited, within these pages.

While its geographic spectrum may be broader than other books dealing with the topic of place, there is a huge amount of commonality between the essays within Spirits of Place. The way our identities and beliefs are embedded in our surroundings; the places we grow up, or live, or come from. Equally, how we interpret and re-interpret ourselves in certain places. How language can sometimes fail us when we try to express the dichotomy of personal experience and shared reality; of things we *know* to be true and things which we can prove, or explain to others. Things embedded in our culture, often at a hyperlocal level. This island, this town, this village, this dirt track, this house, this room; every one has its spirits. A blur of people, of experiences, of lives lived, dreams dreamed, of gods birthed, of loves lost, of deaths died, of journeys across the grass patch.

Stick the push-pins in the map, connect the dots with winding twine like every good movie detective knows you should. A pattern emerges. It is not a pentagram, not a star-sign or constellation, not an arrow or X marking the spot. It is a spiral.

I HAVE TROD SUCH HAUNTED LAND

Gazelle Amber Valentine

I *have trod such haunted land.* Small mountains of my childhood, wrested from Cherokee generations for white settlers' greed. Gritty soil of Florida: shaded by tropical glories of flora, soaked with invisible blood of Seminole and stolen African. Appalachian hillsides with lapsed or hidden mines, where men and women and children have been lost. Grounds of closed factories from Pennsylvania to Michigan; abandoned Soviet Olympic training center in Poland; ancient tomb sites from American Georgia's Etowah Mounds to Russia's Mamayev Kurgan. Cemeteries large and small, prairies and steppes and range-crests unmarked but still laden with past.

Albanian dirt tracks built for Roman chariots, a hole in New York City where World Trade Centers once stood.

When visiting places of known great turmoil, I receive that turmoil emotionally to an extent that is sometimes not possible to contain. For this reason I try to avoid crowded 'touristy' locales of horror. It is one thing to become hysterical in the whispering grasses of Little Bighorn Battlefield National Monument (site of 'Battle of the Greasy Grass' also known as 'Custer's Last Stand') because I feel, hear, see and smell the terrible transition from peaceful encampment with family to brutal massacre. There, I can commune with the spirits in a way that feels respectful and private.

But in populous situations, such as the Vietnam Memorial in Washington, D.C., I find myself inhibited from proper inter-action with the history, and indeed infuriated when visitors nearby are clearly unaffected. For those who don't feel deeply about what has happened in a place or what it marks, battlefields, graveyards and memorials are only brochures to tick off your travel list or backgrounds for a selfie. Perhaps it's the power of such people which creates things like war, slavery and genocide in the first place?

The greatest benefit of nomadic life is an elevated viewpoint. Nature, society, history, politics – all recede as if placed at the wrong end of binoculars, and in so doing reveal their true patterns. By connecting to nowhere you must in turn connect to everywhere, in the course of which becoming wise. Nothing is permanent, but anything is possible. Everything dies, yet beauty and joy endure. We are incredibly powerful and infinitely weak. Again and again these paradoxes repeat, like colors of yarn in an elaborate woven rug. There is a point of sensory overload at which one reels from such a cycle of love and anguish. Buddha was right: to be alive is to suffer. But never mind that suffering stems from desire – the important truth is that so does everything else we know. If our problems originate in desire, our solutions do as well. By discoursing with our weighted past, with our elemental baseness, we find the thread that may unite and sustain us.

I submit that a perfect state such as Buddha described, clean of desire and attachment, is death at its most austere. While I slip easily into this vision as a comfortable way to cease, I can't reconcile it with anything I feel about life. Life is desire, desire is life. And in the end perhaps this grasps the point of the Four Noble Truths satisfactorily. When one is ready to cease, to end the karmic cycle, then it is time to relinquish desire. Until then, for me, it must be relished like a feast.

One of the great literal feasts of my life took place in Warsaw nearly a decade ago. We were playing a show in a drab Soviet-built section of the city, where such not-so-distant past lays a film over everything, seeming even to dim the green of close-cropped grass. Where to follow partly-crumbled sidewalks through small parks flanked by utilitarian buildings feels like transiting the border between two concurrently occurring dimensions: it is easy to believe that one has crossed over into a world where communism never fell – or more chillingly, where fascism actually won. We walked in the dusk with hushed voices.

In the venue we were treated to an entire buffet table filled with distinctly Polish vegan delights. Pierogi and a dozen or more other magical combinations of vegetables and potatoes and bread, with accompanying sauces and sweets that we never competently identified by name but gratefully devoured. The feast was so divine that of fourteen hungry omnivorous travelers (three bands besides ours) only one complained about the lack of meat – and he was quickly chastised by the rest of the group.

To eat in Eastern Europe is to trace its history, written like Braille for the tongue. Poverty food passed down through occupation by Imperial Russia, by Austro-Hungarian Empire, then by Nazi Germany and Soviet Union. The most basic root vegetables, able to be coaxed even from cruelest earth; simple bread; these things creatively combined and recombined a hundred ways with sugar, meat, fruit or salt, then augmented with such post-*glasnost* delicacies as ketchup. Beer and vodka derived also from the earth, and crafted for every purpose from settling babies' stomachs to shuttering miserable adults' minds.

On our first tour in Eastern Germany we played at a squat on the former grounds of the Topf and Sons incinerator furnace company. If that sounds like an alarming business model in context of 20th century horrors, indeed it is: Topf designed and built 66 coal-fired furnaces used at Nazi extermination camps.

We had never played in this venue before, so upon arrival had no idea about its past. Any kind of discomfort or unease I felt, I attributed to the always-unbalancing effect of being stared at and discussed by strangers. We loaded in our equipment, did a soundcheck, and then were guided to the green room. Here was a lovely repast (Germany's Eastern cities have a high concentration of young vegans and hence vegan food is common and varied) complete with wine and beer. We snacked and poured beverages. Our host then revealed the historical nature of this building complex, and pointed out the row of framed photographs on a long wall across from the table. Information contemporaneous to the images accompanied them, describing Topf's patriotic contributions to the war effort and the city's pride in the company's achievements. The sum of this decor was to imprint our psyches with a devastating, stomach-tightening awe which I still can feel.

To create a space that is emphatically "anti-racist, anti-fascist, anti-sexist" on the grounds of so malevolent an enterprise and to fill it with events for young people does seem redemptive. Yet to perform in such a space can never be lighthearted. Silently, numerous times during our set, I dedicated my energy on the stage to the victims of unspeakable atrocity whose end reduction into dust was wrought by devices created here.

Some years passed and we composed an album for which our theme was authoritarianism and (as usual for us) human evil. I wrote about events from around the world which had impressed me with heights of hypocrisy: one of the songs was *Work Will Make Us Free*. This phrase, inscribed around Nazi camps where victims were sent to be mercilessly used until murdered, had to me always appeared especially horrific in its manipulative lie. Work there, of course, would earn not freedom but torture and death. The song became part of our set and eventually, we played it on European tours and in Germany.

On a stage in Berlin, before a packed and darkened house, we built from a slow instrumental intro into the full momentum of our show. As we shifted from the preceding song into the opening chords of *Work Will Make Us Free*, a voice came loudly into my mind accompanied by a word printed against my closed eyelids: *Juden*. In that moment I was overwhelmed with emotion. It was difficult to emerge from this feeling for the remainder of the night. Even as I met fans and casually conversed following the performance, I felt the persecution and sorrow of a people vibrating in my surroundings as if in my very blood. There was no doubt for me that my empathy and attention to their deaths was felt and returned to me with that word, which I had never used or particularly noticed but understood immediately when spoken and written so clearly inside my brain that night. Other times afterward, I again felt them with me through the unbidden appearance of this word.

In 2009 the squat at Topf factory was evicted and the buildings demolished, along with a museum created by the collective which ran the squat. Now, only the vigilance of a small group of people with knowledge of this enterprise and its dark part in history may prevent its role from being totally erased.

Ignorance as historian. This topic is on my mind as I consider the fate of history in the mass-collective hands of Internet; a place whose spirits imbue every story with their own image. Narrow beams of subjective light illuminating only a small corner of a colossal truth which, from this biased perspective, appears as a whole. A sliver of truth doomed to become a falsehood. In my mind history appears a vast expanse of steel turning slowly through space, one thin line exposed brightly, placing into invisibility the darkened 98% of whole. Brutal illustration of futility, that knowledge can be so easily transmuted.

My personal knowledge and my personal history begins with Florida. There I was born, there I crawled my first crawls in warm sand. A suitable cradle like an external womb; warm, humid, lush. There is a sense of peace I feel there, and any time when I am somewhere my bones belong, where I have grown or my ancestors before me. Much of my discovery of that ancestry has been accidental, through my mother and one of my grandmothers, whose interest led them to its study. And always, their new discoveries linked predictably to my feelings of home in certain locations.

Some places draw me without such proof. Yet what I've learned of family history and its dovetails with my instincts implies that

here, too, is likely a place of personal past. Or can it be only empathy?
I hesitate to add to the ignorant cacophony, faux history. Perhaps,
though, history is inextricably twined with fallibility?

From my earliest writing, followed by songwriting, I expelled
dark subjects and couched them in visceral words. The tastes,
smells, textures, noises of life seemed to tell its story better than
any point A to B to C narrative. As I discovered classic Southern authors – especially William Faulkner, Zora Neale Hurston,
Alice Walker – I observed a kindredness in this particular attention to the senses, and in the oppressive quality I felt in my
writing and theirs. Certain suffering and wisdom seems specific
to places. The South casts its own like a net around artists living
there, more especially around artists raised there from birth. It is
a place of distinct flavor, bitter and sweet. For the unorthodox
mind it can be a place to endure and to escape, but which never
leaves our blood.

Travel was also in my blood. I can guarantee both with facts
from my family tree and with every fiber of my being that part of
my ancestry belongs with nomadic peoples. To me it is natural
that my home is a shifting place, like Florida sand, like the wind
in the trees. Like sand and wind it never changes its essential self
(home) but like sand and wind, a primary characteristic of that
self is motion. Such a home requires either complete detachment
from environments, or a commitment to allow them into your
soul, changing you as you move. For me it's the latter.

Existing almost in opposition to this experience of submer-
sion in spirits of place, via transporting oneself to them, is the
other experience I have had throughout my creative life: intuiting the essence of places I haven't yet been. Added to this,
often simultaneously present, is the experience of 'channeling'
the emotions of people I don't know; some completely ficti-

tious, others historical figures. In trying to explain this I have described it as something like, but not quite, automatic writing. I am conscious of what comes forth, and able to edit it. But what comes forth feels dramatically different depending where and who I am channeling.

In my art – creative writing, painting, drawing, and music writing – I have always been led to dark themes, whether intensely disturbing or more gently tinged with malaise or nihilism. When writing fiction (as with short stories, poetry, and three of our early concept albums) I feel utilized by nebulous outer forces of character and place in the exact manner that I feel when writing with reference to history. The facts readily available about events in history create a guiding framework which in fiction must of course be built from scratch. But the process of intuiting feelings and *je ne sais quoi* feels identical. I notice my self recede, as I am inhabited by the character speaking and encounter palpably the sense memory of their environment, *even when I have never been to that environment.*

One example is a song from our album *If Thine Enemy Hunger* called 'Antietam'. The song is based on historical accounts of women and girls during the American Civil War, whose houses were besieged by battles surrounding them, and who through necessity became untrained nurses. One account referenced a large Antebellum home so inundated with wounded that when soldiers died, they had to be piled in the side yard because no one could take time to bury them. The pile of corpses was described as reaching the second story of the house.

When writing and recording vocals for this piece, I felt myself in the place of a teenage girl amateur-nursing there, enduring a level of work and gore and death that is literally unbearable, yet must be borne. During the recording, tears streamed down my face and I shook. This is how powerfully I intuit and empathize, and probably a primary reason I am compelled to make art. I feel both a duty to share such stories, and an empathy that extends to physical reactions.

Throughout my art and music such intuitive understanding either sublimates or bolsters understanding gleaned from actual visits to actual places. For example, on the same album with 'Antietam' are songs relating to the experience of early American period coal and silver miners. The touchstone for writing about this history was a visit to the site of the Ludlow Massacre, which was very moving for both of us (my music writing partner is my husband Edgar) but the songs I wrote did not feature individuals from that event. Instead, I allowed fictional characters to lead my thoughts, while immersing my mind in the history.

The shape of Texas. This was a phrase which came insistently to mind after countless interactions with its subject. Texas was one of the states conquered by our earliest forays away from Georgia, where my husband and I met as bandmates and began our life together. Texas seduced me improbably, as a land reputed for its backward social mores and practical emptiness, but possessed of a stunning visual beauty I could not expect. Imposing flatness such as I'd never seen before then – not a desert or beach but endless silvery land – suggesting infinite grass but rife with secret sandspurs and caches of blue gilia or cardinal flower, yellow mesquite, flapjack prickly pear. I will never forget my first view of real distance in Texas, away from the eastern border mountain ranges, somewhere beyond the edges of urban central interstate pipeline, on a two-lane road cutting through ranchland. No trees, nothing but horizon. And every state highway sign, every rest area, as well as most of the sparsely scattered houses featured some two or three dimensional replica of that shape.

The shape of Texas is something like a stovepipe hat on the top, and something like the underside of a bull on the bottom. Its western border juts aggressively. Its eastern side implies a casual meander. Everything about that shape seems to me symbolic of its place in U.S. history.

During our band's earliest touring days, we roved only a few states to the north, south, east and west. With the reputation of Austin, Texas as an important underground music town came regular routing there via the various booking agents determining our fate. By the early 00s we had seen as much of it as anyone typically reaches by highway, and some parts further off the track. I felt in Texas a deep conflict between beauty and severity of land; between people representing many cultures yet never predictably aligning their political views with cultural origins or racial, ethnic and social groups; between near-frantic ideologies of patriotism juxtaposed with secession advocacy; insistence that uteri be government regulated but guns and industry not; and overweening religious fervor seemingly inextricable from maverick secular *laissez-faire*.

Texas in 2003 was for the American psyche a seat of power. Then-president George W. Bush and his former-president father and his then-governor brother – who, depending what one believes, may have fixed the 2000 election – were Texans. Hardly anyone more accurately embodies with persona the stereotype of a wealthy, bullheaded Texan than does 'W', his presidency carefully accessorized from boots and bluejeans and pickup trucks to his unapologetic attitude when challenged on wrong decisions. For our album *War Bird* I wanted to write about this president both as a human politician and as the absolute archetype of evil, Texas-style. Driving along I-10 I found in myself both the lyrics and song title:

The Shape of Texas

Lungs filled and satisfied
Me and all my beautiful friends
Yeah, we are prime
Bloodshed and alibis
Me and all my means to an end
Yeah, we are oil fed and wings wide
Me and all my
Beautiful friends
Yeah, we are prime

Like many lyrics, these few words can easily be read and even sung without attention to (or understanding of) their meaning. Yet, they are the culmination of many years' exposure to this piece of land, its stark contrasts of nature and its stark way of emblemizing both oligarchy and victims thereof.

Hermit crab teleportation learning? Perhaps another aspect of my creative life that has been impacted by places and the spirits therein is that of adaptation. Like a hermit crab moves through containers, my mind moves through discovered spaces and grows within them to a new shape and size. Even before traveling, I had the ability to transport myself mentally to somewhere imagined or remembered. But certainly, logging hundreds of thousands of miles through the physical world has only enhanced its scale.

For our album *L'Autrichienne,* an expansive double record view of the French Revolution, this mind-only travel was a huge asset. Having studied the Revolutionary period throughout my life, I possessed a good bit of intellectual understanding for its main characters and backgrounds. However, something else was in play during writing of certain songs, that felt more like possession itself.

I am neither an occultist nor a resolute skeptic when it comes to supernatural matters. As with most topics, my innate traits of optimistic gullibility and analytical paranoia create what I find to be a marvelously balanced attitude. I am loath to state that things are entirely one way or the opposite. Usually, they are as complex as my own attitude and more.

When writing, and especially singing, songs from *L'Autri-chienne,* I felt at times entirely suspended inside them. Like a remembered dream, I knew my environs; the scuffle and noise and smells of a rioting mob I was part of; the shadowed stone of Marie Antoinette's prison cell as I see from her eyes; sounds of the jeering crowd and calmness of total despair as Antoinette-me is driven by cart to the guillotine. With queer depth I felt from Louis XVI a guilt so massive it metastasized into numb surrender, and a grief which hinted at gratitude for impending execution.

Though the songs were written over a substantial number of years, the recording session for *L'Autrichienne* was completed over a terribly intense three weeks. In the process I 'lived and breathed' the historical subject matter in a near-literal way. Yet at the point of making this album, I had never been in France. Can we infer that spirits of place, augmented by powerful emotions of events centered there, are so strong as to be capable of transcending physical space for a willing and empathetic receiver? Is this, akin to psychic phenomena, what artists have for centuries understood as the muse?

If I were to surmise cosmic alignments and conjoined paths of fate, I could easily conclude that making this album in the grip of such energies summoned motion in the third dimension: immediately after its release, we were finally able to tour in France for the first time. Since then, we have returned almost annually. Over years the immersive recording experience has faded to memory; yet at times, on certain ground, I feel again a pronounced empathy marked either with comfort or foreboding.

Time seems stronger in the redwood forest. During my first visit there I developed a hypothesis: since redwoods are so enormous, they produce unusually high concentrations of oxygen in the air near them, and this is why when amongst them one feels high. I have done exactly zero research to prove or disprove this hypothesis, but it really *seems* logical to the point of being pedestrian.

Along redwood-bedecked Avenue of the Giants in northern California is a roadside gift shop with adjoining campground. Here we have stopped on every drive through, whether briefly to walk our dogs within the dim charged air – our steps all muffled by needled mulch, our moods all awed by powerful smells of sap and ferns – or to stay a night in the forest's wild humming silence. At the front of the gift shop rests a short segment of hollowed-out redwood log, ideal for climbing inside and documenting human inconsequentiality with a photo revealing our scrawny-by-comparison scale. A bit farther to the edge of the parking area stands the 'Immortal Tree' described by an affixed plaque as approximately 950 years old and having survived, thus far, "fires, floods, and logger's axe".

Imagine! Life, a living creature, which has been steadfast in this forest so long. Ever so slowly growing, counting the cycle of light and dark like blinks of its amorphous eye. An eye perhaps more feel than sight, but nevertheless sensing existence in some way we can never comprehend. Alone, surrounded by family. Created, then creating as seedlings drop. Centuries marking development as decades mark ours.

Among redwoods I feel my place in time's continuum shrinking to insignificance. I stand beside crevices in bark which are larger than my body, between fallen trunks whose diameter is three times my length. I consider how many rings must count a thousand years. *A thousand years.* The concept eludes our brains, except as something abstract, a colored edge of thought. Our bodies can be expected to survive for fifty, perhaps one hundred years. One hundred years to be worn like an anchor, heavy iron mooring us safely to a single century, the century appearing as ultimate limit of time because this is our longest lifespan. Until: redwoods.

I have written nothing directly based on the redwood forest, but am indelibly scored by its distortion of time. Different from the time-sense imparted by ancient buildings or ruins, the redwood speaks language we cannot and need not know. It grows to grandiosity with no concept of grandiosity. Fruitfully, quietly, lengthily. It is as alien as a comet without seeming as ruthless in its detachment from our concerns. It is everything one could hope to become: so powerfully hoary where experience has long worn, so tender with promise in the places it is new. And several are *two thousand* years old.

Like a redwood, some portion of Russia's poetic power rests in sheer size and another in endurance. In my lifetime the Cold War ended and the Soviet Union fell. Twenty-five years have since passed. Yet today on any U.S. news media format we are told the same story as ever: evil dictator, dangerous people, spies, human trafficking, women available to wed if one can afford them (absent any sense of hypocrisy regarding the two latter) and a vastness best left unintelligibly wild. For Americans, Russia's psychological thrust was and is that of forbidden curiosity; as if to look too closely would commit one to some treacherous path. A basilisk!

I shall not address here any actuality of current political situations in Russia. I mention our countries' uneasy relationship only to frame my lifelong affinity for Russia's spirit. As a daughter of artists, I could not fail to be struck by childhood glimpses of her whether landscape or propagandist art. As an aesthete and nature lover I could not fail to respond to her exceedingly effective and imposing vistas and outdoor monuments, whether birch forests, chiseled Soviet heroes or the domes of Orthodox churches surging into the sky. As a feminist from early age – because what is more logical for a person than to know her own humanity? – I could not fail to be interested by the achievements and enduring influence of Catherine the Great.

Beyond this, I was immediately intrigued by a place so large with so long a history (redwood-like) which I was told I must not notice. Irresistible enticement! And so it is that I've been a Russian history hobbyist for the better part of forty years.

My encounters with Russia were entirely cerebral until 2011. In that year, we traveled there for the first time. But prior to the tour, we had already begun making what would become another double album, this time focused on Russia. Since my husband has also spent his life enamored of Russian history, it was inevitable that we'd make an album about this shared interest.

In order to address such a physically and intellectually colossal topic, we knew that we needed to narrow our scope to some

exemplary moment and place within history. Quickly, we agreed
that an important actor in our narrative must be the land itself.
Harsh and unyielding, Russia's terrain has always demanded an
especial toughness which is part of its people's lingering affect.
Also, we wanted to choose a moment which could reveal this
outwardly stern people as human. And we wanted a moment
which would have universal recognition, so that a listener would
immediately feel connection to the subject and be more open to
the story. For these reasons the location of Volgograd, former
Stalingrad, became our crucible.

Indeed, this piece of ground was a crucible not only for our
album but for Russia itself and all Europe. Events there throughout human habitation provide a perfectly distilled view of Russian
history as a whole. In addition, they include an interaction with
other world powers in which Russia defies her typecasting and, at
great cost and sacrifice, stands heroically against fascism. We're
talking about World War II, of course, and how Russia held her
borders against the Nazis during a months-long carnage in which
Russian men, women, and children fought and died as volunteers
alongside enlisted soldiers, to the tune of over a million Soviet
dead. Victory was not won so much as clawed out with a dying
hand – yet victory it was. Arguably the stalwart defense of Stalingrad was a main reason, if not *the* reason, for Hitler's defeat.

As with our French Revolution themed record *L'Autrichienne*, work on the 'Russian album' (titled, with apologies to
Latin alphabet typesetters, за волгой для нас земли нет) was
incredibly emotional. Over the course of the record, I sing as the
land warning of coming attack. I sing from the mind of soldiers
riding high in the bloodthirsty arrogance of war, then confused
and helpless surrounded by chaos and death. I sing as the land
reassuring female anti-aircraft gunners that their deaths made a

difference. I sing as an émigré who reputedly walked from New York to California and eventually, via the Yukon, returned to her beloved Siberia. I sing as the grieving mother of a killed boy. As a tribe of Tatars protecting their shifting territory. As a hectoring member of the 'barrier troops' whose job was to kill any comrades who retreated or fought poorly. As a brother burying his sister. As a female partisan trying to destroy as many invading troops as she can before being captured and hanged. And as a resident of the modern city, heeding the Motherland's call in view of the famous victory statue which crowns Mamayev Kurgan – ancient Tatar burial site, and grave of uncounted Stalingrad dead whose names are not yet known.

Again I am left to wonder how much fate drives the direction of art, or rewards dogged interest with abstract reciprocation. Before we finished recording за волгой для нас земли нет we found ourselves offered for the first time a tour in Russia. The next year, we were able to return for a more extensive tour. Our album still awaited completion, but tour opportunities took precedence and we pushed back recording. On this second Russian tour we were booked in Volgograd.

After more than forty hours sweating on trains, we arrived already exhausted but told our hosts how necessary it was for us to visit the memorial grounds for the Stalingrad battle before reporting to our soundcheck. With these newly-made friends whose lives had been spent in Volgograd, we climbed from the dusty street up and up, a summer sun beating our shoulders, air wavy with 41°C heat, and their two small children frisking beside us. Aloud, they translated inscriptions on the walls which frame the impressively wide and long grand stair; then, markers along a path which leads ever upward to the monument's summit. There are so very many steps to be taken, a test of endurance –

especially in summer – that is fitting to contextualize the long and arduous battle.

Communing with the land and history of Mamayev Kurgan, climbing to the height of the hill, standing at the base of the *Soviet Motherland Calls* statue which towers so impossibly that one's eyes cannot contain it from that proximity – something inside of me tore. But in the tearing I felt a bond made, a pact through pain with this site and its spirits or however you may wish to call that energy which hangs in such places. Silently I promised to carry through our album with utmost empathy and honor. Silently as possible I wept behind sunglasses when passing through the Hall of Glory, beside the silent honor guards, beside the silent flicker of eternal flame, beside what felt like endless rows of names (but which in fact represents less than 1/10th of Russia's Stalingrad dead), a silently screaming gauntlet visitors there must run. Silently and inexorably Edgar and I wept together as we crossed stepping stones through a peaceful pond to lay flowers at the *Grieving Mother* statue's feet.

Graves above ground. Always present here, whether in the foreground or periphery of thought. The cemeteries of New Orleans are a tourist attraction because seeing the fullness of burial is not common in our country, and because of the loving adornment which must necessarily soften such grim and macabre storage of remains. In this city prevails a forthrightness about death, a familiarity which puts you and it shoulder to shoulder at bars or brothels, concert halls or curio shops. Wherever we are, we're gonna party, because we know death, and knowing death requires us to party. Death is at the party, death compels the party, and somewhere down the line, death ends everyone's party. In fact here one sometimes feels that death *is* the party: from voodoo to vampires, in New Orleans death is your tour guide and reliable entertainer. Yet the death toll from Katrina was so unwarranted and of such unimaginable scale that her pall will never completely be lifted from this city or this nation.

Katrina. How is it that a cheerful, youthful-sounding woman's name can evoke such grief, terror and remorse? As summer 2016 draws near its close and I hear once again of floods in Louisiana and hurricanes menacing the Gulf, I am transported as if yesterday to images of New Orleans beneath the devastation of Katrina. Brown water, brown water, brown water covers everything except the sins which caused the poorest and most vulnerable citizens of a beloved tourist city to be destroyed, if not to point of death then as near as may be, whilst those with advantage enough to escape did so, later returning – well past the time of crews fishing bodies under hot and unforgiving sun, well past the time of cameras molesting the sorrowful as they begin to see the depth of their loss – to reap the reward of others' pain; a gentrifying gentry whose love for the unique patois of the Big Easy somehow never extends to the human beings whose culture suffused it with their spirit.

In one intervening decade, 'Katrina' has become shorthand for the loss of entire families' possessions and lives, for the failings of corrupt government, for the suffering able to be wrought by inept infrastructure, and for a structural racism and classism that hums beneath awareness for too many but for those it affects, is harshly inescapable. Because to survive Katrina with lives and possessions intact was a privilege for a privileged class. Those spared by the storm tended to live in a privileged neighborhood, or at the very least enjoy the privilege of adequate money and transportation to leave. Without such an edge, one simply waited for the worst. And assuredly, it came.

In tandem with closeness to mortality, New Orleans holds a bit of contempt for the hurricane. Storm is gonna come, so what. We batten down and turn the music up. In the same way, people who lack finances to change their situation do their best to enjoy the moment with what they've got. So as Katrina bore down on the city, its poor were understandably resigned to letting *les bon temps rouler.* What else can you do, when you can't do anything else? And besides, they'd seen storms before.

To remain after Katrina and to rebuild, or to return after having fled inland, was also a matter of financial privilege. For too many, the temporary shelter of a FEMA trailer became permanent. For too many, there would never be enough money to return home. For too many, home became a car parked surreptitiously under shade while its resident slept and worked a minimum wage job in a new town full of strangers.

My mother always had a certain enchantment with New Orleans. From her I learned a romantic image, owed perhaps in part to literature, and in part to vicinity: as a southerner, I was certainly aware from an early age that here was a *wunnaful* city, a place of wrought iron and jaunty paint, voodoo and masquerades; of fresh seafood, strong spices, wild drinking and wilder jazz; of sturdy religiosity dressed in pagan feathers; of sex in a kind of terrarium which made it respectable to look and even participate... yes, just a *wunnaful* place. The exoticized vision which pervaded my child-hood understanding of New Orleans was magnetic. So when my parents decided to take a holiday there and brought me along (I suspect out of necessity, as by then I was a stereotypically grumpy teen) I was excited to go.

Memories have faded to a few strong impressions: dirty Bourbon Street at night, surrounded by people, music too loud, the stench of puke and alcohol mingling with many strangers' sweat and perfumes; the interior of a restaurant fancier than any I'd yet seen, a menu of dishes I dared not risk (oysters? pate?); crowded souvenir shops flanked by saxophone buskers; old homes, balconies, gardens, colonial stateliness I had not yet learned to recognize as emblematic of slave trade and blood quantum; the fragrant allure of beignets from blocks away as we stumbled toward them heavy with morning; my first taste of coffee with chicory. Surrounded by unfamiliar accents (plushy English embellished generously with fragments of French) I felt I had indeed stepped into some wonderful foreign place. *Wunnaful.*

Not so many years later but aeons away in life's context, I met my husband while playing music, we formed our band, and New Orleans became a regular stop on our ever-expanding tour circuit. It remained as beautiful, contradictory, and intriguing as I'd initially found it. But through the lens of adulthood, I saw an essence there which made me indifferent to shiny baubles and ritual tourist foods. What I saw was survival.

Survival protrudes from New Orleans' veneer like a snapped bone. Dance as you may to current pop hits, ensconced in beads or feathers: this place is survival fought and fighting. Neither the fun here, nor the antiquity visitors come to admire, exists without the marrow of making do at great cost.

Graves above ground.

Traditions were hidden or deformed to survive assimilation into colonists' European cultures, histories coded. Eventual community and family bonds, uneasy yet practical, formed between settler and displaced, enslaver and enslaved – over time, forming the ethnic group Creole. Sex work, entrenched as necessity for a port town, was bedecked with hints of French and Caribbean flair, and alongside it countless other tricky treats were devised and sold to ensure survival of those citizens who stayed and ran the place while others passed through it on their various business.

Graves above ground. In the streets and the eyes and the windows and doors, in the hulking Superdome curved across a sky wobbling with heat, in air so humid that to breathe is a step toward drowning, survival is not the least but the most we can do. And if you dip down from the bridged highways that skim this city with quaint mid-century futurism, if you step off the prescribed tourist grid into the neighborhoods where folks live, where there are no hotels and no chain coffee shops and maybe also no grocery stores and too many liquor stores, you will see that it can be painful beyond belief, but we are here, surviving, and being in this thing together is everything.

In New Orleans as everywhere I am only a passerby, doing my various business. But as someone who lives without security, whose home is able to be hurled by strong wind or derailed by slicked asphalt, whose career is intrinsically uncertain and holds no IRA and no pension, I know about survival and making do. I know the difference between a voyeur and a native. I know the difference between a spectator and one who labors to facilitate the spectacle.

In a stalled moment of met eyes I have shared recognition, many times, of this hard truth no safety life. For the most part we on this edge are kind to one another. It is heartening.

When describing our homeless life, I have grown accustomed to using the metaphor of nests built on woefully dangerous foundations. Perhaps the bald consciousness of subsisting with no promise of permanence leads me to perceive the most ephemeral qualities in every space, to be more of a pessimist and to overlook what is sturdy and welcoming in the world. Yet it is also true that wherever there is wild, I am home. *Wherever there is wild I am home.*

Despite energy from dormant sorrows and torment I feel as I move – whether like seaweed gently brushing legs in a shallow tide, or like unseen glass shards slicing unexpectedly deep – I can find in every place a reason to believe.

When the sky extends beyond possibility of sight, or when tree-clad rock crags convene to confine me, I am free. Lands of this planet we ride always fill me with reverence and the feeling that where there is life, there is hope. People may create oppression and despair, as they are wont to do: yet when I see a small house and yard dotted with chickens or goats, whether Bulgaria or Kansas, Kamloops or Budapest, misanthropy fades. In every span which holds human life there is propensity for darkness and light. Though my artistic vision instinctively delves into darkness, my soul trills ultimately towards light.

And with this dual filter I live, for the most part, perched happily beside the abyss.

Gazelle Amber Valentine was raised in rural Florida and Georgia. From her mother she inherited an early, unrelenting, insatiable appetite for history and for the written word; from her father, innate ability to draw and to play musical instruments by ear, along with a dogged tenacity for problem solving.

After flirting with careers in writing, house painting, eques-trian sport, theater, oil painting, auto mechanics, photography, and agriculture, Gazelle settled on becoming a professional musician as the best way to address her varied interests and skill set. Apprentice-ship entailed fourteen years' waitress service. But since 2000, she and husband/bandmate/conjoined spirit Edgar have earned their meager living solely through music.

As half of **Jucifer**, Gazelle has furthered talents for heavy lifting (the band's infamous 'White Wall' of speakers requires each of the happily-DIY couple to heft 4,000 pounds of equipment per show), structural engineering, comprehending and properly matching impedance, tour booking and management, graphic design, audio production mastering, trailer roof repair, tetris, engine diagnos-tics, video editing, chihuahua herding, record label management at Nomadic Fortress, and truck driving: as the band's main driver, Gazelle captains their 50 foot home/tour vehicle thousands of miles across North America each year as well as shepherding rental vans in other parts of the world.

When not terrifying audiences, being creative, or multitask-ing to defy laws of physics and time, Gazelle can often be found buried under dogs – one hand on a book or Twitter feed, the other on her ever-present, never-ideal-temperature cup of black Cafe Bustelo. Together she and Edgar enjoy playing golf, tennis, basket-ball, riding BMX, junk hunting, and watching trash TV. Last but not least, Gazelle loves dog walks and day naps.

Jucifer can be found online at jucifer.net and on Twitter at @_JUCIFER_.

THE PALACE BUILT OVER A HELLMOUTH

Maria J. Pérez Cuervo

O nly a king or a queen has the power to move the capital of their kingdom to their preferred location. For King Philip II of Spain (1527-1598), this place was at the very centre of the Iberian Peninsula, not far from the city of Madrid, in an area called El Escorial on the southern slopes of Mount Abantos. Here he vowed to build his life's plan: a royal residence that would also be a pantheon, a monastery, a library, a museum and a centre of studies. To bring it to life, he hired a group of architects, experienced masons and theologists, who evaluated the terrain positively but, given the monarch's interest in esotericism and alchemy, probably warned him of an ancient legend: that the Devil himself had lived in a cave at the foot of the mountain, after he was expelled from Heaven and before he opened up seven doors to enter his new abode in the Underworld. The location of one of these doors was El Escorial.

The locals whispered stories of monsters, visions and curses, of frequent electrical storms with lightning constantly hitting the area. Nevertheless, on the 30th of November 1561, the king's experts travelled to El Escorial to make a final decision. Their official chronicler, Father Sigüenza, describes how the group was stricken by a gale that "didn't allow them to reach their destination", which the friar interpreted as the Devil trying to dissuade them from erecting a religious complex over what was rumoured to be a Hellmouth. But the king dismissed the ominous signs in a letter to his men, noting that there had also been a tempest in Madrid. And so the works started a year later, after the court was moved to Madrid, and lasted for over two decades. The complex remains the best-known symbol of Spanish royalty, with its rows of kings and queens resting in the Pantheon. But, in spite of Philip II's Catholic fervour, it seems as though the chthonic currents managed to seep through the soil and leak into the rich marble and gold, into the silver crosses, statues of saints and reliquaries, playing with the senses of the palace's inhabitants, driving them to madness and perdition.

To me, the centre of the Peninsula has always felt suffocating. I grew up on the south coast, in a luminous, heavily-built Mediterranean city where my dad was also born. My mum came from a small village in the north, all high mountains, coalmines and fog. They met in Madrid, almost exactly halfway, when Franco was still alive, and moved to the south after they got married. In the summers, my dad would drive us to the north in his rumbling Renault 14. It was a long journey, and it helped to think of it in two halves: before and after Madrid. In those days there was no seat belt to be worn, so I wriggled in the back seat, kneeling and twisting to catch the best sights on the way. One of the most intriguing was an enormous cross on the horizon, silhouetted and looming over its surroundings: the so-called "Valley of the Fallen". Once I said I'd like to see it up close, and my dad frowned: "That's where Franco and his pals are buried. We're not going there." I didn't know much about the Civil War then, but I knew enough to find the sight disturbing, like a monstrous shadow of the past creeping over us, triumphant. Perhaps on the same trip, or on a different one, I was also told about the most powerful king Spain ever had, who built a huge palace-monastery, not far from that cross, many centuries before the bones of the Fallen had been buried in that soil.

I never liked that central part of the journey – the flat, monotonous roads, the merciless heat, the strange absence of the sea on the horizon, still too far from the fresh green meadows of my mum's homeland. Travelling to the centre of the Peninsula in the summer was like slowly descending into a pit of burning coal, a journey to the centre of the Earth, from which one could only exit either side.

For many centuries, the Spanish court was itinerant and the capital city changed depending on where the monarch was established. Before Philip II's decision, the honour fell on Toledo, a centre of tolerance and cooperation between Christians, Jews and Muslims until the establishment of the Inquisition brought turmoil. By the 16th century, the city was the focus of civil revolts against Philip's father, King Charles I, but it also had one of the most important archdioceses in the Catholic world, second only to Rome. In contrast, Madrid was only a relatively important city, with no ports nearby and no navigable rivers. There was nothing there that could overshadow the king: barely any local aristocrats; no significant religious power. Perhaps he saw this relative isolation as an advantage, as a clean start in the exact centre of the Peninsula, an area with good terrain and benevolent climate.

Philip lived in the shadow of his father, Charles I, powerful warlord, cosmopolitan adventurer, silver-tongued speaker. It must have been a heavy burden to bear, especially because their talents were so different. Philip, the sole male heir, wanted to build a suitable place to bury his father, so there was definitely a component of filial duty in the original idea. But when we look back in history we are often tempted to speculate, so I imagine Philip – the shy, meticulous, taciturn king often dressed in black – consumed by an idea: that the holy palace-monastery he had envisioned and carefully planned must be built over a land that the Devil had claimed as his own for centuries. Once erected, El Escorial would become a symbol, a feat, and, in turn, he would be remembered as the devout, all-powerful monarch who sealed a Hellmouth with a sacred building, making his dynasty and his empire rise over all evil.

The architect he chose to be in charge was Juan Bautista de Toledo, Michaelangelo's right-hand man in the construction of Saint Peter's Basilica. He was to be assisted by Juan de Herrera, who would complete it after Toledo's death. Herrera modified the original designs and was ultimately responsible for the final appearance of the complex, characterised by austerity and geometric rigour, so different to the then *en vogue* Plateresque that it became a style of its own – Herrerian, named after its creator.

In the upper portion of the main façade of the Basilica, the statues of Solomon and David stare at each other, sceptres in hand, flanked by other kings of Judah. The wise king of the Bible was a constant in Philip II's life. When he married Mary I of England, Cardinal Pole gave a speech where he compared Philip to his father Charles I:

> I can well compare him to David, who though he were a man elect of God, yet, for that he was contaminate with blood and war, he could not build the Temple of Jerusa-

lem, but left the finishing thereof to Solomon, which was
Rex Pacificus. So may it be thought that the appeasing of
controversies of religion in Christianity is not appointed to
this Emperor, but rather to his son, who shall perform the
building that his father had begun.

Philip, more introverted and spiritual than his father and less
inclined to a life of action, surely welcomed this parallelism.
Through Solomon he found his own identity as a king. The
comparison was repeated many times throughout his life, and
reinforced in several paintings.[1] It doesn't come as a surprise
that, centuries before Freemasonry's fixation with the esoteric
qualities of the Temple, the Catholic king sought to reproduce
its perfect structure – according to the Bible it was designed by
God – in his *magnum opus*.

As well as its architecture, there are many other Solomonic
details in El Escorial: the central fresco in the library depicts the
Biblical king next to the Queen of Sheba, and both the prior's cell
in the monastery and the entrance to the monarch's bedchambers
display a representation of the episode of the baby, a symbol of the
legendary character's abilities to discern between good and evil.[2]

The complex also served to commemorate the 1557 Battle of
San Quentin, where the king's troops, allied with England after
his marriage to Mary I, defeated the French. It took place on the
10th of August, the feast of Saint Lawrence, a Roman deacon who
was roasted alive for his Christian beliefs, hence Philip's decision
to consecrate his new building to him. Some have said it is
shaped like a gridiron, a tribute to Saint Lawrence's grisly death.
Whether this is true or not, the patron's statue in the west façade
is rumoured to keep another secret: he might be looking to the
burial place of a treasure that has never been found.

The monastery, an essential component of the original plan, was entrusted to the relatively new Order of Saint Jerome, also known as the Hieronymites, reputed for their austerity. It was another proof of the monarch's commitment to Catholicism: not only did he become a patron of the order, he also focused on eradicating Protestantism and strengthened the Holy Inquisition that his ancestors had established in the 15th century. With these credentials it might seem paradoxical that he was quietly fascinated by the other side – the underworld, the occult. These obsessions were consistent throughout his life, and intensified around the time of his death.

THE LEGEND OF THE HELLMOUTH

For all its royal grandeur, there's a peculiar association to the name "El Escorial": it sounds suspiciously similar to *"escoria"*, Spanish for "scum". Perhaps aiming to scrub off its supposedly lowly origins, more modern theories suggest the name might derive from the Latin *aesculus*, the genus that comprises oaks, which grow abundantly in the area. Father Sigüenza, however, believed its etymology was linked to the mining industry and the resultant débris, since the area had been rich in mines of silver and gold.

Oral tradition connects the existence of the mines with the legend of the Hellmouth. Similar ideas appear in different cultures: Hell is underground, and descending into the mine, closer to the centre of the Earth and its core of molten lava, means approaching Satan's dwellings. Whatever lives underground is thought of as evil. Whatever crawls, close to the chthonic forces that come from Hell, is also thought of as evil – hence the association between the Devil and the Ancient Serpent of the Old

Testament. Perhaps a flat journey, from the coast to a central land, conveys the same feeling, as if one were replicating the descent into the abyss.

Not far from El Escorial, in the Guadarrama Mountains, there is an unusual construction known as The Seat of Philip II, a set of platforms and seats carved in granite. Oral tradition tells that the king used it as an observatory to comfortably supervise the works, but its origins are not known. A recent theory suggests it was a pagan altar where human sacrifices were offered to Mars, the god of war. Less than a mile away, another toponym asserts the Devil's claim over the land: La Pisada del Diablo, "The Devil's Footprint", is what looks like a single impression of a cloven hoof on a rock. According to the legend, Satan, dressed as a pilgrim or a peasant, tried to lure a pious young girl to his side, but she didn't give in. In his frenzied anger, the Devil jumped onto the rock – and the hoof-like mark he left can still be seen today.

All these ancient legends about the malevolence of the place became enriched and embellished while El Escorial was built. Father Sigüenza describes how, in 1577, the builders reported having seen "a big black dog dragging chains and occasionally howling frightfully" among the works of the monastery after dark, jumping "as if it had wings". It was said that the dog was Cerberus, the monstrous guardian of the Greek Underworld, who had escaped Hell using the portal the king had attempted to cover. Superstitious fear spread among the locals, and the atmosphere of horror penetrated the walls of the sacred compound.

Sigüenza writes that a black dog sneaked into the monastery – a real dog that supposedly belonged to the Marquis of Las Navas, who must have lived nearby. His howls interrupted the early morning prayers and spooked the monks. Two of them were brave enough to venture out and found it, a flesh and bone animal, not a ghostly one. They hanged it from the cloister, where it remained for days for everyone to see: the beast taken by the monks, the demon defeated by the holy men. But, according to the legend, the Black Dog of El Escorial, like its counterpart the Black Shuck, was a portent of doom – and it would be seen again by none other than the king.

THE PALACE OF THE DEAD

My first visit to El Escorial was on a school trip. We were 16 or 17, mostly girls, travelling with our convent school teachers. We stayed in Madrid, where I had already been a few times, and on a hot afternoon the coach took us to the monastery we had learned of in our History lessons. Its severity and stillness were violated by high-pitched teenage voices and exuberant gestures. It was sizzling, the open space lacking in shade, and we were almost gasping for air. I remember very little about the trip – the façade with the statues, the grandeur of the library and the basilica – but what really stuck with me was the Pantheon of the Kings.

It's a relatively small chamber, with twenty-six marble sepulchres identically designed, all in sumptuous black and gold, each one labelled with the name of its occupant. But, whereas in most churches and cathedrals each tomb has a personality, the Pantheon, like an unbending monk, seems to express revulsion towards portraying the real individuals beyond the pomp that corresponds to their earthly function. I remember it as unnerving, orderly and severe, a bizarre juxtaposition of luxury and sternness. It is as if the building itself prosecuted anything deviating from the norm. Perhaps it was this whiff of repression and intolerance – or perhaps my nervous disposition and overbearing imagination – that made me walk out, back to the sweltering heat, close to having a panic attack.

Mortal remains were paramount in the conception of El Escorial – not only those of the kings and queens of Spain, but also those of the Catholic saints that rest within its walls. Over 7000 relics are kept in two altars in the basilica, in a location close to the king's bedchambers, so he could have easy access to them. In Sigüenza's words, Philip was possessed by a "holy greed" for relics, and in 1567 he was granted permission from the pope to collect them. Whenever a new one arrived in the monastery, the usually self-restrained monarch would kiss it fervently, and examine it before finding a space for it in the collection. Some of them still preserve a label written in his own hand. Of these 7000, around 300 are known as "the authentic ones", since they were sent by bishops and priors, who included a certificate of authenticity. There are 12 whole skeletons, 144 heads and thousands of bones from all known saints, except three: Saint Joseph, Saint John and Saint James the Elder. The altars are displayed to the public only on All Saints' Day, though in the past, these relics – and others that are no longer kept here – played a crucial role in the lives of the inhabitants of El Escorial.

The most notable case is perhaps that of King Philip's son Prince Don Carlos, born in 1545. His early portraits depict a heavy-lidded young boy with an icy, indifferent gaze and the mandibular prognathism that characterised the Habsburg dynasty as it advanced in its inbreeding. An ambassador's report reveals he took pleasure in roasting hares alive, and there were rumours that he enjoyed maiming dogs' genitals and blinding horses from the royal stables. Aged 18, as he was chasing after a maid in the palace, he fell down the stairs and badly injured his head. The wound festered and very quickly the infection spread to his neck and chest, causing his head to swell. His situation was so dire that the eminent anatomist Andreas Vesalius was brought to El Escorial to perform a trepanation, but the prince was given hours to live. Seeing his father's despair, the king's confessor, Bernardo de Fresneda, advised that "since there was no longer any hope for an earthly remedy... they must seek instead for a cure from heaven". His recommendation was Fray Diego de Alcalá, a local miracle-maker who had the peculiarity of having been dead for a century. As Fresneda had probably anticipated, mortality wasn't an obstacle for King Philip, who ordered Fray Diego's sarcophagus to be opened and his remains brought to the prince's room, where they were laid next to Don Carlos. Days later, the boy recovered and claimed to have dreamed of the friar, whose mummy he'd briefly seen before slipping into oblivion. Among the clamour of the people, Fray Diego was canonised. His shrivelled remains are now worshipped in the Cathedral of Alcalá.

The practice of tucking human remains into the beds of agonising monarchs continued for several generations. The mummy of Isidore, later proclaimed the patron saint of Madrid, was kept in Philip III's bed while he was gravely ill. The king's recovery led to Isidore's beatification, who from then onwards enjoyed an even higher status than Saint Diego de Alcalá. In the late 17th century, a locksmith pulled out one of the mummy's teeth to give it to the king: this was the tragically inbred Charles II, the last Habsburg ruler of Spain and Philip II's great-grandson, whose story is the epitome of the bizarre concoction of Catholicism, morbid superstition and fear of Hell that also defined the lives of his ancestors.

THE BEWITCHED KING

Suffering from a debilitating prognathism which gave him a speech impediment and chronic drooling, prone to high fevers and seizures, Charles II (1661-1700) avoided vigorous activity and lived a secluded palace life. After his father's death, his mother acted as Queen-Regent, and even after he turned 14 and was legally allowed to rule without a regent, his health problems kept him away from power, which was exerted by a series of favourites. It was a period of civil unrest and courtly intrigues, and the king was rushed into marriage with the sole object of producing a fit descendant. His beloved first wife died without having provided an heir, and his second marriage didn't prove any more fruitful than the first. The court and his subjects whispered about his weird appearance, his melancholy, nervous temper and his series of misfortunes, and called him "El Hechizado", The Bewitched. He was an outcast in the orderly world designed by Philip II, a changeling-king who could have emerged from the shadows beneath El Escorial.

Charles genuinely believed he had been hexed or, even worse, possessed by the Devil. The English Ambassador Alexander Stanhope notes how "neither his buffoons, dwarfs nor puppet shows can in the least divert him from fancying everything that is said or done to be a temptation of the Devil", and how the king never thought himself safe "but with his Confessor and two friars by his side, whom he makes lie in his chamber all night". It was his confessor, Father Froilán Diaz, who finally asked Cardinal Rocaberti, the General Inquisitor, to investigate his enchantment. Rocaberti knew of a case of possessed nuns in a convent in Cangas de Narcea, in the northern province of Asturias, and resolved that their acquaintance with the Devil would make them a good source of information. Chaplain Argüelles was put in charge of the mission. In a letter to Rocaberti he revealed the result of his inquiries: "Last night the Devil told me that the king has been hexed to rule and to breed". Satan had kindly given him some details: that the king had been jinxed in 1675, aged 14, with a mug of hot chocolate – his favourite drink – spiked with the brains, intestines and kidneys of an executed criminal. The beverage would have been prepared by his own mother, thirsty for power, to remove him from the throne, destroy his health and "corrupt his semen", thwarting the possibility of a descendant.

The story told by Argüelles tapped into the country's milieu, confirming the existence of political intrigues and invoking the powerful archetype of the ambitious witch queen, so it's hardly surprising it became a sensation. To remove the spell, the monarch was treated with questionable remedies that caused his health to worsen. At the same time, hoping for a miracle, he was also sharing his royal bed with the trusty mummies of Saint Isidore and Saint Diego. Meanwhile, the king's men searched for the women who conspired and supplied the dead man's body for the potion, whom Argüelles named as Casilda Pérez, and María or Ana Díez, but the mission was fruitless. In further letters, the chaplain seems to have back-pedalled, alleging that the demons he spoke to were "being rebellious", and that Lucifer had now sworn the king was free from any spells.

In 1699, since the king's health was rapidly deteriorating, Father Froilán contacted an itinerant Neapolitan exorcist, Mauro de Tenda, who was rumoured to be a spy, but who claimed to have travelled to Spain wanting to rid Charles II of his demons. After several private interviews, Tenda discovered that His Majesty carried with him a little pouch he religiously placed under his pillow every night. Suspicious of its nature, he asked the queen to get hold of it. The contents of the pouch – eggshells, toenail clippings and hairs – were suggestive of witchcraft, but the king, who thought them relics and trusted they were protecting him from the Devil, couldn't recall who'd given them to him or when. Father Froilán's first impulse was to destroy the pouch and its contents, but Tenda refused, arguing that this may precipitate the king's demise. He based his decision on an episode that had taken place only some years earlier, when Charles's father Philip IV was dying: similar objects were found in his deathbed, and, just after they were burnt, he expired.

Tenda exorcised the king and queen in a bizarre ritual, both of them naked and kneeling in front of him; and later he gave Charles a recipe to expel the Devil from his body, with instructions that read halfway between a prayer and a spell: His Majesty needed to "cross himself three times over his head or on whatever part of the body hurt him, as soon as he notices any pain, pronouncing the common incantation and asking the Devil to leave in the name of God Almighty".

The Neapolitan was pleased with his patient's progress, but the king's mood was as dark as ever: proof of this is that he was transfixed by the sight of human remains, especially those of his family members, buried in the sumptuous Pantheon of the Kings. Austrian Ambassador Count Harrach spent some time in El Escorial and witnessed how Charles asked for his mother's coffin to be opened. The Queen Mother had specifically demanded not to be embalmed nor her corpse to be altered in any way, yet when her son contravened her wishes they discovered her body remained perfectly preserved three years after her death. Morbidly fascinated, the king ordered the doctors to undress her and examine her entrails, but when they proceeded, the dead queen's complexion turned brighter and redder, as if she was suffering a fit of otherwordly anger. The doctors kneeled down in front of her, terrified, begging for her pardon.

The dark spaces in the palace built by his great-grandfather seemed to have taken possession of Charles II's mind: the Devil crawling out of the soil and into his chambers to poison his soul; the decaying flesh of his family members, sealed under layers of gold and marble, returning to haunt him. None of the exorcisms or bizarre rituals he underwent would convince the unfortunate king that he could live a lighter, less tormented life. He died in 1700, soon after Tenda's interventions; fittingly, on All Saint's Day, when Spain prays and honours the relics of its dead and indulges in eating ossuary-like piles of bone-shaped marzipan. Charles's body, now resting in the Pantheon of the Kings, had to be subject to a post-mortem examination due to the suspicions of malefice. What the doctor saw then was "a very small heart, the size of a peppercorn; corroded lungs, gangrenous, putrid intestines; three large kidney stones; a single testicle, black as coal; and a head full of water". After his death, El Escorial would pass into the hands of his great-nephew Philip V, and therefore to the House of Bourbon.

ESCAPING THE INQUISITION

Even before extreme consanguinity produced the ailments of The Bewitched, the health of the Habsburgs had already been poor. As Philip II got older and felt death nearer, he strengthened his patronage of alchemy. His secretary Pedro del Hoyo was said to have sparked up his interest, which initially seemed to be more practical than spiritual, probably born from necessity, since the coffers of the empire's treasury were in debt after his father's military campaigns and the constant need to please the mutinous

Army of Flanders. After commissioning several attempts that proved futile, the king became sceptical of promises of alchemical gold and claims of metal transmutation. Nevertheless, he was still fascinated by Raymond Lully's work on the preparation of quintessences as medicine, and in 1585 work began to build the laboratory of El Escorial. Independent of the infirmary and the monastery, it would focus on producing essences, distilled oils and the mythical potable gold, and it would gather experts such as Giovanni Vincenzo Forte and Richard Stanyhurst. The latter was an Irish Catholic who wrote several treatises on alchemical medicine, stating it could treat "incurable" diseases such as leprosy, consumption, syphilis or gout. The king certainly suffered from gout, and it's been speculated that he might also have been affected with congenital syphilis, which could explain his personal interest in Stanyhurst's work. In his letters, the Irish alchemist wrote that his work at El Escorial was highly confidential and a matter of state, and, as well as undertaking research, he prepared potable gold, the elixir of long life, to restore the king's health.

Alchemy wasn't prohibited by the Inquisition, but there was a fine line between some practices and what the Catholic Church would have considered appropriate. The library of the monastery also pushed the boundaries of acceptability. In 1574, the first librarian, Antonio Gracián, facing the task of organising the volumes after completing an inventory, advised that "it could be done here as it's been done in the Vatican Library: to have two sorts of libraries, a public one and a secret one." A decade later, the new librarian Arias Montano produced an inventory of books proscribed by the Inquisitorial index of 1584, concluding that they kept around 50 on the library shelves. A natural diplomat, he arranged with the king that the forbidden books would not be destroyed, but would be kept locked away instead. Nevertheless, the secret collection

grew, since, 36 years after Philip's death, a new inventory revealed
a total of 400, although only the prior, the librarian and some dons
were allowed to read them – and the presence of annotations in
their margins reveals that they did so regularly.

ABOVE AND BELOW

In summer 1598 Philip II retired to El Escorial, feeling death
was near. On the 6th of July, in spite of his poor health, he asked
his men to take him on a tour to see all the corners of his beloved monastery for a last goodbye. After that date, his ailments
confined him to his chambers until he met his fate.

Philip II's agony was prolonged and horrendous. Sigüenza writes that he was "consumed by the malignant fire that
had turned him into skin and bones", a combination of fever,
osteoarthritis, dropsy, incontinence and abscesses caused by
gout. The meticulous, dapper king – "by nature the most clean,
neat and tidy person that has ever lived on this earth", according to his valet Jehan Lhermite – literally rotted in his bed,
amidst maggot-infected ulcers and his own excrement. His long
torment was only relieved by the sight of his collection of relics.
They were brought to his chambers and laid out so he could kiss
them, one by one. In spite of his delirious state, he was able to
remember which ones he hadn't kissed yet, and asked the friars
to bring those to him.

During his last years, the monarch had accumulated a
collection of triptychs and paintings by a Netherlandish artist
named Hieronymus Bosch, who had died in 1516.[3] Nominally,
the painter was a Catholic, a member of the Brotherhood of Our
Lady, but his hallucinatory work was crammed with perverse
and terrifying representations of sin and eternal damnation. It's

been said that Bosch and his Brotherhood were secret Adamites, who believed sin was created by God, and consequently approved the pursuit of earthly pleasures as a divine experience. Whatever moved the enigmatic artist, it is clear that his complex visual narratives struck a chord within Philip II.

The Garden of Earthly Delights had been in El Escorial since 1593, and it was moved to the king's rooms so that he could contemplate it in his agony. Even though the painting had been dismissed as heretical, Sigüenza defended the monarch's fascination with it, writing that the three panels "are a satirical comment on the shame and sinfulness of mankind". The first panel is a beautiful, celestial garden; but the lustful scenes of the central panel give way to a dark, haunting hellscape on the right.

Catholicism is dualistic: salvation cannot be understood without the threat of Hell. I often wonder if my Gothic sensibilities were shaped by my Catholic education – to one side, the sight of Jesus tortured on the cross, a stranger's blood sacrifice for all our personal sins, and the unattainable purity of a feminine figure designed to taint and shame; to the other, my paralysing fear of Satan. Order and virtue cannot engulf darkness, much like the orderly design of a holy complex could not seal the Hellmouth opening up underneath.

Philip II's last days are an extraordinary illustration of his beliefs: consumed by fever and intolerable pain, watching mass being celebrated from his window over the basilica, meditating on Bosch's hellish landscapes, kissing mortal remains, the king was rapt in a trance-like state, his body maggot-ridden, his soul in a sort of Purgatory.

Writer Ricardo Sepúlveda collected in 1888 the oral tradition preserved by the neighbours of El Escorial. It was said that the Black Dog was seen in crucial moments of the king's life, specifically, upon the deaths of three of his family members: that of his son Don Carlos; that of his third wife, queen Elisabeth of Valois; and that of his illegitimate half-brother, Don John of Austria. The monstrous beast the monks couldn't take down became a harbinger of calamity for the royal family, howling every time Death claimed one of them. Legend has it that King Philip saw it too, on the day of his demise, by his deathbed, as though it were a reminder of what lay below – what he had been unable to seal, what would torment all of his descendants. Even though he was surrounded by his holy objects and his holy men, here, in El Escorial, he was also closer to the abyss than he would have been anywhere else.

Maria J. Pérez Cuervo (Málaga, Spain, 1980) is a freelance writer based in Bristol, UK. She graduated in Journalism, specializing in history and archaeology. In 2007 she completed an MA in Archaeology for Screen Media in the University of Bristol, and her dissertation on Archaeology and the Occult in popular culture – and her fake documentary on Frederick Bligh Bond and how he resorted to psychic archaeology to excavate Glastonbury Abbey – was awarded the Mick Aston Prize. For over a decade she has worked in television (*Time Team, Tony Robinson and the Paranormal*), print media and social media / e-media.

Maria is a regular contributor to *Fortean Times*, where she writes about weird history, myths and fairytales, and the Gothic imagination. She also blogs about dark mythology on folklore-thursday.com. Even though she's mostly written Fortean essays and articles, she secretly aspires to become a pulp writer. Her first attempt at writing fiction, the folk horror story "The Village Below", set in the north of Spain, was published in Book 3 of the literary magazine "The Ghastling".

She can be found online at mjpcuervo.com and on Twitter at @mjpcuervo.

A COMPENDIUM OF TIDES

Warren Ellis

NORE

There's a ship full of bombs out here.

The S.S. *Richard Montgomery* went down in the Thames Estuary, on whose banks I've lived almost all of my life, back in 1944. She struck one of the many sandbanks that snake under the Estuary waters, and her back broke as she listed over the hidden curve. The vessel went down with somewhere between fifteen hundred and three thousand tons of live explosives inside it. These were determined to be too expensive to retrieve or make safe. So they sit out there in the water. Some three hundred blockbuster bombs on top of the pile, named for their wartime ability to erase entire streets with their blast waves. Thousands of other explosive devices underneath it. If the ship full of bombs went off, every window on the Estuary would shatter, we'd score at least a 4.5 on the Richter scale, the sea bed would get a new twenty-foot-deep crater, and a tsunami sixteen feet high would rush to shore and into London.

It'd be quite a sight. The detonation, it's been calculated, would throw a thousand-foot-wide column of water and dirt two miles into the air.

The Montgomery is still ticking out there under the water, shifting and cracking and degrading year by year and yet somehow still dangerously alive. It even gave its name to our local "pirate" station, Ship Full Of Bombs Radio.

There's graves all over the coastline. The Maunsell Sea Forts, barnacled bones sticking up out of the water. Built as stilted towers to defend London from German attack during the war, they were abandoned by the Fifties. Rusting bodies on sticks. Detourned into pirate radio stations or independent principalities. They're a tourist attraction of a kind now, the Estuary toured like a cemetery full of famous corpses.

Haunted coast. It was out here on the Estuary that Nelson's body reached shore after meeting his doom at Trafalgar, entombed in a cask of brandy.

And the guns still fire. I can hear them again now as I write this section, familiar thunder rolling across the sky from the east. The guns east of Shoeburyness are being cleared. Out there along the estuarine coast is Foulness, which is a real place name. Back in the Fifties, Nigel Kneale and his production team scouted locations on the Thames Estuary for *Quatermass II*, the required locale being the site of an experimental moon-base emulator. In the story, the place they found is called Winnerden Flats, because they thought its real name sounded too fictional. The location's actual name is Mucking Marshes. We are an oddly literal people, out here.

Foulness, east of Shoeburyness is a sealed military test site. It's supposed to be the safest and most peaceful place in the country, aside from the grenades, mines, mortars and missiles – an explosives and firearms proving ground across three centuries. Five working farms, a village, an accidental wildlife preserve, barely changed in over a hundred years, locked up inside the Foulness security ring. Like one of those drowned towns whose rooves and spires occasionally surface from a drained reservoir in summer. Submerged by state security.

It was once known as the Experimental Establishment, trialling "weird and wonderful weapons". I've spent my life listening to the sound of the guns booming down the estuary, fired from a village frozen in time.

Foulness was once only accessible by what is the most dangerous walk in Britain – the ancient track known as the Broomway. The Broomway drifts off the mainland into the mouth of the Estuary for a six-mile loop before touching Foulness. At low tide, it's an extremely disorienting experience, as the mud flats reflect a grey sky almost perfectly. One can suddenly be nowhere, in a floating world almost without landmarks or distinguishing features. Littoral limbo. The tides out there are fast, devious things, and in times past the arc of the track was marked only by tall poles with bundles of sticks lashed to their tops, likened to brooms. These days, we don't even have that. It's still a public byway, but the path is entirely notional now, nothing but a compass heading and an eyeballing of the Black Grounds, the Maplin Sands, the Maypole and Havengore Creek.

People die. People still die, walking the Broomway towards the foul ness where they explode the bombs and fire the great guns that echo down the river.

Seriously. A pathway that kills people which leads only to a military experimental ground on a river that has a ship full of bombs in it. That's where I live.

"I come not from Heaven, but from Essex."

– William Morris

Sunk Head

The first pirate television broadcast that I know of was transmitted from Sunk Head, one of our abandoned and illegally re-occupied Sea Forts.

On 9 November 1965, at around 4:20 in the morning, a hundred-foot aerial atop the four-storey-high Sunk Head tower chucked a signal across eleven miles of water and fourteen miles inland – I like to think that would be the blast radius of our ship full of bombs. The broadcast was reportedly a still image, ghostly and monochrome: a white globe with a star and two Ts atop it, and the name of the nascent pirate TV station: Tower TV.

Sometimes I think that the real world was always moving faster than science fiction: it's just that back then the real future was broadcasting at 4:20 in the bloody morning and no-one was around to see it.

Some say the Mayflower launched with the last of the Pilgrim Fathers from down the road in Leigh-on-Sea. Out here, the future either happens when we're asleep or it leaves on the morning tide.

Thirty minutes' walk from me is the earliest part of my town that I know of. Prittlewell Camp, sometimes known as The Look Out, is a hill fort dating back to around the 8th century BCE. I walk for thirty minutes every day, but in the other direction. The weight of the town has moved, over 2800 years. In the 7th century CE, Prittlewell proper was a Saxon settlement and the seat of kings – a recently-discovered Saxon burial ground has become known as the last resting place of "The King Of Bling", for all his glittering grave goods. It's possible this is Saeberht, King of Essex and the first Saxon king on this side of the country to become a Christian. He went in the dirt with his lyres and Coptic bowls and gold-foiled crosses around 616.

Prittlewell, today, is basically a bunch of supermarkets and a terrible little train station.

The Prittle Brook, which has had people living by it since the Stone Age, rises in Thundersley, the village and one-time Viking settlement where I grew up. It follows me through the West Wood into Southend, where I now live, before striking out for Sutton and Stambridge and finally the river Roach and all its creeks and nesses.

For thirty minutes a day, I run with the river, away from deep time into whatever future tides are waiting.

Coastal experiments.

Sunk Head, by the way, was blown up with more than two tons of plastic explosive in 1967. The light and heat from the blast could be seen and felt more than fourteen miles away.

KNOCK JOHN

Thundersley began as Thunor's Clearing or something adjacent, a settlement in a grove dedicated to the worship of Thor. There's another Thundersley up in Suffolk, and the story was that Thor would fly over both Thundersleys on Thor's Day, to view these more distant of his sacred places. Any of these Essex villages with -ley or -leigh on the end are Viking settlements, clearings and meadows. Apart from Rayleigh, just to be awkward, which is Saxon for "roe-deer stream". The village next door, Hadleigh, is "the clearing where heather grows". There are still patches of heathland scattered around the area, dotted in autumn and spring with marshy pools that were used by the locals for washing water back in the day, and more recently for kids to ride their bikes through or attempt to drown each other in. These are Old English words, speaking to the way Britain assimilates and mutates.

I learned these words from a teacher at my first school in the village – officially, Thundersley County Junior School, but known in the village by the name of the little track it stood at the mouth of Dark Lane School. My teacher, a strange-looking older gentleman called Mr. Lees who had one of those faces that have quite gone out of fashion, spent one long rainy day indoors dripping local history into our heads.

We could see the school crossing from our window. Mr. Lees told us that that thick point in the road used to be a weir. I'm not sure how it could have been – Prittle Brook emerges east of there. Down the hill, of course, there was Rayleigh Weir, source of one of the streams that feed the Roach, long concreted over and turned into a junction on the dual-carriageway A127, which we all know as The Arterial Road. But to think, just out there across the road, there was buried secret water that only ancient people (like my teacher) knew about…

At the ruins of Hadleigh Castle at night, there are strange lights moving under the jagged teeth of the broken tower and around the smashed keep called The Devil's Chair, the ghosts of smugglers holding their lanterns up to find the secret tunnels between there and the sea.

On Rayleigh Mount, looking down at the Weir, there was a Lawless Court held at midnight, unlit, the names of traitors spoken only in whispers, the loudest sound the scratch of coal on slate.

Rough Sands

Radio and ghosts. Electronic sound, another ghost map laid on top of all the others that make up this city.

The first electrical recording issued to the public, made by the scientists of Bell Labs, was of a November 11, 1920 funeral service for the Unknown Soldier in Westminster Abbey, London. The place where the Abbey sits used to be called Thorny Island, which received its first shrine the year Saebehrt died. Thorny Island was described by the charter of King Offa as "a terrible place", and is one of the candidates for the spot where King Canute proved that he couldn't do shit about water. Not long after Canute, the island was tamed, and now contains the oldest garden in Britain, founded by monks a thousand years ago. The place sat between two branches of the River Tyburn, one of London's buried rivers that flow into the River Thames. The Effra, which once joined the Thames from the south, is now encased in a pipe. Under the streets, the rivers. All the little rivers where, up until maybe fifteen hundred years ago, Londoners used to place skulls on the banks, as offerings and boundary markers. Maps made of skulls. Under the buildings and flowers, the ritual sites that existed all around the Thorney Island area.

Time and maps.

All places with histories of human use have a sound. Many of them were even chosen for their acoustic properties. And the ground and the rock and the bone absorb sound.

We speak Estuary English, down here on the shore, a softened localization of the east London accent. It all flows back down to us.

Electronic sound is the fabric of the last hundred years. Early film only feels historical in the sense that it's somehow wrong – it runs too fast, it's black and white or the colours are off. Early sound recording feels like the authentic past – like it's being heard through deep time. It's real in a way that film never is.

Essex is the home of radio. Radio happened about twenty miles from me. Radio was born in a Marconi hut in Writtle, outside Chelmsford. Two Emma Toc, Valentine's Day 1922, right around my (later) birthday, broadcasting music for the first time. When I was young, living down the road from the wellspring of electronic sound, radio came out of wooden boxes, wooden like the early theremins and Moogs. A couple of weeks after Two Emma Toc spoke "Writtle testing" into the air, in fact, Leon Theremin demonstrated the Theremin for Lenin in a private audience. By May he was preparing to take the Theremin on tour to promote the electrification of Russia – much the same time as 2LO, London's first radio station, was launched, from a building that was previously a hotel with a restaurant and a ballroom. The walls still rang with dinner parties and dancing as the new metal cast a new ghost map over the city.

Switches and dials. I liked the way my old radios imposed architecture on a world of invisible waves. A red needle, numbers, a speedometer for signals. Physical switching between Medium Wave, FM and Long Wave. Ramps and streets and windows. To me, it gave radio a structure like the false topology of the Tube map.

Pirate radio had been and gone by then. That was an Essex thing. Sometimes on boats, sometimes on the old Sea Forts dotted around the coast and in the estuary, empty houses standing on stilts in the waves. These were always pirate waters. The creeks of Essex, too narrow for the Inland Revenue cutters to navigate, were the waterways of the classic pirate period. There are still pubs around here that you'd swear somehow remained of that period, that go silent when "strangers" walk into them. Dark-eyed men in heavy boots, reeking of the Blackwater and

Brightlingsea Creek and all the old pirate channels, mud on their soles from Northey, Osea and Cindery Island.

But our radio had moved out of Essex, like anyone else with an ounce of common sense, and floated down the river to London.

SHIVERING SANDS

It was well known, that, on a night when the "atmospherics" were right – that was the term everybody used, whether it was correct or not – strange signals would blow across the water from the continent. If your TV picture fuzzed and prickled a little, some random manual tuning would resolve television from the mainland. Ghostly porn, cop stories that never quite made sense and weird chat shows where everything was black and white and people were still smoking on stage. But, even better, the radio would drift over too, and nights were spent carefully roaming the frequencies, zeroing in on narrow stolen channels of alien music. All imbued with the sound quality of Electronic Voice Phenomenon – the sonics of voices speaking from beyond death. Songs from the Other World. It was a powerfully strange thing, in a time where the informational flow was much thinner and more difficult, on an island country, to receive contextless foreign broadcasts, simply because the sky had aligned itself just so.

'Atmospherics', a new folklore word for a conjugation of natural conditions that nobody really understood. Like "ingine". which was, I learned from certain elder relatives, the word you used when you were talking about broken car engines because it somehow made you sound familiar with their ways. Dad, Grandad and two uncles standing around the big end of a car in the sort of condition that post-apocalypse straight-to-video bad guys wouldn't even have pulled around the nuclear desert by horses. All leaning under the open bonnet with cigarettes in their mouths. "Well, it's the ingine, innit?" One of those last vestiges of east London English before the Estuary drowned it, I suspect. "Ingine" conferred knowledge and comprehension. Magic words and words for magic.

The static washed out of the speakers in tides.

It's 1978. I'm at my grandmother's house in Shoebury. The TV picture is all fucked up. My dad says, "the gasometers must be high. The picture's ghosting".

There was a little road around here called Screaming Boy Lane. The local knowledge has it that some time in the 1700s a young farm boy got himself strangled out there, and for centuries afterwards his ghost would wander the lane and tap on windows. And scream. I don't think the lane is there any more. The atmospherics changed, and it was washed away.

Tongue Sands

Some of us have taken to calling this littoral space "The Thames Delta". It's mostly a joke.

Canvey Island, off the Benfleet coast, is an alluvial deposit, one signature of a delta. It was shored up by the Dutch in the 1600s, which is why something like a third of Canvey streets have Dutch names. I looked it up when I was doing a milk round over there in the 1980s. It was studded with the red hills that denoted Roman salt production, under which were Neolithic axes and Bronze Age bracelets, and the Trinovantes and the Catuvellauni rode around them as a staging point from which to join Boudicca's Iceni rebellion.

Blues bands howled off Canvey in the Sixties and Seventies. "Rhythm & Blues sells more beer than any other kind of music", said (I think) Lee Brilleaux of Canvey vanguard Dr. Feelgood. Pub rock. Later on, "Thames Delta" stuck, in reference to Mississippi Delta blues.

Even in the Eighties, R&B bands ruled Southend. I'd go some nights to an underground space between a bar, which would be rammed with bodies dancing to standards – this was the decadent point in the period, where a lot of bands were just playing stuff you knew from the *Blues Brothers* soundtrack album. And I'd stagger outside at some point for air or a cigarette or whatever, and the side door to the steps would open, and a plume of steam would belch out and rise up into the night, and I could pretend that I was in a real place, a real city with real history and culture where that happened a thousand times a night, every night.

Some nights, people would just stand around and watch that pillar of air and heat and sweat and kisses rise into the sky.

For a space that's been close to a blank slate for as long as it's been here – nothing but forest, settlements stuck to coasts and creeks – even an appropriated identity is an improvement. And not unsuitable for an island that's barely even there and a delta that probably isn't.

Where I'm sitting, in Southend-on-Sea, just used to be the south end of Prittlewell. Not a place at all.

It's hard to find the spirit of a place when it was never really supposed to be a place at all. Random colony points for Vikings. Royal seats that now no longer exist. Royal forests. Dumping ground for the East End diaspora, commuter-belt feeding systems for the London machines.

It's south of the Claudian Roman beachhead, the seat of the East Seaxe, a section of Wessex, a package ceded to the Vikings as part of the Danelaw, a Norman park. No broad history happened here until the Victorians shoved a railway line from London to Shoebury.

There is no deep time here. There is just the river.

Or, put another way: where, in your science fiction, would you put an entire moonbase if you wanted nobody at all to pay particular attention to it? In a place with no history and no future. Right here.

RED SANDS

Ah, but Cunning Murrell, though.

I've told his story before. I told it on stage at a big tech conference in Brighton, once, to contextualize my relationship with time and technology and spirits and place.

Cunning Murrell was the last of the Cunning Folk around here, the hedge witches of old England. He died in 1860 at age seventy-five, having legendarily predicted his time of death to the hour and minute. The same year Charles Dickens started *Great Expectations*, which contains a scene set out here on the Delta, "where the waterside inhabitants are very few". Legend has it that he wrote much of it at the Lobster Smack, a pub in old Leigh that looks over at Canvey Island.

> It was a dirty place enough, and I dare say not unknown to smuggling adventurers... No other company was in the house than the landlord, his wife, and a grizzled male creature, the "Jack" of the little causeway, who was as slimy and smeary as if he had been low-water mark too... The dismal wind was muttering round the house, the tide was flapping at the shore, and I had a feeling that we were caged and threatened.

Thirty-odd years later, Joseph Conrad, who lived down the coast by Stanford-le-Hope, moored the "Nellie" in *Heart Of Darkness* around these parts. The last thing he wrote here appears to have been a short story called "An Outpost Of Progress".

At least one of Murrell's many children moved over into Thundersley from the Murrell family home in Hadleigh. When I was a kid, I had a girlfriend who was a redheaded Murrell, and only realized later that she was probably a descendant of Cunning Murrell.

He lived on a lane that's now called Endway, in Hadleigh, a little outside what bare clusters of settlements constituted the village at the time. He was a chemist, and a shoemaker, and a cunning man. A doctor, a magician, a seer – essentially our regional variant of a shaman. If you looked for him at night – and nobody really did because, like all good shamans, he worried the shit out of people – he'd be found with his whalebone umbrella in hand and upended, to carry the herbs and roots he foraged in the dark to make his medicines with. In 1890, a cache of Murrell's effects was dug up. It included letters from satisfied customers, including this classic: "I have took the powder it made me verrey quear in the stummuk pleas send sum more."

In that same box, I once read, were his iron goggles. I've likened them to Augmented Reality glasses in the past, and they served the same purpose as the hagstones of the West Country. They allowed him to see into the Other World. Iron frames with iron slats in them, iron being the famed anathema to the Devil and his troops. Murrell even called himself "The Devil's Master". Satan was real, back then. It was commonly understood that Satan and his department wandered the world looking for people they could tempt into sin, and God just let them. God was a dick, he was feared, and out here on the Thames Delta, forgotten by history and forsaken by England, when there were barely a couple of hundred people living in Hadleigh, what was a simple person supposed to do when doing any little thing to make your life easier or nicer was a sin that changed your final address to a circle of Hell? Out here in the clearings overlooking the Thames Delta, you went to the cunning man. He was the Devil's Master. He was exactly what you needed when you had to break a deal or put the fix in: a dodgy geezer from darkest coastal Essex, with a copper bracelet on his wrist that was said to detect lies.

Cunning Murrell was a story I didn't find out until I left Thundersley for Southend. Not for many years after, in fact. I wish I'd learned it sooner. If someone had told me as a kid that I was separated by a few miles and barely more than a hundred years from one of the last great wizards of old England, that dismal wind may not have bit as hard.

The first analogue sound recording of the human voice was made in 1860. It was called a phonautogram. It is, punched in paper, the sound of a man singing "Au clair de la lune".

By the light of the moon,
My friend Pierrot,
Lend me your quill
To write a word.
My candle is dead,
I have no more fire.
Open your door for me
For the love of God.

Magical thinking is a terrible trap. Murrell's candle goes out, sound is recorded for the first time, Charles Dickens wanders down the slope from Hadleigh to Leigh to write his book, electronic sound recording begins on the other end of the river, radio is launched half a day's walk from Murrell's house on the

Endway. Aha! I've taken the powders, something is queer in my stomach, everything makes an awful sense, please send some more. I gave my tech talk on Cunning Murrell in the same spot that James Burke, creator of the TV series *Connections*, had spoken one year earlier. Connections make everything somehow have mass, and we reach for them, in some rotten, false way, to impose import. Meanwhile, somebody clambers on to one of the Sea Forts and declares it to be The Principality Of Sealand, a fake country on stilts, and an appropriated blues guitar howls out across the Thames Delta, because there's nothing here to hold on to, just tides, and raising yourself up on sticks and making shit up is the only thing that makes sense. Keep taking the powders.

But. Cunning Murrell. Who looked into the Other World through steel shades and saw all the spirits of our place abroad in the clearings at night. In a placeless place, it felt like Cunning Murrell was the story I was waiting for all along. He was science and fiction: a chemical stillman, a man who wore ghost glasses, working from that radical Essex position of esoteric defence against the dark *and* the clergical bureaucracy. A conman and a wizard. A doctor and a weird bastard who planted iron witch bottles all over the place.

A life of fiction fits with a place that made itself up.

SHIP FULL OF BOMBS

In winter, foghorns still low across the Estuary at night. In summer, I can hear the rails singing as they cool after the last train docks for the night. The trains still sound their horns as they cross the bridge over the hill road down to the sea, and it always delights me. I spent a period living in America, a few years ago, and was surprised every time by the sounds of their trains as they echoed up from the river. American train horns are mournful, haunted and wounded. British train horns are still trumpets of triumph, bright and surging – the very sound of an Outpost of Progress.

We could all be vaporized by a ship full of bombs at any time, but fuck it! Race on down the track with Futurist zeal to the last invented place in England and sound the horn!

And after the last stop on the line there's a secret timeless island and a road to nowhere arcing into the mouth of the estuary.

I live out here on the Thames Delta, still, a ten-minute walk from the shore. It's a placeless place that tells stories about itself because it's rarely existed in a dense enough form to generate its own history. It's nothing but time and tides and salt and mud, and sometimes the mud reflects the sky and you just can't see anything.

I tell stories for a living. I sit by the rivers and creeks with the ghosts of my ancestors, the Viking priests and dead writers and cunning folk, and I see the water run by and count the tides. We launch futures from here, but here we stay, as time flows by and the sea becomes the sky and a ship full of bombs ticks away.

Warren Ellis is the award-winning writer of graphic novels like *Transmetropolitan*, *Fell*, *Ministry of Space* and *Planetary*, and the author of the nyt-bestselling *Gun Machine*, the digital single *Dead Pig Collector* and the "underground classic" novel *Crooked Little Vein*.

The movie *RED* is based on his graphic novel of the same name, its sequel having been released in summer 2013. *Iron Man 3* is based on his Marvel Comics graphic novel *Iron Man: Extremis*. He's also written extensively for VICE, *WIRED UK* and Reuters on technological and cultural matters, and is developing his graphic novel series with Jason Howard, *Trees*, for Hardy Son & Baker and NBCU.

His next book is the novella *Normal*, from Farrar Straus Giroux, where he is also working on a non-fiction book about the future of the city.

A documentary about his work, *Captured Ghosts*, was released in 2012.

Recognitions include the NUIG Literary and Debating Society's President's Medal for service to freedom of speech, the Eagle Awards Roll Of Honour for lifetime achievement in the field of comics & graphic novels, the Grand Prix de l'Imaginaire 2010, the Sidewise Award for Alternate History and the International Horror Guild Award for illustrated narrative.

He is a Patron of the British Humanist Association, an Associate of the Institute of Atemporal Studies, and the literary editor of *EDICT* magazine.

Warren Ellis lives outside London, on the south-east coast of England, in case he needs to make a quick getaway.

He can be found on Twitter at @warrenellis.

AGONIES AND ENCHANTMENTS

Kristine Ong Muslim

"Through my body of writing I contribute to cultural amnesia". This was what I blurted out – in yet another proof of my tendency to not think long and hard first before saying anything – in one of the panel discussions for the 6th Philippine International Literary Festival held in a Davao City hotel's function room in November 2015. The discussion was about placed-based narratives, where I was out of place because I don't write about my roots, let alone write about the regional customs associated with my location. It was my first public outing as an author. I – the woman from the boondocks of Maguindanao and the woman who wrote about weird stuff – sat in a panel discussion along with two other authors, both of whom were pedigreed to the gills with their formal education and attendance at prestigious writing workshops.

At one point during my turn to talk, I even referred to my people's regional mores as 'backward'. One person in the audience rightfully pointed out the insensitivity of using the term. I made the "backward" gaffe in relation to my sharing of an anecdote that I believed was very much reflective of the "sense of place" befitting my geographical location. I told the audience about a man, who appeared to have been chased by kin. Their bizarre entourage ended by the roadside opposite my mother's house. The man was having a fit and was babbling incoherently throughout. He was accompanied by people who were "exorcising" him. I approached one of the spectators. I asked her to tell the woman who was busily driving the "demons" out of the man that he was mentally ill and needed a doctor. She said that wasn't the case at all. Implicit in her answer was the acquiescence to the situation as a cut-and-dried case of demonic possession. So, I left them alone to proceed with the exorcism.

The Philippines is a group of islands with Luzon in the north, Visayas in the middle, and Mindanao in the south. Compared to Luzon and Visayas, Mindanao bore the slightest brunt of colonial influences courtesy of the Spanish and the Americans. Maguindanao, one of the provinces of Mindanao, is the site of two infamous Philippine atrocities. The first, which occurred in 2009, was the Ampatuan massacre that saw the deaths of fifty-eight people whose bodies were haphazardly and hastily buried in shallow mass graves. The graves were dug using a piece of government-owned highway equipment – a backhoe. The other happened in 2015 in the cornfields of Mamasapano, Maguindanao. The Mamasapano clash was a daylong shoot-out that resulted in the slaughter of forty-four cops – outnumbered in the Mamasapano cornfields, mostly crawling on all fours in their box formation, yet still fully exposed to enemy fire, and running dangerously low on ammunition – whose artillery reinforcement had finally been sent out twelve hours too late. At the time the bodies of the policemen arrived in the Philippine capital of Manila and emotions were running high across the country. It was believed that the tragic outcome could have been readily avoided. The former President Benigno Aquino III was pictured grinning his happy toothy smile – the same smile he wore during a press conference after 2010 bungled Manila bus hostage crisis in which eight people were killed – while touring a Mitsubishi car plant mere miles away from where the dead cops were being honoured. Fast forward to May 2016, the presidential election period, and one could just about taste the sickly sweet *schadenfreude* in the air. It was six years of bombastic rage, a massive pot of it boiling and finally tipping over to spew its contents in all possible directions. A historic landslide victory saw the rise to the presidency of Rodrigo Duterte, the first president to have come from Mindanao and the local leader responsible for the transformation of Davao City from a war-torn third-world hellhole of guerillas, bombers, and petty criminals to a metropolis with top-of-the-line security and healthcare facilities for its people.

I grew up and continue to live in Nuro, a rural town located in the municipality of Upi in the province of Maguindanao, the part of the country that had the highest incidences of poverty and illiteracy. The native peoples of Upi are Moros, indigenous people who converted to Islam, and Tedurays. My mother is half-Teduray. My grandfather on the mother side was a Mao Tse Tung fanatic who escaped to the Philippines from China. My father is of Jolowano Muslim descent, an orthodox Islam practitioner. Both of my parents grew up in poor households. In Nuro, Upi, you will find a two-story wooden house at Rizal Street that still stands, although in a much changed state, to this day. That was where I grew up and spent roughly the first sixteen years of my life.

In the early 1980s, the track in front of the house was a dirt road lined with trees, wild lemongrass, and shrubs like hibiscus and *tsaang gubat* (wild teas). A short distance away from the house was a run-down shack made of wood and corrugated metal. There were a bunch of tires stacked in front. The tires are Philippine countryside parlance, signalling the presence of a vulcanizing shop.

In 2016, the dirt road has been properly re-surfaced, the vulcanizing shop torn down and replaced by a *carinderia* (a kind of restaurant), the lush vegetation replaced by a commercial building. Driving along that road, one can often see a *payong-payong*. A *payong-payong* is cheap transportation for traveling short distances — it is a motorcycle with a side-car welded to it, and outfitted with a wide umbrella. There are cars too, which we generally call jeeps or fords. These are not the brand names; they do not denote the vehicle's make or manufacturer. These cars were not fabricated on assembly lines supervised by licensed mechanical engineers. They have undergone no safety or quality testing at the hands of accredited professionals. Just like the *payong-payong*, these cars are welded and bolted together with a grim practicality which is embedded in the Filipino psyche.

In the 1970s, Upi gained notoriety for being the hometown of Feliciano Luces, popularly known as Kumander Toothpick, the founder of the Ilaga militia. The anti-Muslim vigilante Ilaga group was made up of Christians from the Visayas region of the Philippines. They were also rumored to be cannibals, eating or cutting off certain body parts of their victims for use as *anting-anting*, or magic amulets. The brutal rampage of the Ilaga was one of the reasons for the Moro insurgency in Mindanao.

Nowadays, Upi is pretty much rendered fun and innocuous by its Meguyaya Festival, an annual celebration that involves communal feasting on roasted corn to thank nature deities for the bountiful harvest. Roadsides are lined with charcoal-powered grillers on which ears of corn are cooked and then eaten. There is also the omnipresent tackiness of local beauty pageants and public discos during fiestas, but thankfully – and I am hoping it stays this way forever – there are no factories, no banks, no taxis, no movie houses, and no bulky shrines to the demigods of capitalism such as huge shopping malls and department stores.

OTHERWORLDLY TENANT(S) IN THE HOUSE

In real estate, there's this concept of a stigmatized property. A violent crime or a suicide can cause such a stigma. If this happens, then the seller is bound by law to disclose the property's controversial history. The two-story wooden house at Rizal Street where I grew up in had no such history.

There was only one death in that house. It was my grandmother's. She was very old but never bedridden. In fact, she was active for a woman of her age. She never had to be hospitalized, had no chronic pain issues, and was not at all senile. Her eyesight was bad, and that was just about it. And since she liked to sew, and had a nice Singer sewing machine for her sewing routine, she had to ask us each time to slip one end of the thread to a needle's tiny hole. She could do this by herself, fumbling at the needle hole while wearing her prescription glasses, but I suppose it was faster when somebody much younger and nimble would do it for her. So anyway, there was only one death in the house, and it was a peaceful death of an old lady who I didn't even know was ill to begin with. She died in her sleep while we were watching a movie in the room next to hers.

It is interesting to note that in the months before my grandmother's death, she kept the windows in her bedroom shut. She claimed she was seeing relatives who have long passed. She said her long dead relatives were calling out to her from outside those windows. In adulthood, I only learned much later about how psychopomps figure in Filipino culture. In other cultures, these escorts to the afterlife were animals or the likes of the ferryman Charon and the Grim Reaper. In Filipino legends, spirits of the dying person's dead relatives serve as psychopomps.

In the 1990s my cousin (nicknamed Babab) and his family visited Upi when he was seven or eight years old. He and his family lived in Cotabato City, 28 kilometers away from Upi. Babab claimed to have seen a headless ghost in the small and cramped living room of the house I grew up in and spent roughly the first sixteen years of my life. Many years hence, Babab, even as an adult, has never once set foot in Upi again. In get-togethers with his family, he would offer excuses as to why he couldn't visit us. It was because of what he saw – or what he thought he saw – that day.

Long before Babab's memorable brush with his "headless ghost", my father had his. It wasn't a headless ghost that time. You see, whatever it was – or if there really was an "it" to begin with – it was different for everyone in the house. I have a reason as to why it appears differently each time depending on the person, but my rationale sounds really crazy. I'll just let you decide what you make of it. I will simply give an account of what had happened over the years.

My father's strange encounter, years earlier, began innocently enough with a conversation in our sari-sari store (essentially a Filipino convenience store selling groceries and all sorts of cheap odds and ends). The person he was talking to was sitting, reading a newspaper which they held up so that it covered their face and upper body. Despite this, my father felt sure it was my mother he was speaking to. It was past closing hours. Everything had been boarded up. It was just the two of them in there. At some point, he left the store and went inside our house, which were both in the same building. And there, in the house, was mother. You could just about hear a panicky who-was-I-talking to back there squeak from my father. Remembering this now, I find it funny, a sad sort of funny moment, like a bad joke heard by another person who looked just like me but much, much younger. Only that time, it was like being in a B-movie scene with everyone not making any move to check inside the store and find out the identity of the person whose upper body, including the face, was strategically covered by a newspaper. We never had an up-close-and-personal reunion with that entity pretending to read a newspaper while listening to my father talk. There was nobody else in the store.

A few years ago, my mother heard a man's voice chirp pleasantly, "Good morning, ma'am". My mother was busy, hunched in the store counter. It was early in the morning, before the store's opening time. When she looked up to see where the voice was coming from, she saw a man wearing white clothes and that was it – just a "man" in white clothes who was there one moment and was gone the next. Like in my father's case with the silent listener half-hidden by an unfurled newspaper, there was nobody else in the store.

My brother, who was in his early twenties then, used the bedroom my sister and I occupied when we were young. My brother went to sleep using only one blanket then woke up next morning swaddled securely in two blankets. The second blanket was once folded and stored inside a container under the bed. My brother claimed there was no way he could have gotten up in the middle of the night just to filch that other blanket.

Back in the early 1980s the sari-sari store took up almost the entire first floor of our house. The second floor served as our living quarters. And, as I said earlier, it was a place that sold all kinds of things. It can be found almost anywhere in the Philippines, regardless of whether the area is rural or urban. See the bananas, the Tagalog magazines, the sachets of shampoo, the miniature woven baskets. Inside, you can buy homemade *kamote* (sweet potato) cream slices, *ukay-ukay* (used clothes) sourced from Davao City, household supplies, Tagalog komiks for rent, even *tinapa* (dried smoked fish) and *bulad* (dried salted fish).

In 2015, that entity in the house struck again. It sported a wagging tail that made a familiar sound when it brushed against the store's wooden door. My sister and brother-in-law thought that our dog Penny had been accidentally locked in inside the store again. She had been left inside several times before, because she liked to stay under the shelves past closing time. They *knew* it was Penny because each time they called out her name while standing right outside the locked door of the store, the wooden door sounded the same way it did when her tail wagged and brushed it. Walking away from the locked store to retrieve the keys in another location, my sister and brother-in-law saw Penny – wiggling excitedly as usual and steadfast in her belief that the purpose of humanity was to fawn over her – outside the locked store. If Penny were inside, there was no way she could have gotten out of the store because that locked door was her only way out. As usual, we still joke about this incident involving little Penny's harmless, mischievous double. That's how we cope when the scale of the unknowable is tipped against our favor.

KILOMETER 30

Traveling along the 28-kilometer highway connecting the mountainous countryside of Upi to Cotabato City, motorists pass through the scenic Kilometer 30. This section of the national highway is bounded on one side by an eroded mountain rock face covered with trees. On the other side, past the guard rails, is a steep cliff. There were several instances when the cliff figured as a dumping site for bodies of people killed in situ, or in nearby Cotabato City. In May 2013, Kilometer 30 was the location of a politically related road ambush that resulted in one death. It is a strategic spot considering that it is right next to the national highway, as well as remotely hidden from view by trees and thick wild shrubbery.

Kilometer 30 has quite a reputation. The reputation has nothing to do with its mute complicity in the maneuverings of criminal elements. Motorists who leave an available sitting area inside their vehicles – whether they are driving an automobile or a motorcycle – just might *invite* something to join them in their journey. Motorists won't know they have managed to invite something from Kilometer 30, not until someone else who is right outside looking into the car, points out something extra in the backseat.

In two separate instances involving two different groups of motorists I know, a person who was not a passenger in the car, was seen by someone outside the vehicle. Arriving at his destination, Mario, a businessman acquaintance was asked by a surprised member of his household about the female passenger in the backseat. To Mario's knowledge, he had no such passenger. Another incident involved a close family friend, a physician's wife. Parking her car in the garage inside her home, she was asked when her passenger was coming out. And of course, she had no such passenger.

We can always blame it on reflections, the angle of light hitting the car glass window and making shadows that can be mistaken for another person. Or we can blame the small-town small mindedness that breeds superstitious beliefs and urban legends. But what I believe and think of Kilometer 30 and other places like it: a violent death can warp the place where it transpired. The more violent the manner of death, the more powerful the energy that gets dissipated and ends up being absorbed by the place where the violent death happened. The place holds this dark energy forever. It is unnoticeable until it decides to announce itself. And when it decides to announce itself, I believe it has the power to decide on which form it will take. Thus the Kilometer 30 extra passenger appears as a child for some observers looking into the car. For some, it is a woman. And this warping of place, this distortion is not anything that gets manifested in physical terms. It is not simply a blood stain on the ground, a blood stain that just won't fade. The distortion is in the manifold of reality whose nature is not completely known to us. The dark energy generated by violent deaths then becomes firmly rooted in place. It becomes part of the realm of place-specific pure elementals and nature spirits, which comprise the genius loci, the spirits of place.

THE POND, THE BABY, AND THE SECOND LAW OF THERMODYNAMICS

Let's go back to the two-story wooden house at Rizal Street, the house where I spent my formative years. One original feature of the property was a small shallow pond in the backyard. The ground near where the house stood is relatively thin and low lying. The house was constructed close to the underground water table, making it prone to flooding. The ground depression that produced the pond was later filled up. I have searched long and hard for photographs of the pond, but have not been able to find a single one.

It was in the early 1980s that I accidentally fell into the pond. Shortly thereafter, the pond depression was filled in with rocks, gravel, and soil. Now, it is completely paved, except for areas where there are fruit trees like jackfruit and pomelo.

I could not remember much about how I fell in or what I was doing that had me ending up in the water. Here is what I do remember: squatting on the bamboo flooring that lined one edge of the pond. I was watching the surface of the stagnant water, possibly for tadpoles or mosquito larvae, as there were many of those around. The next thing I remember was hitting the water and then another person in the household was helping me get cleaned up in the dark, dreary bathroom right in front of the staircase that led to the second floor of the house. I don't remember drowning or swallowing dirty pond water. There was nothing like that at all. What I remember was this sequence of events: hitting the water face down, being washed in the bathroom, and then Dr. Ampong, the country doctor, checking in on me after the pond gunk had been cleaned off of me.

Now this part is going to sound really crazy, although I assure you that I am not going for the unreliable narrator POV. Many years later, when my falling into the pond was brought up in a conversation, my mother said that no such thing happened, that I did not fall in the pond. Maybe she forgot about it because more than two decades have passed. I will ask other people about this some other time.

I was around ten years old when I encountered the "entity" that looked like a headless ghost to Babab, a newspaper-reading listener to my father, a white-clothed man who pleasantly greeted my mother a good morning, a caring provider of an extra blanket to my brother, and the unseen Penny-double with a wagging tail brushing against the wooden door to my sister and brother-in-law. I woke up in the middle of the night in the bedroom I shared with a younger sister. There was heavy beating on the floor, like a dull thumping sound made by hooves of animals in an excited state. There was no rhythm to the sound, just irregular loud thumping and drumming. The flooring is timber, bare timber regularly polished with wax. I sat up, alarmed. It was half dark. Window jalousies, covering almost the span of two walls, were letting in light from the outside. In my sister's bed, around five feet away from where I sat in my bed, I saw what looked like a baby. The baby-thing was lying on its back in the part of the bed near my sister's head pillow. It was shaped like a baby, as far as I can tell, because I could not fully make out its features. Its small hands were holding what appeared to me as a piece of foil. The foil was shiny and reflected the light from the windows. The baby-thing's tiny hands were moving, holding the piece of foil that made a sound, a crisp *tsk tsk tsk*. All in all, everything went on like this – the hoof beats on the floor and the little baby-thing with its tiny piece of shiny foil that made a crisp *tsk tsk tsk* sound – until I couldn't take it anymore and screamed, rushed to the other room where my mother slept and banged at her door. Days after that, I could not switch off the lights. I could not even go to the bathroom alone.

When I was older, I was able to find a sound enough scientific explanation for this unsettling experience. I find comfort in scientific explanations and neat differential equations as they tend to imply that there is somehow an inherent order and strategy in some aspects of this otherwise strange world. The one-time hair-raising phenomenon had something to do with the onset of puberty, a period in a person's life when the brain, as well as the body, is undergoing radical transformation. This is the reason for poltergeist activities occurring solely in the presence of pubescent kids or young females. The paper "Some conjectures about the mechanism of poltergeist phenomenon", archived online and in full by the Cornell University Library, was published in a 2008 volume of the journal *NeuroQuantology*. The transformation in the brain of a pubescent person is geared toward creating order or entropy reduction. This is counterbalanced by the brain dissipating greater entropy to the environment. Greater entropy in the environment can split some of the molecules of the component gases in the air, producing the weird noises I heard. For example, in normal conditions, like in room temperature and in the altitudes where we live, when an oxygen molecule is split, we end up with two atoms of oxygen. If we go high up to the stratosphere, then we might have to deal with three oxygen atoms for each molecule of ozone. The more oxygen molecules are split, the more oxygen atoms are there inside a room, which acts like a semi-isolated vessel for these gases. These atoms can collide with one another and with other atoms of air's component gases whose molecules were presumably split, thus increasing the air pressure. Rapid increase in air pressure could generate a rapping or drumming sound. The latter is a good justification to account for the weird hoof beats. On the other hand, a slow increase in air pressure is not likely to produce sound but it can trigger movements – an explanation for the baby-thing making soft noises with its brandishing of the shiny foil. I hope – and I wish – that I am dead-on correct. It happened around the time when I had my first menstruation, so it made sense to me that drastic electrochemical changes in my brain can temporarily alter my immediate environment. The alternative is just too disturbing for me to contemplate.

THE SCALE OF THE UNKNOWABLE
AND THE IRREPARABLE

The human body is equipped with sensory aids that function only in certain conditions. We can only see roughly between wavelengths 390 and 700 nanometers. In relation to the entire span of the electromagnetic spectrum ranging from the regions beyond the infrared and beyond the ultraviolet frequencies, our window of visibility is sorely limited. One can only imagine the colors that are invisible to us. The auditory range of the human ear also comes with its own narrow threshold. Our bodies cannot tolerate the very hot and the very cold. And so on and so forth, like a re-enactment of Plato's cave allegory. Understandably, this affects how we perceive our environment and how we decide which details we zero in on when we make conclusions about our environment. This selectivity skews our understanding of the world. Is the supernatural a psychological response? Or is it the other way around? Are archetypes, which are found to be common in various myths from cultures separated by time periods or geographical locations, enough proof of humans being wired a certain way? Meanwhile, memory, which is crucial to knowledge acquisition and learning, is locked in by associating it with place or a time period, according to the results of a study conducted by researchers at Dartmouth University and the University of North Carolina. And place, most especially the place where we spent our formative years, is where a good deal of our cultural conditioning occurs.

We can only do so much to curate the features that define our respective places and spaces. We can curate by setting boundaries, by surrounding ourselves with inanimate objects and living things that give us pleasure and comfort, by interacting with our environment according to our moral compass and ethical foothold. I believe that in so many ways, literature and the entire spectrum of creative arts are based on content curation. In literature, we select narratives we consider important. In selecting these narratives, I suppose we select them with the mindset of either an observer or a participant. One is not necessarily better than the other. It's just that an observer would pose different selection criteria from a participant's.

Many of my stories carry the recurring motif of the archetypal child. The child archetype plays a part in ten out of the sixteen stories in my book *Age of Blight*. In my other short story collection, *Butterfly Dream*, the count is four out of eight stories. I did not plan it this way. Perhaps, when I do my rounds of content curation, I intuitively deem that narratives about the archetypal child, from its exegesis to its excoriation, are important.

In addition, my attempts at mythologies woven across my various books are sometimes needlessly misanthropic. Human civilization is almost always depicted as a systematic, ever escalating wave of destruction. I'm not saying that this view is inaccurate. We all had a hand in putting the world in the state that it is in today, and the damage is irreversible. It is not going to get any better. The planet has ventured past the global temperature threshold, many times over than it has done so in the past, which was way before we got our hands on the cake and ate it, too. We even ate the proverbial hand holding the proverbial cake, including the proverbial body where the proverbial hand holding the proverbial cake was attached. The Amazon rainforest that was supposed to take in atmospheric carbon in its soil or trees is so overtaxed that it is now emitting more greenhouse gases than it can absorb. The permafrost in Alaska and Siberia has melted. Methane, a potent greenhouse gas, is underneath the Siberian permafrost. Methane makes the warming of the planet totally irreversible. It's like how characters in American movies would put it: "We're fucked." Then it gets better – or rather, worse – because the melting of the ground cover unearths pathogens. There was an anthrax outbreak in Russia – in Siberia, where permafrost had melted because of deforestation, among other causes. The anthrax spores came from reindeer carcasses that were once frozen under the permafrost. There are plastic wastes ending up all the way to the Arctic Circle. Then there's the depressing fact regarding the extinctions of many species in many places across the world. People violently subjugate other people, as well as other sentient creatures that had as much right as us to live on this planet. So, it is not surprising that place – its natural terrain and its distinctive markings – is relentlessly configured over and over according to whim, by people. At some point, nobody's going to be around anymore to artificially configure the landscape.

Most days, I think only about these things. I think about the latest new disease, the mosquito-borne Zika virus, because it has finally found its way to the Philippines. I think of smallpox buried in Siberia. I think of heat waves, rising sea levels, dynamite fishing, tortured bears and dogs and elephants in Asia, tortured bulls in Spain, trophy hunters and poachers and illegal loggers, captive animals in stupid circuses and petting zoos, tortured animals everywhere. I think of the brutal displacement of indigenous tribes just to get to the oil or metallic ores underneath their homes and farms. I think of the endangered species endemic to the area surrounding Liguasan Marsh in Mindanao. I think of the untapped oil and natural gas reserves long buried underneath the marshland. I think of what will become of these rare living creatures – creatures that pre-date human civilization – once good old Filipino-style greed gets to the oil, the oil that should not even be touched in the first place because it is just going to pump more and more greenhouse gases into the atmosphere. I think of my place here in the mountains of the Philippine south, where the lightning storms of August bring out delicious wild mushrooms in decaying banana stalks, corn fields, and rice fields. I think of my place here in the mountains of the Philippine south, where I condescend on city people cuisine that uses coconut milk in powder form. Here, real coconut meat found inside a real coconut is squeezed by hand to get real coconut milk. I think of my place here in the mountains of the Philippine south, where there are still lots of trees that may stave off the inevitable. There are times when I believe it is better off not knowing. This is one of those times.

Engkantos comprise some of the main characters in the pantheon of elementals and nature spirits in the Philippines. Filipino folklore tells of the *Kapre* (giant deity living in a tree), the *Tikbalang* (a creature with the body of a man and head and feet of a horse), the *Duwende* (an elf living in caves, rocks, anthills, termite mounds, or under the shade of old trees), and the ethereal *Maria Makiling*, a forest nymph considered to be a protective spirit of the mountain. I hope we'll never get the chance to trespass upon and mess up their pristine realm with our synthetic hormones, oil spills, plastics, and polymer microbeads.

Kristine Ong Muslim (b. September 1980, Kidapawan, Philippines) is the author of eight books of fiction and poetry: *Age of Blight* (Unnamed Press, 2016), *Butterfly Dream* (Snuggly Books, 2016),

Meditations of a Beast (Cornerstone Press/University of Wisconsin-Stevens Point, 2016), *Black Arcadia* (University of the Philippines Press, 2016), *Lifeboat* (University of Santo Tomas Publishing House, 2015), *A Roomful of Machines* (ELJ Publications, 2015), *Grim Series* (Popcorn Press, 2012), and *We Bury the Landscape* (Queen's Ferry Press, 2012).

Her fiction and poetry have appeared or is forthcoming in *Sunvault: Stories of Solarpunk & Eco-Speculation* (Upper Rubber Boot Books, 2017), *Ghost Fishing: An Eco-Justice Poetry Anthology* (University of Georgia Press, 2017), *Dadaoism (An Anthology)* (Chômu Press, 2012), *The Moment of Change: An Anthology of Feminist Speculative Poetry* (Aqueduct Press, 2012), *Confrontation Magazine, New Welsh Review, Existere, Southword, The State,* and *Weird Fiction Review,* among others.

She serves as poetry editor of *LONTAR: The Journal of Southeast Asian Speculative Fiction,* a literary journal published by Epigram Books in Singapore, and was co-editor with Nalo Hopkinson of the *Lightspeed Magazine* special issue, *People of Colo(u)r Destroy Science Fiction!.*

Widely anthologized and published in magazines in North America, Canada, and the UK, Kristine Ong Muslim grew up and continues to live in rural southern Philippines.

She can found online at kristinemuslim.weebly.com and on Twitter at @kristinemuslim.

THE GREAT MONGOOSE

Vajra Chandrasekera

I grew up in Rajagiriya, which is a suburb in Greater Colombo, just outside the border of the city proper. My maternal grandparents had moved onto that plot of land in the 1950s. By the time I was a kid in the 80s, it had been divided between my mother and her siblings, so I lived in a cul-de-sac with a dozen cousins. It was a dense neighbourhood, all trees and houses. I used to spend a lot of time off the ground, climbing both. Climbing trees (ambarella; bilimbi; king coconut; alligator pear; even bamboo, though carefully avoiding the culm sheaths, which were coated in fine black hairs that itched like the dickens), climbing roofs, climbing from one to the other. Clambering about barefoot on corrugated asbestos sheets burning hot in the sun – if you moved fast, it didn't burn so much – breathing in carcinogenic fibres like pollen, I would consider death-defying leaps between roofs and then for the most part decide sensibly not to defy death that day. (I only fell out of a tree one time, an otherwise cooperative *Pisonia alba*, and walked away with nothing but bruises. My ribs ache just remembering it now.)

I also grew up in nested, competing etymologies. Names and meanings tend to be contested here. Ceylon, Lanka, Eelam – is that too easy an example? I've heard four different explanations for why Colombo is called Colombo, and only one of them was a joke. Even Rajagiriya has a complicated etymology. What seems like the literal and most obvious meaning of Raja-giri is *the king's hill* or *the royal hill*. Rajagiriya is indeed a low hillock, and the story is that the king in Kotte in the early 16th century, bedevilled by the Portuguese, had the hill used as a vantage point for his sentries, overlooking the way between the port and the city. My house used to be at the top of the hill, never flooding in the rainy season

My parents dismissed this overly literal etymology and supported another theory: that *Rajagiriya* actually meant Great Mongoose (the *giri* being actually *kiri*, shortened from the Tamil word for mongoose), named after a particularly exotic specimen – a white mongoose – that had been sighted in the grounds of the local manor-house sometime in the late 19th or early 20th century.

This manor-house sat directly across the street from our family cul-de-sac, and it has a complicated history of its own. It was built in the 1820s during the British occupation, as a residence for the governor, Lieutenant-General Sir Edward Barnes. It was later bought by Ananda Coomaraswamy, the historian and philosopher of art. Later still it was owned by the Hewavitharanas, the family of the Anagarika Dharmapala (my mother taught at the neighbourhood school they founded). And finally by a wealthy family known as the Obeysekeras, a large extent of the property flaking away over the decades and ending ignominiously in lawsuits and disrepair. All four owners named above have streets or neighbourhoods named after them today. When I was a kid it was just a big old house in the neighbourhood that some rich people lived in. When it was new, though, its grounds encompassed *all* of what is now the dense suburban town of Rajagiriya. For a year or so recently, I lived in Rajagiriya again, renting a house on Madinnagoda Road and working in an office off Cotta Road, my daily four-kilometre commute never leaving what was once Edward Barnes' estate.

Rajagiriya is most probably a new name, then, perhaps less than a century old. It replaced an older, stranger name: *Yakbadda*, a name still very occasionally used by older residents when I was a boy. The easiest translation of this is "the Devils' Forest", though of course this is not accurate because the names for the otherworldly – the spirits of this place – were translated awkwardly during the British occupation and made to fit into mappings that don't suit them. The *yaka, naga, rakusa, pereta* are all generic devils or demons in English. The 1901 W.H.D. Rouse translation of the Jataka tales renders the half-human, half-bird figure of the *kinnara* variously as "spirit", "sprite", and "fairy". But a *kinnara* is not a fairy any more than a *yaka* is a demon. The problem isn't about what would be a better translation – would the *pereta* be more accurately described as a hungry ghost, or a vampire, or an unquiet spirit? – but rather that they are being translated at all. In this kind of translation, there is always an imperial mapping of the one to the other, which sets the "demon" as the more general, universal category, and the *yaka* as a particular, local category that may be considered to belong in its entirety to the former. The problem is the framing of the *yaka* as a *kind* of demon, and the sheer persistence of this framing.

A better way to read the *yaka* is to read it as itself: a *yaka*, a primary category in its own right. That would leave us room to look for the root of *yaka* perhaps in the word *yajna*, to worship, and that both the *yaka* and the *rakusa* – the *yaksha* and *rakshasa*, to give them their older names – come from a now obscure creation myth. They were the first to come into being after the creation of the primordial waters and represented, in some ways, the first choice: some chose to worship the water, and were called *yaksha* (meaning "worshippers"). Others chose to protect the water, and were called *rakshasa* (meaning "protectors"). These are their ancient functions. But that's not how we see them today, because their re-framing as demons and devils has been altogether too successful.

We're reminded only in the margins that there's a world outside that framing: for instance, in the adivasi usage of *yaka* to refer to gods – e.g., the *kande-yaka*, the god of the mountain – or in half-forgotten phrases like *nae yakku*, where the prefix means "kin" or "family", and *yakku* is just the plural of *yaka*. The *nae yakku* are, of course, the beloved dead. But this is another idea that's difficult to translate because there are so many better-known traditions of ancestor veneration. It runs the danger of being subsumed. I hesitate over the words to explain it: do I say *"spirits"* when this seems to have Christian connotations that would be irrelevant here? It's not an *"afterlife"* because reincarnation is a given. If there are many worlds and many lives and many states of being, then every life is already an afterlife, and a before-life. The *nae yakku*, then, are the recognition of a kin relationship across the boundary of death and rebirth. In its own way, it is an assertion of kin-relationship with all that has ever lived.

I moved out of Rajagiriya after my mother died; my father lived in the same house for a few more years until he, too, died. I sold the house after that, because I couldn't face the thought of living there again. Grief takes its due and for me all of Rajagiri-ya was a wound. I told myself I would never live there again. I spent years living in the city of Colombo, or in other suburbs like Nawala and Pita Kotte. Of course, eventually circumstances dictated that I move back to Rajagiriya for a while, because this is the sort of thing that happens. The house I rented required me to commute past the house I'd grown up in – which no longer existed by then, since the new owners had demolished it and built their own, which respected not at all the childish mytho-logical relationships I had built with the stones and the trees of that place. This is a trivial example, but I don't mean it facetiously. This is pretty much how all territory works, as I understand it: alienation, renaming, grief.

At my mother's funeral, my uncle – her younger brother – said something generically Western-sounding about feeling her spirit close by, which made my father very angry.

This was after the cremation, when we'd all come back to the house for what is known as the meal of the dead. (It has a particu-lar menu, with dry fish and a pumpkin curry, although I have no idea why.) In villages like the one my father was from, cremation is a very personal affair. A large pyre is built on the village crema-tion-grounds and lit with a torch by a nephew of the deceased, who must face away from the pyre while they light it. I've done this for uncles and aunts; I suspect one of the reasons it's tradi-tionally a nephew is that it leaves the immediate family in peace to grieve. The pyre takes a long time to burn down, and you watch it with the heat lapping at your face, the ash in your hair, the great fire roaring.

In the city, cremation means going to the crematorium like the one at at the Borella Cemetery and pressing a button. In an awkward adaptation, it's still a nephew who presses the button, facing away from the machine. There is no heat, no fire, no ash: just faint wisps of smoke, too high up to smell. Some people still react emotionally to the smoke when it rises: it's the only way to know that something is happening.

(Later, the crematorium attendants will sift through the ashes and give you some in a clay pot so that you can scatter them into flowing water. You have to bring your own clay pot. Crematoria are inefficient, so sometimes these ashes include shards of bone. When it was my father's turn some years later, I found myself handling a piece of his skull. We gave it to the river just the same.)

The meal of the dead is usually not so sombre an affair. It's a breaking of tension, after the emotional intensity of the long vigil and the climactic cremation. Everybody feels a little better after eating. In my experience, this is also a moment when people sometimes relax too much and say unwise things that they might not have otherwise said. I don't know how my uncle came up with the thing about feeling my mother's spirit, but my mother's family were very urban Buddhists who grew up around Christians, so it must have seemed like a natural borrowing. I recognized the form of the statement from TV shows, at least, and ignored it as quaint but harmless.

To my father, though, my uncle was saying something unthinkable. He didn't watch those TV shows and his Buddhism was more old-school. Only *peretas* ("hungry ghosts") could be nearby enough to be felt – the beloved dead don't haunt us, because haunting is for wretched spirits that lack the virtue to move on. He heard it as an accusation, and it made him furious. It raised the devil in him.

You see how I talk about place instead of walking in it. I start with the layers of names and the tensions between them, because I want to say that since the Treaty of Tordesillas, when Spain and Portugal first divided the world between them, there is no *flânerie* in the divided world.

Consider walking. I first read Thoreau's *Walking* in my father's library; it was included in a collection of essays, one in a big pile of books my father inherited from his uncle, who lived in a village in the north-west named Yakvila, which ordinarily would be translated "the Devils' Lake" – there are devils everywhere. When I first read *Walking*, I wondered if my great-uncle had felt that way about the woods in the back of his own garden. I doubt it, though. I've been in that forest as a boy and it's not exactly a pleasant stroll: it was spiky, unwelcoming jungle, thick with thorny undergrowth and lacking paths. I remember being shown, as a boy, how exactly to break a branch to placate the god of the forest – or the devil, depending how you translate it.

Thoreau wrote *Walking* in the 1850s, a few years after the Matale Rebellion. (Matale is up in the mountains: my paternal grandfather's family supposedly came from there, moving to flatter country in the north-west sometime in the generation after the Rebellion. The Matale Rebellion was violently suppressed by the 7th Viscount Torrington, who also has a street named after him in Colombo today.) Thoreau comes up with two folk etymologies for the word to "saunter" – to be a "*sainte-terrer*", a holy-lander on pilgrimage, or to be "*sans terre*", without home "in the good sense... having no particular home, but equally at home everywhere". But of course, Thoreau is not talking about the peoples who were systematically displaced from the land

that he and his ilk consider empty and free to be experienced –
to be explored.

I find it difficult sometimes to read exploration as other than a
euphemism for empire and exploitation. The first-contact stories
of the age of empires (Vasco de Gama, James Cook, Lorenzo
de Almeida) make much more sense if we frame them as alien
invasions whose consequences shape the world to this day. One
of the smaller consequences is how public space was constructed
in the post-apocalyptic world that those alien invasions created,
and how that public space became navigable by different groups
of people.

Most of the formerly occupied territories of the world are
formally independent now, even the settler colonies. But this
independence is a quaint and peculiar nationhood often stated
explicitly in European terms: it often sits awkwardly on a polity
that is separated from its original time-line by five centuries of
war and occupation. The nationalisms that grow out of the urge
to *be* something – to find a thing that we are, that we can be proud
of, that we can lay claim to, something that we can no longer
remember – are invariably virulent, often violent, and almost
never sane. It's difficult to even talk about culture and heritage at
all, much less from an anti-imperialist position, without accidentally giving aid and comfort to burgeoning fascisms. Looking
back and not looking back are both dangerous now, leaving us
stuck in a side-eye from a half-turn.

How do we walk, under nationalism or under occupation? I
can't count the number of times I was stopped by police on the
streets of Colombo during the war years, and I was never even in

the target demographic. On a particularly memorable occasion, I was stopped "randomly" three times while walking halfway up Horton Place, from Wijerama to Town Hall: a distance of about seven hundred metres.

Horton Place is named after Robert Wilmot-Horton, who was governor sometime after Barnes and sometime before Torrington; all of their streets are in the same posh neighbourhood, part of what's called Cinnamon Gardens because it used to be Dutch cinnamon plantations in the 18th century. At the start of that century during the Dutch occupation, a little over half of Colombo's population were slaves, mostly transported from South India or Southeast Asia. (Sri Lankan slaves, meanwhile, were similarly transported elsewhere, such as South Africa: Dutch policy was that slaves were easier to control when they were always strangers in a strange land.) Slaves walking in public were required to avoid jostling or getting in the way of Europeans, a crime for which they would be whipped; they were not allowed to use the side-walk at all, unless in attendance on their owners. Slaves were also not allowed to have long hair or wear hats, as this made it easier to identify them.

This was not a mechanism successfully transplanted to the 21st century by the militarized and paranoid state security machine, much as they would have loved it – this is why I always needed my national identity card to prove to the police that I was Sinhala, not Tamil, and therefore (taking a moment to underline the blunt grimness of that *therefore*) not a target for harassment, arbitrary arrest or detention. In our periodic riots, Sinhala mobs in search of Tamil or Muslim people to assault but still unable to identify them on sight (because we all pretty much look the same) would demand that potential targets perform their Sinhala-ness or Buddhist-ness with shibboleths: pronouncing particular words to test for accents, or reciting Buddhist prayers that people of other religions were unlikely to know. For example, the ඉතිපිසෝ, which in a great irony is a recitation of the virtues of the Buddha, probably including suitably incongruous things like kindness and compassion. I say *probably* even though I know it by heart (I suspect my not-particularly-pious parents insisted on me learning these prayers by memory in anticipation of future riots) because the prayer is in Pali, not Sinhala, and I've long since forgotten what the words mean: to me, it's just a string of sounds that represent thuggish fanaticism.

Of course, without justifying this militarized police state, one can also point out that one of the other dangers of public space in the war years was being blown up by a suicide bomber. My seventh-grade classroom was shaken up pretty good the day the Joint Chiefs exploded across the street – our school building held up, though it was declared unsafe after that day – and what I remember most clearly (apart from being smacked on the head by pieces of ceiling) is that the kids cheered even before the debris settled, because we knew a bomb that nearby meant that school would have to be closed for a while. (A few weeks, as it turned out, the delay mostly being to find different buildings for the seventh-graders to have classes.) I cheered too. I mean, I was twelve. I'd like to say I didn't know any better, but I think I did: it's just that by that point we were all quite used to the idea that the city around would occasionally explode, and that people would die.

Consider public space: volatile, hostile, explosive, already full of ghosts.

I dislike walking in the city even more than I dislike walking in the forest. The forest belongs to old gods who might be demons; I know how to placate them. The city is a contested ground, full of claims, full of ghosts. By definition, wherever you may wander in the city, somebody's already been there, lived there, died there. They may be my *nae yakku* too, at whatever remove – we're all 50th cousins at most, so they say – but they are not so easy to placate as mere gods.

Behind gods, ghosts, and people squats the state, which asserts total access to both public and private space: the Prevention of Terrorism Act allows police the right to enter and search any premises without warrant. I once had my house searched by armed police bright and early on a Saturday morning in late 2011. They never explained what they were looking for, and I have no idea why it happened unless it had something to do with my work. The war was over by then, but post-war Sinhala triumphalism was stronger than ever, and I'd been working with anti-war human rights activists for some time, perhaps long enough to be tangentially included as a footnote on somebody else's file. Who knows? Maybe a suspicious neighbour thought I was a drug kingpin like Walter White. The raid was particularly surreal for me because my brother had died six weeks before that, and nothing had quite felt real since – nothing ever did again, but this was so early into that state of irreality that I half wondered if it was some kind of anxiety dream brought on by too many painkillers.

Grief is a nation, like the dead are a nation. These are the nationalisms I can get behind.

In 1915, the British used Maxim guns on civilians in Colombo to suppress a series of riots. The story of the riots themselves is quite complicated and I won't go into it here. What I'm looking at is the shaping of public space: the British installed Maxim guns at the choke-points of ingress to the city. To the north, a Maxim gun was placed at Victoria Bridge, which was the only bridge over the Kelani until 1959 (despite being eventually superseded by two newer bridges, the original Victoria Bridge remained open until 1998, the year I graduated secondary school). Another one in the south at Wellawatte Bridge, a similar choke-point at what was then the other side of the city. Within the city, one at Kuruwe Street, now Hussainiya Street; another at Messenger Street, now M.J.M. Lafeer Mawatha, and so on: the intent being able to control Wolfendhal Street (a Dutch translation of *Guadalupe*, after a Portuguese church of a previous century) on the one side and Sea Street on the other, commanding the core of the city at that time. Entrapment, enclosure, control: this is the mechanism.

The guns were fired, of course: at least a hundred died, and hundreds more injured in those early days alone. A few days later, martial law was declared: first in the western province, and then gradually in most of the other provinces as well. People who broke curfew after 6pm, knowingly or otherwise, were shot. Brigadier-General Henry Huntly Leith Malcolm instructed his soldiers to "not waste ammunition, but shoot through the heart any Sinhalese that may be found on the streets". The following year, Malcolm (by then transferred to France for World War I) was made a Companion of the Order of St. Michael and St. George.

This is a pattern. It repeats, note for note, in the Amritsar massacre in 1919: where Colonel Reginald Dyer trapped thousands of civilians in the Jallianwala Bagh in Punjab and then had troops fire on them. The number of the dead is contested, as it always is, but at least hundreds, perhaps a thousand. In both cases, there were pretexts (clashes between Sinhala and Muslim communities in Colombo in 1915; a British woman, Marcella Sherwood, attacked during a riot in Amritsar in 1919) and a reason underneath (fear of revolt in the occupied territories, possibly backed by Germany.) There are differences in the pattern, too. Dyer didn't get a medal and was mildly censured by the British authorities; he did get £26,000 raised by a benefit fund run by a British newspaper, though. And Dyer did manage a particular shaping of public space that Malcolm did not: about a week after the massacre, he issued an order that all Indians using the street where Marcella Sherwood was attacked were required to crawl its full length, about 180 metres.

Consider public space. Consider walking in it, or crawling. Perhaps all *flânerie*, all sauntering, should begin in crawling. Perhaps the first step in discovering the truth of place is to abandon all pretence of being separate from the world, of being able to assert any control over it – to be the civilized saunterer, Thoreau's Walker Errant, to be the one who observes and experiences – and to get down on our hands and knees, to put our bellies against the ground, our faces against the earth. There is something restful in being brought low, in breathing in the dirt, in feeling all the little sharp discomforts of gravel on skin.

I'm wary of touching the city: I'm wary of the ease with which meaning can be imposed on it. Growing up in wartime – in many ways, growing up *with* the war, maturing as it festered, only slowly learning that war wasn't normal, or permanent – left me with a sense for the fragility of history. How contested history can be, how easily the past changes under pressure. A minor example: during the war, any Wikipedia page about Sri Lanka's history was constantly edited and re-edited by partisans of either side, in ham-fisted attempts to legitimize one myth or another about our roots: while the war itself was fought over a quarter-century, the conflict of mythologies played out on a scale of twenty-five centuries in an effort to establish whose claim was primary, or who was the original aggrieved party. And of course, these mythologies are always at least proto-fascist: it's always ancient glories and lost wonders, chosen peoples, and sacred homelands. It's always shit that never ends well. It's always shit that never ends.

Yaka is a verbal commonplace in Sinhala. People use it to refer casually to each other, as if it meant bloke or blighter. The Sinhala equivalent of "I'm so hungry I could eat a horse" is යකෙක් කන්න බඩගිනියි – I'm so hungry I could eat a devil. To say that someone lost their temper, we say යකා නැගලා – someone's raised the devil in them. Devils everywhere. Their depiction in art or in sculpture – in the famous devil masks, for instance – is traditionally grotesque, distorted humanoid faces with bulging eyes and distended fangs. They are at the same time figures of exaggerated horror, and easy, familiar presences in our lives, both apart and not.

(Ironically for Sri Lankans, who love nothing more than contesting who was here first, one thing that has never been contested is that the *yakku* have an ancient right to this territory. They were here before we were: our own origin myth tells us so.)

The place where that comfortable familiarity overlaps the horror is the devil dance. There are some variations of this, but I'm talking about the classic *daha ata sanniya*: the eighteen devils of sickness. I haven't seen it done since I was very young, and I have to admit my reaction at the time was mostly boredom. The *daha ata sanniya* goes on for a long time and is quite repetitive.

Each devil represents a kind of illness, either physical or mental: each has a particular type of mask, and the dancers wearing the masks appear in turn, so that the demon can be appeased, mocked, or cajoled to remove their malign influence. The play is about methodically demystifying the devils: they appear first to be frightening, but then are humbled. Devils brought low, made to crawl.

There are devils of boils, of vomiting, of epilepsy, of cholera, of malaria. There are devils of insanity and of nightmares. The specificity of the "eighteen" is something of a misnomer: there can be more, or fewer. There are regional or contextual variations between which ones actually are performed on any particular occasion. New ones are sometimes invented as needed: I've heard of, but never seen performed, the devil of bullet wounds. I imagine that existential dread probably ought to get a devil. A devil of post-colonial angst. A devil of complicated grief.

In *Walking*, Thoreau remarks that there is a harmony "between the capabilities of the landscape within a circle of ten miles' radius, or the limits of an afternoon walk, and the threescore years and ten of human life. It will never become quite familiar to you."

It's remarkable how well that fits me, as much as I hate walking. I've completed a little over half my threescore and ten, and barring brief excursions, I've lived all of it in a circle of that radius from the place where I was born. I wouldn't even remotely claim that I knew that circle well. I barely know it at all. There is far too *much* in it. People; history; overlapping, contested, nested loops of power and ideology. Ghosts and devils.

I don't object that the space is so occupied. What I object to is the mere thought of "exploring" it in a lifetime's worth of after-noon sauntering: that exhausts me, and bothers me besides. I would rather crawl belly to the earth right here, and accept that the circle shall remain a total mystery. Stomping about thrusting oneself into the world to experience it is not intrinsically better than lying down in it and letting it take you in its tide. But this caveat aside, there is still a fundamental true thing here: there is a scale at which a lived life can map to landscape. Very few of us ever operate at a bigger scale, and that only at the loss of fine resolution.

Let's come back to Ananda Coomaraswamy for a moment, who used to live across the street from the house in Rajagiriya where I would grow up some decades later. Writing about the *yaksha* in the 1920s-30s, Coomaraswamy talked about their origin story, what he called the water cosmology. The *yaksha* are power-fully identified with the primordial waters that they worship, and so with rain, vegetation, abundance, and life. Coomaraswamy considered them a pre-Vedic life cult, later assimilated into more familiar theologies, and as such that they were originally tutelary spirits that might be associated with rivers and trees, or with clans and kingdoms.

The gap between this ancient life cult and the dark comedy of the *daha ata sanniya* is tens of centuries deep. Virtually anything would change in that time, especially given how eventful the last few centuries have been. But I don't think it's changed beyond recognition. We still recognize that there are devils everywhere, even if it's now mostly in language and fading place-names, rather than in dances or shrines. The devils are in us, of us: they connect us to the primordial waters, to the rain and the river, to the sea, and the growing things. Or rather, they are a sign that we were never apart from those things.

Belly to the dirt, then–

Without exploration; without discovery; without observing; without experiencing; is it possible to simply *occupy* a place? So much of our negotiation with place is about seeking out *other* places. Better places to live and work; stranger or wilder or richer places to exploit and experience; afterlives of more comfort and solace than this one. But at the centre of the circle, always, there we are.

Perhaps the entire over-engineered concept of endless rebirth only recapitulates the much smaller, simpler idea that nothing material is destroyed – we already know that the matter of our bodies is reincarnated endlessly in both organic and inorganic form. We have continuity with everything that our bodies will ever be or have already been, shit and stars alike. How this differs from the conventional notion of rebirth is only in the lack of individual selfness in this transmission. It's not the world that's transient: it's us. The matter of our bodies is accounted for – the pattern of our minds, though, is not, and this is why we grieve. Information is the only thing that can be lost in an imperishable universe. Mind is the only thing that truly dies.

Human history is a crushing litany of loss by this measure, but like landscape, it's also too big to consider: we are bounded by our point of view. There is a harmony between the holding capacity of our threescore and ten, and the depth of grief we are asked to carry within it. Or at least, I hope so. And if I'm wrong, I hope that my *nae yakku* will carry me through.

Vajra Chandrasekera is a writer from Colombo, Sri Lanka, and his favourite etymology for "Colombo" is not kola-amba-thota (the port with green mango trees), not kolonthota (from Kelani-thota, the port at the mouth of the Kelani river) and not Christopher Columbus, but rather a dad joke where the punchline is කබෝඳළමට බැත්, which means "barking like a fool". See, a white man asked a local what this place was called, but the local thought they were being asked for an explanation of why the dog was so noisy...

Vajra's short stories have appeared in several dozen speculative fiction magazines, podcasts, and anthologies since he started writing in 2012, including *Black Static*, *Clarkesworld*, *Lightspeed*, the *Apex Book of World SF*, and *Strange Horizons*; and have been translated into (so far) Chinese, French, Italian, German, Spanish, and Dutch. In 2016 he joined *Strange Horizons* as a fiction editor and is now finding out what it's like on the other side of the table.

He blogs occasionally at vajra.me and can be found on Twitter at @_vajra.

DEATH IMITATING ART AT CASTLE AN DINAS

Joanne Parker

I t is not your average commute from work. In the summer months I drive, pilot-like, above islands of low-lying white cloud enshrouding every valley, and past constellations of tiny white flowers that wave on the verges. But it is in the winter months, when the A30 is near-empty in Cornwall, that the journey home up the nobbled back of Bodmin Moor feels most unearthly. Most nights I make my way through an oblivion of fog that obliterates even the rocky top of Brown Willy and the glowing lights of Jamaica Inn. It is a place where I dread the thought of a flat tyre or a burnt-out clutch. This high land of twisted tors and peaty pools is wreathed in myth and folklore. There is, of course, the leg- endary Beast of Bodmin Moor – the panther-like creature spotted at least sixty times in the last thirty years. But there is also Jan Tregeagle, the corrupt magistrate who is pursued by hell-hounds across the moor on dark nights, and poor Charlotte Dymond who wanders the slopes of Rough Tor where her body was found in 1844. There are more reputed smugglers' haunts than you could shake a bottle of rum at. And, just one mile from the tarmac of the A30, there is Castle an Dinas.

From the road, Castle an Dinas does not look impressive – certainly not enough to lure any of the column of camper vans and heavily-laden family cars that pass it every summer to briefly detour from their goal of sea, sand, and ice-cream. And there is no brown heritage sign to encourage visitors. Just a small roadsign pointing down a narrow farm track, a little, rough-surfaced car-park at the end of it, and beyond that a narrow grassy footpath. But close up, the scale of Castle an Dinas cannot fail to impress. Measuring 850 feet across, this Iron Age hill fort has three concentric ditches and ramparts – the highest sections of the embankments standing almost seven feet high. Walking between those towering turfed walls the nearby road and the new homes and shops at Indian Queens feel a world away. It is a place to hide – a place to lose yourself in.

Climb to the top of the hillfort, though, and the world spreads before you. Castle an Dinas is not only one of the biggest but also one of the most impressively sited hillforts in Cornwall, standing in an imposing position on the exposed summit of Castle Downs, 700 feet above sea level. Its original occupants would have commanded views across central Cornwall that stretched on a clear day as far as both the North and the South coast. There is evidence that this site has been considered important for as long as the area has been inhabited by man. The hill fort we see today was built in the second and third centuries BC, but a pair of barrows in the central enclosed area suggest that the hill was used earlier, in the Bronze Age (2500 – 800 BC). And a flattened platform between the outer and inner banks has been interpreted as the remains of an even earlier structure, from the Neolithic period (4000 – 2500 BC).

In its days as a hillfort, Castle an Dinas's earth and stone ramparts were probably topped by a wooden palisade, while the centre would have enclosed wooden roundhouses. It would have been a focus of community pride – a symbol of its tribe's power and wealth – and a place where trade, ceremonies, and rituals took place. The cobbled entrance to the hillfort speaks of a time when a constant traffic of hooves and feet would otherwise have turned the ground into a quagmire. At that time, Castle an Dinas must also have been looked upon fondly by its tribe, as a place of security. Although Iron Age hillforts were not used as permanent dwelling places, they were secure strongholds that could be retreated to in times of inter-tribal conflict. And with a natural spring in its centre, Castle an Dinas could have sheltered its tribe for prolonged periods.

From being a place of shelter and safety in pre-history, though, Castle an Dinas became one of the darkest sites in Cornwall – a place that would be linked with betrayal and violent death across more than five hundred years. There is no archaeological evidence that Castle an Dinas was used after the Iron Age – though there have only been limited excavations at the site, in the 1960s. However, it's been suggested that the existence of stories about the hillfort from medieval times might point to the site's continuing importance and significance in the Post-Roman and the Early Medieval periods.[1]

The earliest surviving written account of Castle an Dinas is in William Worcester's 1478-1480 *Itineraries* – his account of his travels through Britain, including Cornwall. According to

Worcester, Castle an Dinas was "where Tador, Duke of Cornwall, the husband of Arthur's mother was killed".[2] The story of Arthur's mother was first related in Geoffrey of Monmouth's influential *History of the Kings of Britain*, which had been composed more than three centuries earlier, by 1138. According to that, in the late fifth century, King Arthur's father Uther had ordered all the nobility of Britain to meet in London to celebrate a festival. There he caught sight of Igerna, the wife of the Duke of Cornwall (here called Gorlois – Arthurian names in all the early sources are as slippery as a West Country eel). She was, he tells us, "the greatest beauty in all Britain".[3] Uther was smitten, and made little attempt to disguise this fact. Consequently, Gorlois packed up and returned to Cornwall poste-haste, afraid of losing his wife. Uther sent messages commanding him to return to court, and when Gorlois (understandably) ignored them, the lascivious king marched into Cornwall with an army, setting fire to any towns and villages that had the ill luck to be in his path.

Gorlois, William tells us, sent Igerna to "Tintagel, upon the sea-shore, which he looked upon as a place of great safety. But he himself entered the castle of Dimilioc, to prevent their being both at once involved in the same danger, if any should happen".[4] Tintagel Castle was known to be impregnable, but Merlin (here described as a 'prophet') used remarkable medicines to give Uther the appearance of Gorlois so that the old saucepot was admitted to the castle, enjoyed the delights of Igerna, and fathered the future King Arthur. Poor Gorlois, meanwhile, charged out of Dimilioc to fight Uther's army and was killed.

We can never know why William Worcester assumed that Castle an Dinas was Dimilioc. Where did he read this? Or – perhaps more likely - who told him? Scholars today consider that the village of St Dennis near Newquay, which has a large conical hill, now church-topped but once fortified, is more likely to have been the site that Geoffrey of Monmouth was thinking about, since William the Conqueror's Domesday Book lists a manor there by the name "Dimelihoc".[5] However, Castle an Dinas with its large banks and moorland setting undisputedly looks more impressive. And there is also evidence that the area around it has long been associated with the Arthurian legends. In 1123, the Canons of Laon in northern France went on tour around Britain, carrying with them a miracle-working shrine of Our Lady, as a way of raising funds to rebuild their cathedral, which had been burnt in a riot in 1112.[6] In 1146, Hermann de Tournai wrote an account of the trip, in which he described how, in the vicinity of Bodmin:

> A certain man having a withered arm kept a vigil at the shrine to recover his health. In just the same way as the Bretons are accustomed to argue with the French about King Arthur, the same man began to bicker with one from our community by the name of Hangello [...] saying that Arthur still lived. Then there arose not a small tumult; many men rushed into the church with arms and if the aforementioned cleric Algardus had not prevented it, it would almost certainly have come to the spilling of blood.[7]

By the twelfth century, then, the inhabitants of Bodmin Moor were fiercely proud of their local area's legends of King Arthur – enough to fight to the death with dubious Frenchmen. So it is not at all unlikely that around that date or soon after, Castle an Dinas might have been claimed by locals as the site of Gorlois' death, and that three centuries after that the story might have passed into local folklore so that it was then relayed to William Worcester on his visit to the area. Certainly, by the start of the sixteenth century, the association between Castle an Dinas and the Dukes of Cornwall seems to have been well established, because in the 1504 miracle play *The Life of St Meriasek*, there is a character known as the Duke of Cornwall who states that he owns a castle "called Tyntagel" but also lives in "the castle of Dynas".[8] It was perhaps descriptions like this which led later visitors to expect not a hillfort, but rather a grand, stone-built castle when they visited the site. In 1538, when the antiquary John Leland toured Cornwall, he was somewhat disappointed to discover "no building" at Castle an Dinas but only "an hille bering that name".[9]

Today, Bodmin Moor has many Arthurian place-names and folklore – most of the traditions undateable and untraceable in the mists of Cornish history and folklore. There is Dozmary Pool, believed to be bottomless – a dark, unnaturally still water into which King Arthur's Excalibur is believed to have been tossed. There is King Arthur's Bed – a man-shaped indentation in the granite summit of Trewortha Tor, where Arthur's body is said to have been lain. There was once a stone bearing the hoofmarks of Arthur's horse – though that has now been lost. And there is King Arthur's Hall – the impressive 47-foot-long remains of a rectangular, earth and stone Bronze-age ceremonial site. The area around that earthwork is known as King Arthur's Downs; Goss Moor, around Castle an Dinas, is reputed to have been the hunting ground of King Arthur; and Castle an Dinas itself is sometimes claimed to have been Arthur's hunting seat. While this geographic folklore gives to Bodmin Moor a spirit of romance and mystery, none of it has reverberated down the ages like the tragic story of lustful jealousy said to have taken place at Castle an Dinas.

Whether or not the Duke of Cornwall really did die outside the great earthen banks of Castle an Dinas, the hillfort was to be associated with other deaths – all of them connected to women

– in later centuries. Two hundred years after William Worcester wrote about the death of Gorlois at the hillfort, the monument reputedly witnessed a yet more gruesome demise. John Trehemben was a local boy – from St Columb, less than three miles from the banks of Castle an Dinas. Turning carefully through the huge pages of the St Columb parish records, now housed on the outskirts of Truro, I found the record of his birth on 7th August 1651, and his baptism four days later. The next mention of him in the records comes on 23rd June 1671, just six weeks before his twentieth birthday. It states:

> Anne daughter of John Pollard of this parish and Loveday the daughter of Thomas Rosevere of St Enoder, were both most barbarously murdered the day before in the house of Captain Peter Pollard att [sic] the bridge, by one John the sone [sic] of Humphrey and Cissily Trehemban of this parish, about 11 of the clock in the forenoone [sic], upon a market day.

The records leave many questions unanswered. Loveday, we know from her baptism entry, was 18 when she died. But what relation was Anne Pollard to Captain Peter Pollard? Why were the two girls together in that house? And what led young John to kill them, mid-morning, in the middle of a busy St Columb. This tragedy, though, is only the beginning of the story. In the parish records, at some point in history, somebody has drawn a large square bracket around the account of the murder to draw attention to it among the other births and deaths.

The mark may perhaps have been made by a Plymouth librarian in the nineteenth century. Certainly, Arthur Jewers seems to have paused over the record, because in 1881 when he published

an edition of the register, he added a note under the account of
the Trehemban crime which states: "traditions relative to the
murder still exist in the parish". Frustratingly, Jewers does not
say what the "traditions" are. But two months after his edition
of the register appeared , on June 4th 1881, a note appeared in
the *Weekly Mercury* newspaper, published in Plymouth, in a new
column titled "The Western Antiquary", which had just begun on
March 12th of that year. The note had been submitted by a Richard
Cornish of St Columb and was titled "Murder at St Columb, 210
Years Ago". It began by quoting from the parish register of St
Columb, but continued:

> The following tradition is given in connection with the
> above: "A bloodhound was obtained and set upon the trail,
> which it followed up a narrow lane, to the east of the union
> house, named Tremen's-lane; at the head, the hound made in
> an oblique direction towards the town, and in a narrow alley,
> known now as Wreford's row, it came upon the murderer in
> his father's house, and licked his boots, which were covered
> in blood". The sentence on Tremen [sic] was "that he be
> confined in an iron cage on the Castle Downs, 2 miles from
> St Columb, and starved to death". While in confinement
> he was visited by a country woman on her way home from
> market. The prisoner begged earnestly for something to eat;
> the woman informed him that she had nothing in the shape
> of food but a pound of candles; this being given to him, he
> ate them in a ravenous manner. It's a saying here, in refer-
> ence to a scapegrace, that he is a regular Tremen.[10]

It seems likely that Richard Cornish submitted his story in
response to the new edition of the parish records, with its myste-

riously vague reference to local "traditions". He does not actually state that John Trehemban was hung alive on Castle an Dinas – only on the Castle Downs of which the hillfort forms a part. But in later retellings of the story, the punishment always takes place actually on the exposed hillfort with its earlier, Arthurian associations with death. Intrigued by the gruesome story of John Trehemban's crime and punishment, I visited the National Archives in Kew to learn more about him. There I discovered, in the Western Circuit Gaol Books, that John Trehemban had been sentenced to death for the murder of the two girls at the Cornwall Autumn Assizes in 1672. His parents were also both tried as accessories to the murders, but both were found not guilty.

So was John Trehemban really starved to death in a cage at Castle an Dinas in 1672? Many districts in England have gruesome tales of a man being gibbeted or "hung in chains" while still alive. In Derbyshire they say that a tramp who murdered a woman by pouring hot fat down her throat was hung alive in chains behind Chatsworth House in the seventeenth century – his screams so disturbed the Duke that he then campaigned for an end to live gibbeting in that county. In Cumbria it is said that a notorious highwayman, John Whitfield, was gibbeted alive in 1777, until the guard of a passing mail-coach put him out of his misery by shooting him. In Durham there is a tale of an Andrew Mills who was gibbeted alive for murdering his master's three children while they slept. It is claimed that he was kept alive for some time by his sweetheart, who pushed a milk-soaked sponge through the bars of his cage. And in Norfolk there is a story of a man named Watson who, in the eighteenth century, was sentenced to die in a cage on Bradenham Heath for throwing his wife and child down the stairs.[11]

Most of these tales, however, begin to fall apart when names, dates, and details begin to be probed a little. In Merrington churchyard, on the tombstone of the three little children murdered in their sleep are the words: "He was executed and afterwards hung in chains", but by the 1890s the words "executed and" had been nearly obliterated by deep, deliberate chisel marks – perhaps to create the story, or else in an attempt to corroborate local legend, who knows? Likewise, in the late nineteenth century, when the Victorian adventure novelist Rider Haggard set to with a spade on Bradenham Heath at the site of the old gibbet, he discovered to his delight the iron cage which had once hung there. Inside, he recorded afterwards, was "a portion of the skull of the murderer who, so says tradition, killed his wife and child by throwing them downstairs". On the skull Haggard discovered "a mark of the searing of a hot iron [...] showing that the smith had set them there after death". He concluded that the legend of the live gibbeting could not be true, for "even during the last century hot irons would not have been welded onto a living man".[12]

In fact, the only certain cases of live gibbeting in Britain occurred during the reign of Henry VIII, when a small number of rebels were executed in this manner. The most famous case was Robert Aske, the leader of the Pilgrimage of Grace – a popular uprising in Yorkshire, protesting against Henry's break with the Catholic Church. Aske took days to die, hanging from the walls of York Castle in 1537. In his 1577 *Description of England*, written as an introduction to Holinshed's *Chronicles*, the Tudor historian William Harrison claimed that the punishment was also used in his day for premeditated murder, with murderers being "either hanged alive in chains near the place where the act was committed, or else, upon compassion taken, first strangled with a rope".[13] And in 1603, the poet Henry Chettle (in *England's Mourning Garment*, written to commemorate Queen Elizabeth), recounted how the late queen had introduced "one generall punishment of murder", whereas before that there had been "extraordinary torture, as hanging wilfull murderers alive in chains".[14] Both claims, however, may be folkloric. Holinshed was not a man averse to a fairy or two, and the *Chronicles* that Harrison's *Description* introduced are essentially 'mythical history'.[15] Certainly, though, by the period of the Stuart monarchy, a century later, when Trehemban was sentenced, there is no evidence of live gibbeting.[16] It is most likely that the St Columb resident was hung at Launceston or Truro, although this is not confirmed in the court records.[17]

Live gibbeting, then, is mostly a legendary punishment in England – a tale told around firesides on winter nights when the wind could easily be imagined to carry tortured screams from the hilltops; a story to discourage children from adventuring too far across moor or heath after dark. On the other hand, though, gibbeting after death was a sentence that was sometimes used for murder and other serious crimes in England and Wales in the seventeenth and eighteenth centuries – as an additional punishment, due to belief at this time that the body would only be resurrected on Judgement Day if it had been properly buried. In the seventeenth century, it was fairly common to leave the bodies of murderers simply hanging from the gallows after death, but in the early eighteenth century gibbet cages were increasingly used. These were iron, birdcage-like contraptions, forged by blacksmiths, into which the body of a convicted criminal would be placed after death. The cage was sometimes welded or soldered onto the body itself, and it was then hung from a gibbet pole in a prominent position close to the scene of the crime, where it often remained for decades.

The practice of gibbeting was regularised in 1751, when the Murder Act was passed in England and Wales. The Act was a response to the increasing number of crimes which carried a death sentence – everything from damaging the bank of a canal

to stealing from a rabbit warren – and was an attempt to distin-
guish the most serious offenses by additional punishment.[18]
From the following year, when the Act became law, the bodies
of those executed for murder could not be buried but had to be
either given to anatomists for dissection, or "hung in chains". The
process of creating a gibbet cage was costly, though – they were
made to fit each individual and couldn't usually be re-used – and
so in practice far more bodies went to the anatomists than ever
were gibbeted. On average, between 1752 and 1834 when the
practice was abolished, just two bodies a year were hoisted onto
gibbet poles across England and Wales.[19] Despite the relative
rarity of hanging in chains, though, the image of a body suspended in a creaking cage impressed itself deeply on the British
imagination.[20] A newly gibbeted body would often attract crowds
numbering tens of thousands, and stalls and sideshows would
spring up around it, like a crop of ghoulish mushrooms. Gibbets
were sketched by the well-known naturalist and artist Thomas
Bewick (they appear, rather bizarrely, for instance, in his 1797
History of British Birds) and his work made them a characteristic element of picturesque paintings of the English landscape.
They appeared in poems by William Wordsworth, and later in
the nineteenth century by A.E. Housman. And it was perhaps out
of the ghastliness of these real gibbeted bodies in the countryside
that the folklore of live gibbeting arose.

Recent research suggests that no bodies were gibbeted in
Cornwall between 1752 and 1834 that might have inspired the
story of John Trehemben's fate – although there were six or seven
cases in Devon.[21] However, the legend might owe something to
hazy folk memories of a far earlier gibbeting. In 1549, the Prayer
Book Rebellion or Western Rising took place in Devon and
Cornwall – a popular, Catholic revolt against the introduction

of the Book of Common Prayer and the suppression of traditional processions and pilgrimages. It has been claimed that nearly
7,000 men and women took part in the revolt, clashing with
government forces in a series of battles in the villages around
Exeter. Around five and a half thousand rebels were killed in the
rebellion and after its suppression, when government officials
pursued those who had been connected with the uprising. Many
suspected leaders were executed – among them William Mayow,
the Mayor of St Columb who was hung outside a tavern in the
village. And across Devon and Cornwall, accounts from the time
state that the bodies of hundreds of rebels were gibbeted at prominent sites, as a warning to their communities. There is no record
of whether William Mayow's body was among those gibbeted –
but it is possible that local memories of such a terrible event could
have coloured stories about the surrounding landscape of Castle
Downs for centuries to come.

The story of John Trehemben's sorry fate, related in "The
Western Antiquary" in 1881, also probably owed much to a more
general fascination in the late nineteenth century with historical
crime and punishment. This seems to have been a response to
the passing of the Capital Punishment (Amendment) Act on 29th
May 1868, which ended public hanging and required all future
executions to be carried out within prisons. Over the next two
decades the absence of capital punishment in public areas seems
to have generated a lurid nostalgia for public executions and
punishments from earlier periods. A.E. Housman's 1887 poem
below, with its sense of dislocation from the past, is just one
response to this change in death culture (the reference to "sheep"
here refers to the colloquial term "keeping sheep by moonlight"
which used to be a term for gibbeting):

And yon the gallows used to clank
Fast by the four cross ways.
A careless shepherd once would keep
The flocks by moonlight there
And high above the glimmering sheep
The dead man stood on air.
They hang us now in Shrewsbury jail
And trains all night groan on the rail
To men that die at morn.[22]

The late Victorian fascination with 'olden punishments' colour-ed the content of the "Western Antiquary" newspaper column, which was rife in the early 1880s with contributions from readers about ancient ducking stools, stocks, and public whippings. Some contributors sent in as many as six articles over a number of months – each one more lurid than the last. And in 1881, the editor W.H.K. Wright (another Plymouth librarian) appealed to readers to send in any "illustrations of the various instruments of punishment formerly in use" that they might have lying around at home.

Among the articles on historical punishment in "The Western Antiquary" was a string of contributions about a gibbet that had once stood in Plymouth in the late 18th century: a story that Plymouth residents had been too afraid to walk past it alone at night; another tale that a man had hitched a lift down to Plymouth, only to find himself in the same wagon as a body headed for the gibbet; an account of the hundreds of birds that used to nest in the gibbeted bodies; and so on. In April 1881, an invitation was printed from W.H.K. Wright, stating that "the Editor will be glad to receive similar notes from contributors".[23] Two months later, the account of the live gibbeting of John Trehenban appeared in the column.

It is impossible for us to know when the story of John Trehemban was first told – though when the Cornish historian Fortescue Hitchins visited Castle an Dinas in 1824 and wrote a long, detailed account of the monument, nobody seems to have told him the tale. It's also impossible to guess at how well-known the story was in St Columb and the surrounding area by the 1880s. Did the local children look gingerly up at Castle an Dinas and imagine a man starving to death in a cage there? Did they think twice before they walked over the Castle Downs at night? Three years after Richard Cornish submitted his account of John Trehemban's live gibbeting to "The Western Antiquary", though, an account of another, more recent live gibbeting at Castle an Dinas was sent in by a reader to the *Illustrated Police News*. It read:

> My grandfather has often told me that when he was a youth he used to walk to work with some miners over a lonely moor in Cornwall, near Castle an Dinas Hill, and that he well remembered the horror he felt in passing a place where there was a "gibbet". It was on the top of a high pole, and there was a cage of iron bars in which a living man was imprisoned who had been legally condemned for some serious crime, and left exposed to the weather to starve. The poor wretches used to cry out to the passing miners, in the most piteous tone, "Throw a crowst [crust] or a candle". The miners in passing would throw up to the poor wretch a candle or two from those they used in the mines, and when, sometimes one fell down, the wretched prisoner would entreat them not to leave it on the ground, but to throw it up to him again to stay his hunger.[24]

There are no records of gibbeting in Cornwall in the early nineteenth century – let alone live gibbeting. So what this seems to be is a strange, modernised version of the John Trehemben story (complete with candle-eating). And what it suggests is that a variety of grim tales of death and decay were circling around the mound of Castle an Dinas in the late nineteenth century.

Does it matter that the residents of a small Cornish village liked to believe that their local hillfort had been the scene of terrible retribution in the distant past? Or that even further in the past it had been the site of another death, motivated by lust and jealousy? Sometimes stories can give to a place a spirit more indelible than any history. And sometimes stories generate their own histories. It was about half past seven on a fine Saturday evening on 11th June 1904 when two bothers named Tabb, from the farm at the foot of Castle an Dinas, spotted a young couple pushing their bicycles up the lane to the hillfort. Leaning the bicycles in the hedge, the couple set off to climb the hill. The young man, it afterwards emerged, was Charles Berryman, a carpenter whose father had been the postmaster for St Columb until his death. Just twenty-years old, the lad had high hopes of emigrating to America.[25] Several days earlier he had bought himself a revolver and fifty cartridges. The dark-haired young girl was seventeen-year-old Jessie Rickard, the daughter of a local farmer, who had set out that evening, telling her father that she was visiting her music teacher. When her body was found between the high ramparts of the hillfort the next morning, her face was so riddled with bullets that it was initially impossible to identify her. She had been shot five times in the face and once in the arm.[26] After five days of searching the area, Charles Berryman's boots were spotted sticking out of a pool at the foot of the hillfort and he was discovered lying face-down in the water. He had shot himself in the head. In his pocket was a photograph of Jessie and a farewell letter to his mother, written on the day of the murder.

The "Cornish Tragedy" as it was dubbed was reported in dozens of newspapers across Britain, and also in Australia and America. Interest in the murder was fuelled by the press's quick assumption that Charles Berryman must have shot Jessie Rickard in 'a fit of jealousy'.[27] According to the report in the *West Briton and Cornwall Advertiser*: "There was a suggestion that Berryman was jealous of the attentions paid to Miss Rickard by a man from St Columb, and that is given as the motive of the crime".[28] There was no certain evidence for this at the inquest. Rather, it seems that commentators' understanding of the event as a crime of passion was influenced by the hillfort's own legendary history. The *Western Argus* newspaper in Australia, for instance, reported:

> It is not often that a tragedy takes such hold upon the public imagination as has been the case in the Castle an Dinas murder. [...] St Columb is in the heart of that famous half-mythical country of King Arthur and his knights of the Round Table [...] From a letter he [Charles Berryman] left it was clear that the crime was premeditated [...] and there is little doubt that it was love for the dead girl which threw his reason off its centre. The story and the scene is easily reconstructed in imagination – love, an ill-balanced mind, unhinged reason, and tragedy.[29]

While the reporting of the murder was certainly influenced by legendary tales of Uther, Igerna and Gorlois, though, a chilling question remains – one which can never now be answered. Did Charles Berryman choose very deliberately to take Jessie Rickard to Castle an Dinas that sunny evening? Yes, it may have been a practical decision – once the couple passed between the ramparts of the hillfort, they were lost to the view of the Tabb brothers and others. But in Bodmin Moor's rolling landscape of granite outcrops and ferny hollows there are many discreet corners, but only one place wrapped in legends of lust, envy, and violent retribution.

Eleven years after Jessie Rickard's violent death, a new chapter in Castle an Dinas's life brought commotion of a different kind to the hillfort. In 1915, Britain's only Wolframite mine was opened at Castle an Dinas, producing the ore needed to create Tungsten – the hard, brittle metal in high demand at that time for artillery shells, and afterwards used in everything from lightbulb filaments to jet engines. Just to the north of the hillfort was the mine shaft, to its south lay the processing works, and directly below the monument itself lay the seam of precious Wolframite. As part of the development, level platforms were cut into the ramparts of Castle an Dinas to support an aerial ropeway, used to transport around 200 tons of Wolframite every year from the mine to the processing works, which were next to the current small carpark.

For forty years, amid all of this industrial hustle and bustle, the old legends of Castle an Dinas seem to have become dormant – they are not mentioned in any accounts of the parish written during this time. In 1957, however, the mine closed, the machinery was dismantled, and Castle an Dinas returned to its quiet life as a ruin. And amid this return of silence and stillness, the monument's old atmosphere of doom began to impress itself once more upon those who visited its ramparts. The old stories of John Trehemban began to breathe again. In 1961, Marshell Arthur visited the area in order to write an article for the September issue of the *Cornish Magazine*, aimed at encouraging tourists to explore inland Cornwall. In his account of Castle an Dinas Arthur related:

A young farmer named Tremon murdered his sweetheart, and was such a Judas that he pretended to help in finding her murderer. While searching, riding on horseback behind the bloodhounds, his hat blew off and the dogs wouldn't leave it. Eventually he confessed, was tried and condemned to die of starvation in an iron cage on this hilltop. Someone threw in a pound of tallow candles, which he ate like a ravenous beast. The story still lives on in the folk-lore of the district.[30]

Arthur's account of the murder has several new elements: the hypocrisy of the man, the tale of the hat blowing off, and the notion that John Trehemban murdered his "sweetheart". The story of the hat seems to be borrowed from folklore. Murderers and other criminals are identified by lost headwear in a number of English songs and ballads – for instance in Robert Southey's 1796 ballad, "Mary the Maid of the Inn" (which ends with the gibbeting of a de-hatted bodysnatcher). The addition of the sweetheart may also be folkloric – but it seems more likely that this was a merging of the John Trehemban story with the real murder of 1904 (which is not mentioned in the article).

This rewritten version of the story from "The Western Antiquary" was just the beginning point, though, for a new century's myth-making at Castle an Dinas. In 1979, in *The Book of St Columb and St Mawgan* written by the St Columb resident and local historian Ivan Rabey, John Trehemban's story ends with the murderer being found by bloodhounds "trapped in a cage among the old mine workings on Castle an Dinas, having died after subsisting finally on one or two tallow candles. It transpired that the murderer was the very person who had earlier suggested that the perpetrator of this crime should be starved to death".[31] Once again, the killer is a hypocrite, but in this version, the entrap-

ment in a miner's cage and the subsistence on candles has been
radically re-imagined in an age no longer obsessed with 'ancient
punishments' – but instead haunted by the decline of Cornwall's
mining heritage, including the closure of the Wolframite Mine at
Castle an Dinas.

Ivan Rabey returned to the subject of Castle an Dinas seven
years later, to write "The Legends of a Famous Hill Fortress" for the
West Briton and Royal Cornwall Gazette.[32] In this version of the story,
he gave the Trehemban story a radical new date. Rabey related:

> There have been two murders on Castle Rings within the
> past century: one about 1889 when a woman was killed and
> her killer was subsequently found starved to death, having
> been trapped there, thus meeting a death he had public-
> ly suggested for the miscreant. In 1904 pretty, dark-eyed
> Jessie Rickard, aged 17, was shot in the head six times by
> her lover, Charles Berryman, in a fit of frenzied passion. He,
> too, was subsequently found dead, shot by his own hand.

John Trehemban was sentenced for murder in 1672. And between
1880 and 1910, there were no unusual deaths documented in the
record of births, deaths and marriages for St Columb, and no
notices of murder or accident at Castle an Dinas in the Cornish
press – besides an unfortunate farmer's son who in 1884 was
accidentally impaled by the handle of his own pike. That date of
1889, however, is just a few years after the story of John Trehemban was first published in "The Western Antiquary".

So while fifteenth-century chroniclers imagined an Arthurian death at Castle an Dinas, and nineteenth-century historians
invented a seventeenth-century live gibbeting at the hillfort,
twentieth-century historians concocted (perhaps uninten-

tionally) a Victorian murder and fatal accidental there. Today, Castle an Dinas remains shrouded in those myths – their grubby fingerprints sully even official publications about the hillfort. Historic England's most recent Archaeological Survey Report of the monument, from 2011, for instance, informs readers that:

> In the late 19th and early 20th century two crimes of passion at Castle an Dinas brought notoriety to the area. [...] Around 1889 the murderer of one woman was found in the old mine workings having become trapped and subsequently starved to death. In 1904 the body of 17 year old Jessie Rickard was found in one of the hillfort ditches.

And in 2012, the current owners and managers of the site, Cornwall Heritage Trust, told their members that "two murders are recorded as being committed on the site, one in 1889 when a local woman was killed, her assailant being found dead of starvation after being trapped in the mine".[33]

If Castle an Dinas sat in the midst of rolling arable farmland on the South Downs it would maybe have cast aside its pall of legends by now. It would perhaps never have become entangled in them in the first place. It might be remembered instead as the welcome sanctuary that it originally was, two thousand years ago. This is what I tell myself as I drive past the hillfort on dark winter nights. But amid the mists, the tortured rocks, and the dank pools of Bodmin Moor, who cannot easily imagine a little cruelty, a few howls of despair? And the hillfort is also a place that seems, like some dark lodestone, to attract death and tragedy to itself.

The last time I visited Castle an Dinas, on a blustery October day, I stopped off at the Cornish Studies Centre in Redruth afterwards, to look through the most recent archaeological reports about the monument. As I sat at my desk in the silent reading room, a librarian knelt quietly beside me and asked in anxious, whispered tones whether I was interested in the history of Castle an Dinas? When I nodded, she offered to bring me a folder of press cuttings about a horrible event that had taken place there. I expected reports of Jessie Rickard's death in 1904. What she brought me, though – laying the cardboard folder discreetly on my desk with a silent nod – was a collection of roughly cut-out newspaper reports from a far more recent catastrophe.

On 15th December 1995, at 6.30 in the evening, a low-loader carrying a digger had been driving along the A3059 to its depot in St Columb. Its exhausted driver had been working for 15 hours and, it later emerged, had not correctly secured the digger's arm. As the vehicle passed a column of oncoming traffic, the arm swung across the other side of the road, peeling open the tops of cars like sardine cans. Four passengers suffered terrible head injuries. And four drivers and one back-seat passenger were instantly behead-ed. I returned the folder silently to the librarian. The tragedy had nothing to do with Gorlois, John Trehemban, or even Jessie Rickard. And yet, as I drove home afterwards, I couldn't help thinking how odd it was that the accident was referred to in all those haunting reports as having happened "at Castle an Dinas" – a monument set well back from the road – rather than on the A3059. It was as though the hillfort's old associations with dreadful fatalities – both real and legendary – were somehow naturally associating it with this tragic event. And since then a new mythology has been weaving itself around the monument, with locals claiming to have seen spectral low-loaders on the road in front of them, as they have driven past the hillfort.[34] So Castle an Dinas remains a monument to terrible deaths and a place that people avoid thinking about. And it is a landmark that still sends a chill of horror down my spine as I drive past it, alone, on dark December evenings.

Joanne Parker is a senior lecturer in the English and History department of Exeter University in Cornwall. She is interested in British literature, history, landscape, and folklore (and the relationships between those things). Her last book, *Britannia Obscura: Mapping Hidden Britain* (Jonathan Cape, 2014; Vintage 2015) introduced her to leyhunters, druids, and airline pilots, and sent her tramping over moors in pursuit of stone circles, poking through undergrowth to find lost canals, and searching for leylines in the middle of London. The book was paperback of the week in both the *Guardian* and the *Mail* and was one of twelve books longlisted for the Wainwright Prize for nature and travel writing. Her other work includes *England's Darling: The Victorian Cult of Alfred the Great* (Manchester University Press, 2007), two edited books – *The Harp and the Constitution: Myths of Celtic and Gothic Origin* (Brill, 2015), and *Written on Stone: The Poetry of Prehistory* (Cambridge Scholars, 2009) – and numerous articles. Her features on walking Britain's historical, archaeological, and literary landscapes appeared monthly in *Trail* magazine from 2004 to 2009 and she edited the Dartmoor newspaper *The Okehampton Times* from 2006-7. She lives on Dartmoor with a Morris dancer, two daughters, an overweight cat, and nine black sheep.

MALLEUS SPECULIS

Mark Pesce

ONE: ROOTED

A generation ago, one of my virtual reality colleagues suggested that – in the future – people would pay good money to spend time an empty virtual world, holidaying in an environment free from stimulation, distraction, or activity. On this side of our information revolution, what once seemed dry sarcasm about the spare nature of early virtual worlds – expensive to create, they remained largely empty – now feels perfectly prescient. The real world of the mid-21st century, symbolically dense, overstimulating, and panoptically aware of our presence within it – always watching – totally crowds out any innate sense of ourselves. It's gotten to the point that we openly long for (and secretly dread) any brief encounters with a world that simply exists on its own terms, empty and asking nothing of us.

If I covered my eyes with a display

that projected only a perfect black, and my ears with headphones that cancelled even the smallest ambient noise, I could visit a space of sensory deprivation. With nothing presenting itself to my senses, my interior landscape slowly relaxes into whatever it believes is its natural shape. As soon as my attention wanders, that brief moment of freedom vanishes. I find myself in another reality: memory. The empty stage quickly populates with experiences, new and old, that have somehow left their mark on me. This could be a profoundly therapeutic moment: Freudian psychoanalysis uses the analyst's couch in a similar way. The patient lies down, relaxes, the mind wanders, and – with some guidance – unconscious forms emerge. Confrontations with the unconscious tend toward the unexpected and unpleasant, psychic wounds seeking the healing properties of light and air. So, unless directed, I will wander away from the uncomfortable, dromomaniacally bumping up against more of my mind's unconscious architecture, repeating this process until I either seek refuge in sleep, the quiet anxiety of boredom, or consuming panic. My experience of nothing paradoxically forces a confrontation with everything within me. The virtual world – like a funhouse mirror – twists and amplifies invisible qualities of being, stretching my psychic dimensions into hyperbolic forms, reflecting them back in a way that allows me both to see and ignore the truth. I am unreal, but recognisable, revealing parts rarely seen, rendered at monstrous scale. Because it is empty, the virtual world becomes the ideal screen for the projection of my self, making the unconscious, if not conscious, at least visible. All of the neurosis, narcissism and psychopathies that lurk beneath my skin in the real world find their way into the virtual world as tangible expressions, because the virtual is entirely psychical. Its manifestations are projections of me. As a psychic microscope, the virtual world should be the greatest tool ever offered in what Philip Rieff called "The Triumph of the Therapeutic." The virtual world can expose the unconscious in an almost predictable and systematic way. I can get a look into myself that would be nearly impossible by other means. Yet, with the exception of works by a few pioneers like Sherry Turkle, there have been no psychoanalytic approaches to a space that is definitionally psychoanalytically composed. It's as if we have created an MRI for our souls, but are too afraid of what we might see to slide ourselves into this psychic machinery and begin the scan. Why? In the unconscious, observation means destruction. Once exposed, my automatic enactments of psychic injury lose their capacity to command me, that being the entire point of the psychoanalytic project: self-actualisation advancing through an erosion of the unconscious into consciousness.

As a culture, we practice precisely the same avoidance we observe in individuals. We don't want to look inside ourselves, alone or together. This is a great loss, because the potential for a global therapeutic capacity – using a tool that could make us collectively more sane - has never been part of our expectations for the virtual world. At every moment, our cultural unconscious presents itself for view in the virtual world, but our culture ignores that as unconscious. An ignored unconscious does not disappear. Instead, it swells and occupies more and more of the psychic space of culture until little room remains for anything other than avoidance of the unacknowledged. We're running away from what we can not admit to, and we've nearly come to the end of our tether. Individuals dominated by an unexamined unconscious exist in a continual state of mechanical reaction, seeking something – anything – that will help them look anywhere other than at itself. For many that means sleep, for others boredom, and for some a rising panic. The same is true for this entire culture. All of us, connected as one, spending all of our time avoiding together. This pervasive, collective, connected unconscious has become the unspoken foreground of individual and cultural life in the middle of the 21st century. Unseen and unacknowledged, we slide into avoidance, avoidance becomes neurosis, and all cultural activity unconsciously amplifies the presence of the unconscious. The longer we ignore this quality of the virtual to expose our inner selves, the more it dominates and controls us.

Two: The Sea of Fecundity

If the virtual world existed in its own plane, entirely separate from the real world, we could entertain the option of a tactical withdrawal, closing the door and sealing off its psychic amplifier. But the moment to make that choice has passed. Long before humans visited the virtual, intellects vast, cool and unsympathetic had colonised virtual space, bending it toward their own ends: the markets. When William Gibson casually noted, "Cyberspace is the place the bank keeps your money," he said less about the ephemeral nature of cash in a connected world and more about the nature of the entities already long present when Gibson got around to naming that space in the early 1980s. It makes a perfect sort of sense that the money economy – purportedly the 'rational' basis for our culture – inhabits a space that amplifies our neurosis and psychopathy. Money makes us crazy, so where better to keep it than a space that makes us crazy? In its own way, money – and especially paper money – represents our first encounter with anything that is virtual. Money is the placeholder for all other goods and services, but represents nothing in itself. The allure of money lies in the imaginative leap it demands of its bearer. When you hold a bank note in your hand, you never see it for what it is. Instead you look through it to all of the possibilities it opens onto. Just like the virtual world, money acts as a projection screen for our souls. The virtual world contains money, and money contains the virtual world. And it's been this way for a lot longer than we might be aware. Long before Gibson named anything 'cyberspace', the storage of wealth in the virtual world generated its own attractive force, almost gravity-like.

Secured (for the most part), invisible (for the most part), and rarely spoken of, the origins of the "black hat" hacker – the 21st century equivalent of the bank robber – grows out of this earliest purpose for the virtual world. Put enough invisible money into the virtual world and individuals will begin to treat both that money and the virtual world as thoroughly real. It's as if we placed one funhouse mirror against another: reflected distortions become the only visible feature. Money found its ideal partner in the virtual world, each making the other seem more real than either could ever be on their own. Before long, others beyond the community of bankers and thieves confused virtual and real. Each looked into the virtual world and saw money reflecting their heart's desires. Those desires, projected onto the virtual world, made it seem real. The rest happened with astonishing speed, the virtual world bursting through into the real world, glowing with the colour of money. In the early days, this could only happen under tightly controlled conditions – large computers with fast and sophisticated communication links into the virtual world. But the glamour of the virtual world quickly grew so strong – because of money – that it bent the material world toward it, like matter falling into a black hole. In accelerating succession, a series of technologies brought the virtual world and its riches ever closer to an ever larger number of humans, culminating (as of this writing) with the intersection of the smartphone and the

World Wide Web.

I have a smartphone, and chances are high you have one, too. We think of them primarily as devices for connection, but in reality love of money is just as much of a factor. Through smartphones, the vast majority of adults on the Earth have quickly been gathered into a single, global space of commerce, connecting a triumphant, universal virtual world, each of us drawn there by the love of money. The virtual world ("over there" just a generation ago) has, via money, become interwoven into the fabric of the real world. It has become difficult to imagine life without its virtual aspect because the virtual world, through its relation to money, has become identified with the most material aspects of the real world. People look to the virtual world and see the real world. People look at the real world, but more and more look through it, into the virtual world. That's given the real world the consistency of a Swiss cheese or highly leavened loaf of bread: full of voids, containing nothing. "Here" or "over there" makes no difference any longer. Neither has any particular meaning. The real world invaded the virtual world, placed its money there, but that invasion made the virtual world irresistible to the real world. We opened five billion doors (one for every smartphone) to this conquest and colonisation by the virtual world. For us, the virtual world has become the real world.

THREE: ARTS AND MINDS

With money comes people. Everyone connected to the money economy has a reason to be deeply involved in the virtual world. We mind our own business, and – because we are human – we naturally involve ourselves in the business of others. This brings a new and unexpected dimension to community. In addition to the face-to-face of the real world, another space for connection now exists. Born from commerce and the love of money, cyberspace has been overwhelmed by our all-too-human drive to communicate. We could not claim that people do not love money, but we know that the vast majority love one another more than money.

The virtual world, originally and still stubbornly commercial, has become the chosen ground for relating to one another. As soon as we spied one another – peeping out from behind the curtain of transactions – we engaged. We find ourselves compelled to connect because other people are infinitely complex, unknowable, and the only truly interesting aspect of the virtual world. Each of us gets the opportunity to peer into the fascinating depths of others – or at least imagine we see depths in others. There remains the very real possibility that these funhouse mirrors of cyberspace exaggerate human depths. Things online seem more dramatic, ironic, or profound because the online world distorts and amplifies those qualities. We come across full of sound and fury, signifying only that we imagine in one another depths we pretend to ourselves. Yet this pretence has endured. It dominates conversation. Connected through the virtual, people appear extreme – we seem smarter or stupider, fairer or more prejudiced, happier or more miserable. Reflected in these mirrors – and in the gaze of countless others – human strengths and human foibles amplify to absurd endpoints, an overstimulated emission of emotion. In the virtual world, every human act of consequence tends to arc toward the absurd. Constant exposure has led us to believe these absurdities are reality, and not just reflections off funhouse mirrors, products of a virtual world which tends to distort real modesty into virtual profanity. In comparison to the excite-

ments of cyberspace, we find reality flat and unexciting. Now
habituated to virtual over-stimulation, we focus on and connect
through the virtual because it delivers the hit of absurdity we
crave, and with every dose reality seems somehow less real. We
prefer wild exaggeration to a dull truth, and the virtual world
offers this choice, providing – in seemingly inexhaustible supply
– a steady diet of outrages and sympathies needed to feed a
growing appetite whetted by the extremes of human feeling. To
feel in the virtual world means to feel together. Feeling together
can create common ground for understanding, sympathy and
empathy. Sometimes, outrages can produce their opposite. We
who connect to mourn an outrage often find something in one
other that endures beyond a brief moment, persisting even as the
outrage fades. Our worst human qualities create the opportunity for other, higher parts to appear. Make hate to make love. The
opposite appears to be equally true. When we rub up against one
another intimately in the virtual world, we can see through the
mirrors, into something closer to reality. The qualities we project
onto one another become translucent, then fall away. That feels
like a huge insult to our self, which narcissistically imagines
all others as our ideal reflections, a disappointment leading to
rage as these others never conform to expectations, nor do they
comply with demands. Our inevitable (if infantile) disappoint-
ments, shared through these new networks of communication,
become the seed for new outrages. So it goes on, endlessly. In
the age of the virtual, we cycle ever-more-rapidly through peaks
of love, disappointment and outrage. We seem oblivious to the
source of this cycle – emotional attachment. We get such such a
charge in the virtual world that it makes us blind to its capacity
to bring out the worst in us. The drive to connect that serves us
so well in the real world – as evidenced within families, tribes,

villages and cities – unexpectedly produces its opposite in the virtual world. The closer we come together, the further we feel driven apart.

These emotionally overwhelming moments of community in the virtual world inevitably bleed over into our real experiences, as we pin the feelings experienced in these funhouse mirrors of ours souls to the people we meet in the flesh. The virtual world so completely informs our expectations for the real world that where they don't agree – and that's at almost every point – we experience frustration. Why isn't the real world like it is online, we ask ourselves, further confusing the confected outrages of the virtual world with the petty annoyances of the real one. After spending time in a space of emotional over-stimulation, everything assumes too much meaning. This delicate and ridiculous balancing act – between the grounded and the absurd – frames our lives as we head into the middle years of the 21st century. Hypnotically entranced by our own shadow-play, intoxicated by our own uncontrolled emotions, and narcissistically unaware of our utter absurdities, we make faces into a funhouse mirror – and frighten ourselves.

Four: The Lies of Others

The virtual world provides a place to put everything. Where the real world clutters with collections and curios, the virtual world accommodates everything from the first clay tablet to the latest text message on an equal basis. In the real world things become permanent through a combination of intent and accident; the important tends to be preserved – if incompletely – and the unimportant lost, but rarely completely. In the virtual world, only accident applies – a random power outage shorting out some vital electronics. Everything endures because the virtual world, untarnished by the entropy of apathy, keeps on keeping on. Everything that has been known in the real could at some point be recorded in the virtual world. But where the real world continually edits itself according to taste or need or history, in the virtual world all bits hold the same value. On a comprehensive diet, the real maintains its size, while, continuously fed, the virtual grows to elephantine proportions.

Because it gets trimmed to size, the real feels superior to an obese virtual world. Something holds greater importance because it has not been culled, where something else holds less importance as part of an ever growing collection. Our curations of the real world reflect our priorities and truths. In the virtual world more signal means more noise, leading eventually to the triumph of another kind of chaos; the entropy of acceptance. We've gathered so much data it signifies everything, and therefore nothing. Because we constantly prune it back, the known in the real has always been in short supply, valued because of its rarity, like flecks of gold. We've built temples to the known, then universities, endowed priesthoods and established traditions to preserve and maintain the known. And though specific titles may change, these forms remain the same, consistent across civilisation, throughout the world. Orwell's "memory hole" can only exist in the real world, where the physical productions of knowledge can be tracked, altered, or destroyed. In the virtual world, an inverse quality arises in the "Streisand Effect": the attempted deletion of anything produces widespread duplication and dissemination. Things can be forgotten in the virtual world, and easily misplaced, but destroying something has turned out to be quite difficult. Suddenly, we confront this tsunami of "all and everything". The virtual world makes its claim to be both alpha and omega, accepting all, becoming the ultimate reference point: this is how Wikipedia overran Encyclopedia Britannica. Increasingly the virtual world encompasses all we know. This will only ever be approximate, as we continue to narrow down the few facts that haven't found their way into the virtual world – but it's true enough. Knowledge outside the virtual world still has tangible value – embedded in our bodies and experiences, but only a dedicated few of us will endure the difficulties associated with knowledge in the real world to locate and make use of it. We've got everything, and that's made us fat and lazy: providing all knowledge in a great cornucopia has become the great gift of the virtual and its most harrowing curse. Bill Gates once promised "knowledge at your fingertips" would change everything. It did. Anything known by anyone is now known to everyone. With this, the "burden of omniscience" (a paranoid delusion that someone in authority somewhere observes and understands all) has become a universal expectation. Not a sparrow falls to the ground unseen.

As we make this transition from the scarcity of knowledge in the real world into the endless, meaningless abundance of virtual world, we navigate between Scylla and Charybdis. The breadth and ease of knowledge creates a dizzying sense of possibilities, a utopian prospect of a world perfected through a universal franchise of knowledge. But we've learned one thing above all others: the known and the true need not necessarily move together. Much of the known bears no relation to the truth. "Knowing is doing, and doing knowing." Where we are informed by truth, knowledge extends our capacity to do what we will. But where knowledge is not true, and we act on that, the result can only be an eventual catastrophe. "Reality is that which kills you when ignored long enough." The power of the virtual world comes from its absolute acceptance of any knowledge on an equal basis, but we must not see acceptance as an assertion of truth. The virtual world lies as easily as it speaks the truth, and because it lacks any discernment, it can not judge between the two. The virtual world does not know when it lies to us, so it can not stop lying.

Those corners of our lives most infiltrated by the virtual world have seen truth replaced by "truthiness"; reassuring lies we find, share and broadcast as we tumble through this vast sea of meaning without guide or editor, pouring through an unfiltered melange of fact and fiction. So much of history has been filled with the telling of tall tales it seems perfectly natural that we continue to tell the tale. But the lie commonly agreed will be insufficient to the demands of the future.

Five: Dark Fomo

The virtual world, crowded with our voices, a billion-throat chorus of chaos, chitters unceasingly, whispering sweet nothings, shouting alarums, resolving into a steady hum of something left undone. That continual siren's song speaks of what may be and what, for some – right this moment – is. We see photos and selfies and snatch brief descriptions of wonders we will never experience as it dazzles and tantalizes and seems utterly substantial and believable. Its glamour carries it along, weaving it from mouth to mouth until the fabric of fascination takes on its own character. We can't believe it ourselves, so we share it with others. Almost too good to be believed, almost too specific to belong to anyone in particular, we see these moments captured, captioned, and shared, as each gets shared and forwarded and amplified beyond all recognition. These distillations of desire fly like arrows through the virtual world, piercing anyone who looks upon them with lust in their heart. They are like hungry ghosts, sweeping the virtual world for souls organised around desire and thereby ripe targets for possession. If we have nothing within ourselves, we find ourselves powerless to resist, for this nothing fills us with with the promise of everything we want. It whispers all the lies of every dream fulfilled. It offers nothing, yet promises all. Filled with nothing, these desires so severely warp our souls that the real world can no longer be seen. Instead we find ourselves transformed into unthinking, irrational creatures of no sense and all hope, faithfully expecting a complete and sudden change of circumstance, without recognising the impossibility of our beliefs. Hollowed out by our hungry ghosts, we prefer annihilation to illumination, avoiding the truth for as long as we can live in someone else's dreams. Other voices, speaking not of impossible longings, but instead extolling the virtues of the ordinary, things that bind us to the real, preference a boring truth over an exciting lie, and the comforts of home as a defense against the extraordinary tales luring listeners into prisons filled with hungry ghosts. After such an enormous, collective dose of extraordinary – billions of moments from millions of others – something more ordinary would come more naturally to us. It might even help to balance this sudden move into a virtual world that lies about its promises so comprehensively.

Breathing space, that's what we need. Can we put aside the alluring chitter of a billion voices, just focusing on the sound of the breath – in and out, in and out – reflecting, mindfully in single voice and from a whole self? Even here, hungry ghosts seek to lure us with sweet promises of individual will *über alles*, a romantic fantasy of living alone and acting alone and performing alone – above all others. Down this path, narcissism and selfishness dominate us in each proclamation of our eternal, inalienable freedom, producing the ideal conditions for an eternal possession; true freedom comes only after we see the chains, and accept that we have been enslaved. Danger lies everywhere, alone and together, and only the rare soul has not seen a visit by hungry ghosts. For that reason our immediate concern might best focus on the techniques of exorcism: how does one expel these demons? Being modern, scientific folk, we lie beyond the reach of the traumatic interventions of ritual and prayer. Instead, we must practice mindfulness, filling ourselves with something other than the desires of others. Hungry ghosts need to feed constantly on the desires of the living, and where those energies have dried up, they immediately decamp, seeking the richer pastures of a more susceptible soul. If we can keep our focus firmly located in the world, it will provide the 're-mind-er' to be mindful. But a reminder is not a reason. That must come from within us, driven by a desire of a different order; not the lust of fantasy we can never realise, but a real love received and accepted from the highest part of ourselves. That moment of "gratuitous grace" – as Aldous Huxley well named it – offers us the choice of liberation. Do we choose to be free, or do we find our dreamy desires too tempting? Each of us faces our own moment of decision every time we open a door onto the virtual world and gaze upon its glamours. Is this all we are? Is this all we wish to be? Multiply that interrogation by billions and we come to a greater moment of decision, a crisis which will force us into either clarity or confusion, ascending into something more like ourselves, or descending into an increasingly narrow envelope of unquenchable desire. The virtual world puts this question to us at every moment; puts this question to all of us.

SIX: BEGGAR THEY COME

Everything about the virtual world promises successful outcomes – rich, happy, well-connected, well-informed. All knowledge made available freely to all, and all wisdom follows. Each act we take, fully informed, expresses a perfection of influence approaching the Absolute. Illuminated from within by this culture of knowledge, all things appear as lights: "*Omnia quae sunt, lumina sunt.*" Yet our eyes see less than the whole, perceiving only what they can understand. We look upon our works and declare them good, for we are good and good can only create good. We judge ourselves leniently, one approval leading to another, then another, and another in an endless sequence that acquires authenticity by virtue of its own continuity. Seeing only good in ourselves, our works must be good.

The funhouse mirrors of the virtual world have their antecedents in each of our souls, for nothing can exist in the virtual unless we put it there, and we can only draw from our knowledge. This knowledge reflects the parts of ourselves that seem good – all the rest suppressed into the unconscious – so the warps and blindnesses within us look normal when we see them within the virtual world. They are our most familiar features. Pretending dark is light, we infuse all we look upon with that same darkness, ignoring our real essence – unpleasant and unfamiliar – replenishing it with nothing. The real world has been undermined by this progressive darkness, giving way to the negative absolute of utter virtuality. Triumphant, nothing surveys its kingdom, seeing nothing everywhere. We sleep. Dreams disturb this strange slumber – the only way in through egos so hardened by delusions of their own perfections that they admit no light. Revealing hell in rage and fire, these dreams shout us into another kind of wakefulness: the dark night of the soul. Woke. Aware only of heartbeat and anxiety, the world seems too small and too tight and too short and nothing too close for comfort. Light and dark reverse for a moment, illumination fades to black: has it all ended so quickly? All over, and nothing to show for it. In this moment we confront a choice: do we turn over and go back to sleep (in reality spending endless hours worrying into a timeless night), or do we rise up, and walk a different path. Sleep ends in fire and nothing, while a walk eventually comes to the Bo tree, and a moment's touch. Look hard enough – as Buddha did – and perfection disappears in reflection. The perfect, ever the enemy of the good, evaporates back into nothing. If we choose to look, we see it really does not exist. Once we see that, and are revealed to ourselves as broken and incomplete, we can approach the Absolute on its own terms, in its own time. Of this little can be said except that the attempt contains within it all that can ever be achieved.

Of anything else, what should we say? "When a monkey looks into a mirror, no god looks out." Lost in the funhouse, panicked, beset on every side by wrathful demons who pursue us out of pure, mad love – emanations of our souls and thus forever bound to us – flight consumes all and leaves us nothing. If we run, we might never stop running. If we stop, we will always need to calm ourselves – because we will always want to run. If we wait until the very end, that sudden and unexpected stop when the prison doors open of themselves, what can we do? If we have spent our lives running from ourselves, great liberation produces the greatest fear. Then we begin again, recycling darkness back into light: that's life!

SEVEN: CRONE OF THORNS

At this moment in time, we awkwardly straddle two worlds – the virtual and the real. Entranced by visions, our heads in the clouds, we ignore our bodies – until we stumble and fall. The Norse god Odin had a solution for this; blinded in one eye, he could always see within, looking upon the virtual landscape of everything within us. A modern Odin might find that landscape populated with all of the qualities we've imported into the virtual world, old sins given new life in a realm unconstrained by the sharp rebukes of social forces that see these for the chaos they portend. For if enough of us function from fear, greed, anger, deceit, envy, pride, everything falls apart. The centre can not hold. Yet Hope endures, even in chaos, because our self-wrought Hells bring with them the refiner's fire. We can burn, feel the pains of our dross consumed utterly, and then arise, phoenix-like, born anew. "It is impossible to achieve the aim without suffering."

Each day brings its own troubles, and each time its own tortures. The problems of our present precisely match the needs and the capacities of we who face them, like hammer and anvil. These problems – our problems – emerge from the gift of the virtual world: a universal, unconscious collectivity. We are connected but do not yet understand that, nor what it means for us. Instead, we thrash about like a blinded Cyclops, powerful and terrified, smashing all to wrack and ruin. Who has done this? "No man." We never find the fault in ourselves, blaming others for our circumstance, until the ruin of our world. But we can not bestow the gift of seeing on one another. I can not force you to see the world through my eyes any more than you can force me to see it through yours. This gift can not be given. It can only be received. Here's the test for each of us – all of us – one that is

being administered continually at an ever-accelerating rate, until
we learn the lesson. In this moment it consumes almost all of our
attention, because what lies on the other side of this test can not
be understood until the test has been passed. The land just ahead
of us is unknowable to ourselves today, invisible and impossible
and just beyond arm's reach. We feel a rising frustration, and a
growing sense that perhaps too much has been asked for – more
than can be delivered. *"Mene, mene, tekel, upharsin."* The terror
of being weighed and found wanting, perfectly natural in the
circumstance, the dark fantasy of choking during the exam. How
we confront our terrors during this test makes up at least half of
our grade. If we surrender to fear and greed, we end in Hobbes'
"war of all against all". If we give ourselves over to pride and
arrogance, we drown in our own filth, and, through our deceits,
believe all along we have covered ourselves in glory.

The consequences of our choices could not be drawn more
clearly, even as the lines begin to blur between our our inner lives
and the outer world. The virtual world acts almost like a sea-bath,
healing the weeping wounds of our souls – but mostly because
it provides the space for madness to boil up through every pore
of ourselves, pouring out of us like disease from a lanced boil.
Some mistake that disease for themselves, and scramble after
it, grasping at fearsome, hateful, ghosts. These worst examples
become a warning to the rest of us, of how not to be. Turning
away from that damage, toward something whole and healed that
is being called forth from us, in this moment right now, we catch
a glimpse a different way of being – wondrous and unfamiliar
and fleeting. With everything on the line, everything matters, for
everyone. We struggle with this, clinging onto the devil we know.
Yet if we hold fast to our past selves, we will tumble into the abyss
of hallucinations, lost forever in the funhouse.

An angelic Other offers itself, but at a price: "A condition of complete simplicity / (Costing not less than everything)".

"Sell all your possessions."

"Surrender your attachments."

"Let go of your hate."

Whatever happens, nothing will remain the same. The forces brought to bear in this moment of trial can not be sustained indefinitely, for it would not be long before the refuge of madness would become universal. Illumination – or annihilation in a colder fire, unwarmed by the hearts of others, an airless, endless night on haunted, dead worlds. Our oldest myths speak of the journey of the soul as it rises up, its story a retelling of the tale of life: feeding, then copulating, then driven by hunger, then consumed with fear, then obsessed with the thoughts of others, then cool insight into our own being, then aspiring to the absolute. These stories speak to the things that made us human, and to the things that will take us beyond, into the posthuman – naked but unafraid, awareness unbound, all in unity. Better to enter the fire willingly, eyes wide and heart open, ready to be consumed utterly. Et in Arcadia ego.

Hammer smashes mirror.

Mark Pesce is an inventor, writer, entrepreneur, educator and broadcaster. In 1994 Pesce co-invented VRML, a 3D interface to the World Wide Web.

Pesce has written six books, including *The Next Billion Seconds*, exploring how connectivity amplifies human capacity, and *The Playful World*, which used toys such as Furby and Sony's PlayStation to illuminate the interactive world of the 21st century.

As an educator, Pesce founded postgraduate programs in interactive media at both the University of Southern California's world-famous School of Cinema Arts and the Australian Film, Radio and Television School. Pesce currently holds an appointment as Honorary Associate in the University of Sydney's Digital Cultures Program.

Throughout his career, Pesce has had the opportunity to collaborate with talents as diverse as Sir Tim Berners-Lee, Terence McKenna, Alexander and Ann Shulgin, Erik Davis, Douglas Rushkoff, Jimmy Wales and Danah Boyd.

Pesce immigrated to Australia in 2003, where he has become a sought-after explainer of all things digital for both print and broadcast media, writing a fortnightly a column for the internationally respected tech publication *The Register*.

While working his contribution for this volume, Pesce released his latest invention, Mixed Reality Service, an Internet-wide system that seamlessly knits together the real and virtual worlds, adding a new dimension to both.

BECOMING ELF – BECOMING WITCH

Bryndís Björgvinsdóttir

(with contributions and translation
by Marteinn Sindri Jónsson)

It can be quite bothersome these days to harvest Icelandic
elf-belief for academic research or for creative inspiration.
Mentioning just one word about elves can provoke the interest of foreign journalists – as well as Icelandic tourist
companies, many of which are eager to show the elves to visitors
from abroad – or at least something original and different. Many
lose interest, however, in the work of the scholar or the artist when
it becomes clear that she has not been successful in proving the
existence of elves – and is, to be honest, quite indifferent to seeing
elves or communicating with them, whatsoever.

Icelandic folklorists have so far not been
intent on proving or disproving the
existence of elves – no more than the
existence of ghosts, trolls, aliens,
or the blonde of dumb blonde
jokes. Research is rather
focused on recording and
interpreting   elf-belief,
based on the presump-
tion that such belief

might shed light on the society of people who hold these beliefs –
that is to say: ourselves, our culture and our society. And despite
the folklorist's attempts to make this point, she is still being asked
if she has seen an elf, has ever seen anyone who has seen an elf,
and so on and so forth. A more academically interesting question
would be: how does modern elf-belief manifest itself and what
does it say about us? What effect does belief in elves have on our
environment and our identities? Can these effects be studied?
Can these effects be seen? And could it be maintained that elf-belief affects our daily lives?

Even though very few of us might actually see elves, the
manifestation of elf-belief in Iceland is often in plain sight: a case
in point would be how purported elven-stones and enchanted
spots affect the appearance and location of buildings and roads in
the country. In the past two years I have, together with photographer Svala Ragnarsdóttir, catalogued and located over fifty places
around Iceland where elf-belief has either impacted the appearance or location of human constructions or stood in the way of
new buildings, playgrounds or other human interventions. It is
believed that these places, associated with the elves, are not to
be disturbed in any way. One could also argue that the effect of
elf-stories and other folk-tales can be seen in literature, poetry,
cinema, music and art as well as in the news. This most definitely
sheds a light on our identities, how we think about ourselves in
relation to "others" and how we contrast humans with wild nature.

ON THE BORDERLINE OF HUMANITY

My mother has been reluctant to acknowledge one particular
ancestor of ours, while idealizing other ancestors. This unpop-
ular person is one of Iceland's most infamous serial killers,

Axlar-Björn, a farmer in Snæfellsnes in the 16th century. Canni-bal, people would call him, "a vampire in human form", as one academic writes.[1] My mother refuses to be descendent of such a man who, by the meaning of the names we call him, has been exiled to the borderline of humanity. Just as the elf or the ghost, Axlar-Björn is not considered entirely human.

Elves, ghosts and vampires are not animals. But then again these creatures are in no way properly human – although they might be related to humans or even to have once been men. These beings differ from human beings as their perception of time and space is different to that of mortal people. They can disappear into thin air and lead lives that by far exceed the time given to us humans. They are however not completely alive and therefore rid of the myriad predicaments and pleasures of human exist-ence. Elves, ghosts and vampires belong to the category of "the undead". What is in their best interest, is far removed from what is in our, human, best interest. While they are closely related to us, they are still alien and different to us, which also makes them perilous. Their intentions are beyond our grasp: we don't know what they want, what they think or what drives them. Calling Axlar-Björn a vampire emphasizes that we don't understand the intentions, will, thought or urges that drove him to his fell deeds. That may indeed be fine, one might conclude, for thus we distin-guish him from "us".

People might disagree on the point, whether vampires really exist, but the human existence of Axlar-Björn is an historical fact – although his life's choices and legacy might inspire a compari-son to vampires. This begs the question: are tales of supernatural beings perhaps originally accounts of people? Could they be an attempt to account for the legacy of those people and even, simul-taneously, an attempt to account for whole historical periods?

Many are familiar with the term "The Dark Ages". The term indicates a certain medieval period in Europe. Why dark? We can be certain that the sun shone in those days as it does now (more or less). We also know that the people of these ages produced magnificent literature and made amazing discoveries, all around the world. The darkness denoted by the term is spiritual or symbolic. It indicates the state of a society in a period before, supposedly, brighter periods of renaissance and enlightenment. But the allusion to medieval darkness might actually reveal more about ourselves and our historical period than about medieval times. We believe that our days are brighter, more enlightened and more developed than medieval days. In turn we are prone to distancing ourselves from certain things – making them a little more mysterious, alien and different. Dangerous even.

Eerie tales of ghosts, trolls and elves were collected in Iceland in the 19th century by the folklorist Jón Árnason. When he published his collection of folktales in 1862, he and his associate had already categorized all the supernatural beings figuring in the tales, in the taxonomical manner of Carl Linnaeus and other naturalists who studied natural history in the 18th and 19th centuries.[2] This undertaking was an attempt to construct an orderly system for those supernatural beings in much the same way that naturalists had attempted in their categorization of animals and plants, not much earlier. This was done despite the fact that supernatural beings were impossible to observe in the same way the naturalists observed nature. Jón Árnason divided them into four categories – ghosts, elves, trolls and sorcerers – even though medieval texts often denoted all four kinds with the same word: "troll". When medieval texts are studied it comes to light that an elf can be a ghost, a ghost can be a troll, a troll can be a sorcerer and a sorcerer can be a man.[3] An elf could also be a man, worshipped after death as a benevolent or malevolent spirit. A case in point would be the story of the Norse king Ólafur Guðröðsson, who haunted his own grave-mound as an elf and thus became known as Óláfr Geirstaðaálfr.[4] This correlates quite accurately to what most elves are expected to do in modern day Iceland: to watch out for their dwellings in nature – their abodes in hills and fells, and make sure that no one disturbs their peace. They guard hills and meadows in very much the same way the ghost haunts his grave.

Another example, a few hundred meters from where I sit in a coffeshop writing this article: In Hafnarfjörður, where I live, there is a hill. It is very central, very elevated and offers an amazing view. However, construction is forbidden up on this hill which usually is called Jófríðarstaðir. Historical sources attest that a yet older version of the name pertains to this place, Ófriðarstaðir. The name can be taken simply to mean battle-ground and the most probable reason for such a name is that a battle between English and Hanseatic merchants, who traded and docked in Hafnarfjörður in the 16th and 17th centuries, took place on this hill.[5] The 17th century scholar Jón Guðmundsson lærði wrote that men were killed in this battle, a fact that gave rise to the expression "to be at Ófriðarstaðir".[6] Thus, this enchanted spot which more recent sources associate with elves, hosts the graves of anonymous foreigners.

When more recent sources are considered, one finds the story of a farmer named Hendrik, who lived at Jófríðarstaðir at the turn of the 19th century. He was said to have split open a stone on the hill to mine construction material for a new house. This he did, despite being warned by his neighbours of a supposed elven dwelling in the rock. Shortly thereafter Hendrik's daughter fell ill to a mysterious disease and passed away as the family moved into the new house. According to the legend, Hendrik sold the

land to the Catholic Church, and the buyer, Marteinn Maulen-
berg – the first Catholic bishop in Iceland since Lutheran reform
in 1550 – ordered that "no one should be so bold as to disturb
the peace of those, who possibly dwelled in the rock and neighbouring rocks".[7] These orders seem to have been obeyed up to
this day, as nothing has ever been constructed on this hill. In this
enchanted spot, there is nothing to be seen but a few rocks – one
of them split open.

A human person seems, under certain circumstances, able
to become a supernatural being, such as a vampire, a ghost or an
elf. We reflect the mysterious, the daunting, the uncertain and
what we are frightened of, in supernatural beings. The stories we
tell about those beings often convey knowledge about historical
events that have faded from our collective memory and been
forgotten. They might also describe aspects of our humanity that
we wish to suppress, by naming these aspects unnatural or alien.
By way of such storytelling we project, on to these supernatural
"others", what we don't want to find in ourselves, what we don't
understand, what we don't want to understand and what we are
forbidden to understand in ourselves. These supernatural beings
stand on the borderline of human experience, and consequently
cast what is considered natural and acknowledged in relief.

J.R.R. Tolkien and the Icelandic elves of the 19ᵀᴴ century

Most contemporary Icelandic elf-tales depict elves as guardians
of nature who almost exclusively appear to oppose urban sprawl
and the proliferation of constructed roads that disturb nature,
whenever they feel threatened. Today's elf-belief reflects, to a
great extent, ideas about urban development and urban landscap-

ing and the dividing line between the urban and the natural
– man-made environment and nature.[8]

Elf-tales from the 19th century, those collected by Jón
Árnason, seem to have had a more diverse range of topics. Some
stories tell tales of love between humans and elves and other
stories recount humans coming to assist elves in the giving of
birth. Yet other stories concern evil elves, in particular change-
lings (in Icelandic , *umskiptingur*), an old elven hag or a hideous
old elven man who replaces a human child that the elves have
abducted from its cradle. These shape-shifters resemble the lost
child so accurately that the child's mother would sometimes
notice nothing amiss until much later.[9] The habit of elves to
abduct children is reminiscent of the witch of the forest in Hensel
and Gretsel – or the witch of the movie *The Witch* (2015) who in
the opening scene carries an infant child away into the forests,
where she then devours it. The same might be said about trolls,
who in Icelandic folklore are reported to steal children and eat
them. The most infamous of those children-devouring trolls is
without doubt Grýla who, beside cannibalizing, is the mother to
the thirteen (or more) Icelandic Yule lads (Santa Claus's mischievous Icelandic counterparts).

In the folk tales of Jón Árnason, quite a lot of ink is spent
on describing elves and their societies. They are said to resemble humans and to do a similar line of work as did 19th century
Icelanders: raising domestic animals and fishing from small
boats.[10] The elves attend church on Sundays as the elves of the
folktales embraced Christianity at some point in history. Iceln-
dic elves are nonetheless believed to originate in heathen belief
and they are mentioned in Norse mythology.[11] The few obvious
things that set elves apart from humans is the more fair appearance of the elves, as well as them being taller than humans. Their

homes are illuminated by far more light than human abodes, and
their clothes are more rich and colourful than human garments.[12]

These tall and fair elves would later come to figure in the
work of the British writer and academic J.R.R. Tolkien, in both
The Hobbit (1937) and *The Lord of the Rings* (1954-1955). Tolkien
was fascinated with the otherness of elven time perception,
something that differs radically from human temporality:

> For the Elves the world moves, and it moves both very swift
> and very slow. Swift, because they themselves change little,
> and all else fleet by: it is a grief to them. Slow, because they do
> not count the running years, not for themselves. The passing
> seasons are but ripples ever repeated in the long long stream.
> Yet beneath the Sun all things must wear to an end at last.[13]

Tolkien sought inspiration for his ideas about elves from many
different sources, as well as employing his own imagination to
endow them with life.[14] Tolkien's elves closely resemble humans,
but are fairer and more wise. They live in a closer connection
with nature than most beings of Middle-Earth. Legolas, from
the Woodland Realm, would be a case in point; he who perceives
anger and peril in the Forest of Fangorn when a man and a dwarf
notice nothing.[15] Tolkien's elves are wise and mostly benevolent
but also dangerous, magical and cunning. They never hesitate to
slay an enemy and take cold revenge on anyone who crosses them.

In *The Lord of the Rings* and *The Hobbit* the ambiguous nature
of elves is apparent, an ambiguous nature that Icelandic folklore
also portrays. The elves are not only fair but also perilous.[16]
Their demeanour is usually ostentatious but still they belong
to the ancient and the past. Their time is about to come to an
end in Middle Earth as the elven queen Galadriel well knows.

Ármann Jakobsson, a scholar of literature and medieval studies, writes in his book, *Tolkien og hringurinn* (*Tolkien and The Ring*) that Galadriel has, along with the power of divination, a strong will and powerful desire – she is driven by her feelings, no less than her moral sense. The nature of her desire is revealed by her temptation, when Frodo Baggins offers her the Ring of Power and thus appeals to her darker aspirations. Suddenly her inner struggle comes to light.[17] This begs the question, is Galadriel by nature good or evil? Is she akin to the witches and the hags? Yet she withstands her temptation, turns down the offer and confirms her benevolent elven nature. Icelandic folklore, very much in the same way, recounts an elven emotionality that is not always dictated by reason, especially if children or grownups have wandered too close to elven homes, with clamour instead of politeness and care. Elves are also annoyed when humans desire what the elves believe to be their own properties. The elves, both of Tolkien's works and Icelandic folklore, demand unconditional respect, if nothing else.[18]

Sustainability is a certain keyword when elven believers make themselves heard nowadays. Sustainability has never been as important or as widely discussed as today, especially in the context of environmental destruction, climate change and ocean acidification. At the same time that we are informed about the importance of an unconditional respect for nature we also want to *enjoy* what consumerism, technological progress and natural destruction brings us: effective travelling, fast food, affordable furniture, inexpensive clothes etc. This gives rise to the suspicion that the elves of today reflect human guilt, as the elven hill is opposed to tarmac, bulldozers and urban sprawl. Fair and tall elves in rich clothing are opposed to raving and unfit consumers, craving fast food and wearing unendurable H&M garments.

"When a society or its particular groups share concerns
or conflicts of some kind, this comes to be reflected in folklore,
whether it is in jokes, rumours or graffiti – or in tale, such as
elf-tales",[19] writes Valdimar Tr. Hafstein, scholar of folklore, in
his article *Hjólaskóflur og huldufólk: Íslensk sjálfsmynd og álfahefð
samtímans* (*The Elves' Point of View*). This might explain the persistence of elf-tales today, especially in the cases of road or building
constructions that disturb nature close to human settlements –
disturbances that are hard to ignore as these are, so to say, in one's
backyard. Therefore it could be concluded that mentioning elves
in the context of environmental destruction relates to our guilt
– the consumption, the excess and the disrespect. Maybe we ask
ourselves questions like: Where and when will we stop transform-
ing nature into tarmac and roundabouts? Must we not stop before
something bad comes to pass? These questions are ever upon us,
especially in the shadow of terrible climate changes and daily
news reports on natural destruction on sea or land – but this also
begs the question: is our guilt soothed and our bad feelings kept at
bay by occasionally leaving an elven stone unscathed?

THE OTHERS

In his aforementioned paper Valdimar Tr. Hafstein analyses
how contemporary elf-belief reflects our ideas about traditional Icelandic farmer's society.[20] Valdimar looks at contemporary
elf-belief in the context of the rapid changes of Icelandic society in
the 20th century. Icelandic society figured, around 1900, amongst
the poorest and most destitute countries of Europe, but through
occupation by British and U.S. armies in the Second World War
with a lasting impact on economy, urban development, transportation and culture, it was transformed into what it is today: a

fully modernized society. "Contemporary elf-belief recounts no social change in the elven world, whatsoever", writes Valdimar, making the point that the elves of today are mostly occupied with guarding the land and preventing the submission of nature to the human world.[21] "The hierophanies of the supernatural, when the elven world takes its stand, brings that which stands outside our society, into a sharp relief, that which belongs to others, and not to us – while at the same time confirming our sense of identity, what belongs to us and who these 'we' are".[22]

The otherness of elves is easily recognized by their strong connection to nature, reminiscent of what we imagine to have been part of human nature in past times, antecedent to a Biblical expulsion from paradise, that severed human ties to nature itself. And thus, humans instead began gaping over reality-TV in specially designed TV rooms and spending their time surfing the Internet. All the while, elves have been our neighbouring others, but still *our* others. The places that belong to them are unsettled land – the wild and untamed nature close to, or even within, human settlements, on the borders of cities and towns. These elven homes are enchanted; they cannot be disturbed or made to change.[23] In this respect the elves belong to past times. Like ghosts, the otherness of elves is rooted in their peculiar understanding of time and their different settlements – not only do they belong to a different time but also to a different spatial dimension.

Otherness pervades our lives. We can analyse news reports for othering – the "others" are for example made explicit in contemporary discourse about a supposed "refugee crisis", that only appears when "others" need to seek refuge in "our" countries. People are terrified by the effect of the arrival of "others" in our homes, but when "we" need to leave our homes we talk about "emergencies", "settlers", and "New World Icelanders".

The othering of women made way for Europe's witch hunts when gynocides were justified by labelling some women as "unnatural" or placing them on the borders of humanity: these women were reading books, learning, experimenting, artistically creating, etc. They threatened conservative social values and thus became terrifying, the perilous neighbours – and eventually "the others".

The insane have also suffered social exclusion, isolation and torture throughout the ages on account of a supposed otherness. The idea that the insane are unclean has had a lasting impact on occidental minds; a case in point would be the German idiom *psychohygiene*, which denotes sanity. Another persistent idea that others the insane, is that they are not *healthy* or *whole* and therefore that each insane person is *many*. A case in point would be the man Jesus encounters in the region of the Gerasenes as is recounted in the Gospel of St. Mark. This man lives outside of society, dwells among the tombs and would cry out and cut himself with stones. Attempts have been made to chain him like an animal, but every time he tears the chains and breaks the tethers. Jesus asks him his name, to which the impure spirits answer: "My name is Legion, for we are many."[24]

The man of the tombs is solidly placed at the border of humanity: dirty, bloody and bound, he lives among the dead like a ghost. This parable portrays the tendency of western societies to categorize people in terms of "healthy" and "unhealthy", "sane" and "insane", "whole" and "divided", "wholesome" and "dangerous" while the truth is that we are, each of us, many opposites at the same time, prismatic and contradictory. That is to say: no one lives his entire life clean, whole, good and undivided. We are all many – which is brought into sharp relief in our folklore where people's ideas about the hidden worlds reflect first and foremost themselves and the societies wherefrom the folklore springs, and where it belongs.

Elves, ghosts and trolls are all beings that we have employed as our counterparts or to emphasize what counts as "normal" at a particular time in history. We thus use other worlds to delineate our world and what it contains.[25] Elves might be considered, by some, to be more "normal" and therefore more desirable than trolls and ghosts – or even refugees, some might say – even though elves, according to most folk tales are ill-tempered, revengeful, conservative and magical. But elves are all the same more cherished in 21st century Iceland than their supernatural relatives, as the elves are, first and foremost, beings of nature. But elves have not always been fair representatives of an idyllic nature. And they can truly be dangerous, just like ghosts and trolls – not only because of their otherness, but also because of their strong connection to nature itself – a nature hostile to human existence.

DANGEROUS NATURE

In 2014 a new road was constructed through the lava field of Gálgahraun, that lies between the local municipalities of Álftanes and Garðabær. Nature conservationists protested against the road construction as the lava field is considered a valuable and beautiful place with its unique lava formations that have figured, for example, in the paintings of a prestigious Icelandic artist, Jóhannes Kjarval. It was no coincidence that a few elf-seers, humans who see elves, were among the protesters. In the lava field there stood two supposed elf-rocks, one of which is a big elven church called *Ófeigssteinn*, that under no circumstances was to be exploded, bulldozed or destroyed in any way.

The nature conservationists criticized the ideas of the local city council, consisting of simple solutions, protesters said, harmful to nature, without a long-term perspective. They prompted for a reconsideration of the new road's design or a renovation of an old road that was already there. They wanted to conserve the lava field unscathed as a public reserve on the edge of the city. They also considered the road construction illegal and filed a lawsuit against the contractors.[26] The elf-seers also wanted to help their friends – the elves. "They summoned me there, the elves, and expressed their concerns", said elf-seer Ragnhildur Jónsdóttir, in the newspaper *Morgunblaðið* on the 28th of October 2013. "The call for the preservation of the lava field echoed in the rocks. I was deeply affected by this emergency call from the elves", she added. According to folklore the elves often take revenge on those who disturb their homes.[27] That is to say: according to elf-belief the disturbance will be avenged sooner or later.

The Office of Public Road Construction, Vegagerð ríkisins, decided to heed the demands of the elf-seers and relocate elven stones while ignoring other conservationist protest, as the demands of those protesting the general destruction of the lava field conflicted with the Office's interests, based on political decisions and the investments of businessmen and city councils. These interests did not however conflict with relocating two stones. This gave rise to a curious news report: "The Office of Public Road Construction relocates elven stones". Curious, especially in the eyes of foreign media – but maybe not so curious considering the effort by The Office of Public Road Construc-tion to accommodate the demands of protesters without having to seriously alter their own plans. Some people might have sensed a certain relief, knowing that the elves would keep their homes, albeit on a new place in the lava field. And thus one might conclude, there was a feeling that some agreement had been made, between elves and men – nature and humans.

As I have argued, we civilized human beings distance ourselves from the nature-loving elves to establish our own identity. In the case of the road construction in Gálgahraun, civilized society is represented by the uniforms of police officers and bulky construction vehicles in the lava field, and subsequently in High Court when protesters were fined for "resisting police intervention"[28] – an accusation that in our time seems to have become interchangeable with the constitutional right of protesting. This evokes the binary opposition between culture and nature. Culture is then considered the locus of science, technical progress, masculinity, public institutions and rationality while nature is filed with unscientific belief, archaic ways of life, femininity, superstition and emotionality, such as the "love of nature". These binary oppositions are reflected in the basic credo of the Bible where God commands man to dominate nature.[29] Shortly thereafter, man's domination over nature is complemented with male domination over women, which might explain the strong cultural tendency to associate women with nature – and supernatural powers – against the masculine. This might sound far-fetched, but these are the ancient binary oppositions that structure tales and stories as recurrent themes. Cases in point would be the movies *Antichrist* (2009) and *The Witch* (2015). Both these movies associate the feminine with nature, as opposed to the rationality of man (as masculine) who has science and the power of definition at his command (please note: spoilers follow).

The movie *Antichrist*[30] by the Danish director Lars von Trier is driven by binary oppositions corresponding to femininity and masculinity: the main characters, whose names are simply *Her* and *Him*. The movie sets out with an intense sexual scene where neither is properly present when their infant son climbs a window, falls down to the street and dies. She is explicit-

ly emotional in the aftermath of her son's death but He clings
on to rationality. He is a psychologist – the specialist in their
relationship – and starts to doubt her ability to recover without
his help. They change their environment, head for the forest, to
a remote cabin where He intends for her to get better. But soon
enough He starts to spot curious animals, a doe with a stillborn
calf hanging by her side, an aggressive raven and a talking fox.
He sees nature in an uncanny light. He has trouble sleeping
when the acorns start falling from the trees in their thousands
to hit the roof of the house. He wakes up with his hands covered
in leeches. The fox addresses Him and announces that "chaos
reigns". At the same time She is turning on him. He recalls how
their late son came home with a broken leg, last time She took
him to this place in the woods. He even starts to suspect that She
intentionally hurt the child. Their communication keeps getting
worse. She doesn't obey Him and doesn't heed His advice. His
concerns grow heavier and he starts to doubt Her sense of reality, and Her innocence, unaware that his own sense of reality is
slowly slipping away. Her aggression grows and they conflict
physically. He has no other option than to slaughter her, as if
she were a witch of medieval times, when she finally attempts
to murder him in outrageous violence. Their struggle ends with
His victory, who then abandons Her in nature.

"We will conquer this wilderness, it will not consume us!"
says the head of the family in another movie that also deals with
man's struggle with nature, and the supernatural: *The Witch*.[31]
But everything comes to nought. In the film we follow the
expedition of a religious family in New England, banished from a
pilgrim settlement on account of the father's extremely orthodox
religious beliefs. Because of his religious conviction the family
seeks out the borders of an ancient forest, where they build their

home. From within the forest, supernatural powers in the forms of witches and beasts conquer the Christian and human family, bit by bit. The whole family is killed, apart from the teenage girl, who has been made a scapegoat by her own parents of all that went amiss. They were convinced that she had inflicted the ill fate her family suffered with a malicious intent – she must be the witch. Eventually the young girl is offered the chance to join the witches in the forest, laughing and levitating she finally is freed from the millstone of her family and their wrongful accusations. She was never a witch – not until now.

What is so exciting about *Antichrist* by Lars von Trier is its openness to interpretation. The film emphasizes Her physical and natural existence – His spiritual and cultural existence. She is emotional and without self control – He is virtuous and rational. She does not find any ordinary cure for her ailments – He is a psychologist and believes in the power of its therapies. Thus the binary oppositions are faithfully reproduced, according to millennia of cultural reinforcement, in the first half of the movie. The second half proposes a shift, as they move into the realm of nature. She refers to this realm as "Satan's church" and thus alludes to the idea that wild nature is something outside of, and opposed to, culture. Suddenly we see with His eyes the ground of "Satan's church" coming alive, nature pulsating, becoming lush and green, withering, rotting, decaying. The animals take part in these processes. They are made disturbingly wild – until they address Him. But at that point the dualism of Him and Her has been so strongly underpinned, that one doubts if his perceptions can be taken literally: they must be cinematographical metaphors! When He has executed Her and leaves the forest, suddenly a legion of women appear from out between the trees. They appear in a spectral way, like ghosts or the spirits of past times. Maybe these women are the victims of witch-hunts. The victims of the dualities that He and She represent. But He is blind to their presence.

It is interesting in this context to mention that both Icelandic elf- and troll-tales more often employ women figures than males. Elves and trolls, just like witches, can be magical, curse people, inflict diseases or cause people to lose their minds (the Icelandic word *trylla*, means to make someone lose their mind, and has clear etymological ties to the word for *troll* or *tröll*). These beings are at times benevolent and tender but can also become suddenly angry and hurt people for no obvious reasons. Their actions come across as irrational. These beings reflect our ideas about the generosity and cruelty of nature. Nature gives and takes and is dangerous as it is unpredictable, cruel and merciless.

With this in mind, we could say that when we Icelanders assert our humanity in opposition to elves, we are actually making attempts at identifying with civilized and virtuous nations that are known to make rational decisions and can be trusted to act on those same decisions. We don't act violently, we don't act on emotion. We are neither dangerous nor crazy. We are a nation that has left the mud houses of the bygone farmer's society – away from the untamed and cruel nature.

But still we think of relocating occasional elven stones, so long as these relocations are framed in terms of history and cultural heritage. "The Office of Public Road Construction doesn't believe in elves", G. Pétur Matthíasson – the PR agent of the Office – said when I interviewed him in 2015 on occasion of the, then current, road construction in Gálgahraun. "But we consider such an event [to move elven stones] a part of Icelandic cultural heritage",[32] he explained, when I asked him about the relocation of the stones in Gálgahraun.

In his paper, *Menningararfur: Sagan í neytendaumbúðum* ("Cultural Heritage: History for Consumption") the afore-mentioned Valdimar Tr. Hafstein puts forward the notion that the discourse on cultural heritage affects people's actions and perceptions.[33] It was, in this respect, so interesting that G. Pétur mentioned cultural history and cultural heritage. His reference to cultural heritage draws a sharp dividing line between the modern man and the past when Icelanders used to respect the elven stones on the terms of the elves themselves and on nature's terms, not on the terms of culture and cultural heritage. Relocating the elven stones as a culturally sensitive gesture breaks the chain between the stones and the superstition, nature and "others" – and importance is given to the relationship between the stones and a civilized, modern, rational human being. Relocating an elven stone in this sense is therefore a modern and rational, not to say an enlightened, decision.

Becoming elf – becoming witch – becoming "crazy"

What foreign journalists have found most fascinating about modern Icelandic elf-belief is that the Office of Public Road Construction is still spending money and efforts on conserving elven stones when roads are being constructed. The cases in point are not so few, and they can be observed decades back in time. The modern elf-tales often speak of curious vehicle malfunctioning, accidents, nightmares of workers or people around the construc-tion area and messages relayed from beyond, through dreams.[34] These events are then associated with elves or hidden people who are intent on delaying or disturbing the construction by threat-ening dire consequences to anyone who crosses their will.

As nigh always in tales of supernatural beings, elf-tales
are employed to explain something that can not otherwise be
explained: things get lost but are found later in an obvious place,
unusual malfunctioning of people's devices, fear or an uncanny
feeling towards a certain landscape, certain actions etc. In my
hometown of Hafnarfjörður many elf-tales circulate and quite
a number of elven stones and fells can be found, where elves
supposedly live. Hafnarfjörður stands in a lava field and the
formations of the rocks can be strange and function as some kind
of markers in the landscape. It is usually with such landmarks
that the elf-stories are associated.

I never gave the elf-stories of Hafnarfjörður any serious
thought until the new road through Gálgahraun was constructed. The discussion about the elven stones soon turned into
a polemic accusation that some Icelanders – and especially
elf-seers – were insane, but still a lot of people disagreed with
the construction of the road, as it ran straight through a beautiful lava field that until 2015 had been left untouched. Electrical
blackouts occurred a few times in the neighbouring town of
Álftanes during the construction period and stories about
vehicle malfunctioning circulated. Constructions were delayed.
An elf-seer visited the construction site, natural conservationists protested and the police made arrests. Among those
arrested were many senior citizens that the police handcuffed in
the lava field, one of them a famous and cherished comedian and
TV personality, Ómar Ragnarson. All these events made the
discourse on insanity uninteresting. There was something else
going on, something that speaks volumes about the identities
of people and the society, its history and popular conceptions,
nostalgia, guilt, conflict, capitalism, generations and definitions
of otherness.

I spent a few days with members of a Japanese film crew who wanted to learn about Icelandic elf-belief because of the road construction in Gálgahraun. When I started rambling on about my thoughts, they asked me to please talk less and move closer to the elven stone we stood by. Finally I was asked to lean against the stone, lie on top of it and stroke it – knock on it as if I were expecting someone to answer the door. Maybe the Japanese TV spectator was supposed to think that I thought that there was an elf in the stone. And then suddenly it dawned on me: I had myself been transformed into an elf in the eyes of the members of the film crew. I had been turned into an alien being in a distant, remote place, a being so connected to the unspoiled and wild nature that she knocks on stones and waits patient for an answer while others connect to the world around them through Facebook or Twitter.

The cameraman gestured to me and the director, that he was content with my long blond hair and my blue coat with its fur collar because of its "old-fashioned" manner. I had turned into some kind of 19th century elf and I was to be portrayed as such on Japanese television. In these circumstances I even tried to explain that the elf-belief was similar to the ghost-belief that the Japanese knew from their home country. It would definitely be an odd sight to have someone figure as a ghost on Japanese television – why then have me figure as an elf?

As I lay on the elven stone in front of the Japanese film crew I realized for the first time why so many of my acquaintances, that have done academic research on elf-belief or used it as an inspiration for artistic creation, stopped answering the questions of foreign journalists, stopped meeting them – decided to occupy themselves with other things. Wind from the ocean, swept over the lava field and blew in my hair.

"Yes, great, look at the stone now!" the American interpreter working with the film crew exclaimed. "Keep on stroking it and ... and look as if you were looking *into* the stone!"

I had been conquered by the binary oppositions. They crept upon me from behind. Probably just like they crawled upon the myriad witches who were burned in past times, or all kinds of people who have been labelled insane. Suddenly I had become one of these naturally connected women, an emotional being in the realm of nature. Insane even. Me, that had always rolled my eyes when people asked if elves could be seen in Iceland, I had become a very visible elf indeed, in a documentary about Iceland. Elf-belief is certainly always developing and now I had been made a part of that development. Like the "witch" that buries her nose in books, learns about the world and mediates her knowledge to others – but ends up becoming *one of "them"*.

Bryndís Björgvinsdóttir (born March 24, 1982) is an Icelandic author and folklorist. She started her writing career at fifteen when she co-authored the book *Orðabelgur Ormars ofurmennis* (*The Wordballoon of Worm Wonderman*). In 2011 she returned to writing with the children's book *Flugan sem stöðvaði stríðið* (*The Fly Who Ended the War*) which won the Icelandic Children's Book Prize (2011). Three years later she published the young adult book *Hafnfirðingabrandarinn* (*The Local Joke*) which won both the Icelandic Literary Prize (2014) and the Icelandic Women's Literature Prize (or Fjöruverðlaunin 2014). In 2015 she co-authored the book, *Leitin að tilgangi unglingsins,* with two teenagers, Arnór Björnsson and Óli Gunnar Gunnarsson. *The Fly Who Ended the War* will soon be published in Korea, The Untied Arab Emirates, Turkey and France.

Currently Bryndís is working as a folklorist, host and a screen writer for the TV-Series *Reimleikar* (*The Haunting*) on ghosts, elves, trolls and other supernatural beings in Icelandic folklore. The series will be broadcast on National Television (RÚV) this autumn. Bryndís has written several theoretical articles on elves, folk-tales, jokes, cultural heritage, performance-theory, and the artistic work of Kurt Vonnegut and Kurt Cobain.

Bryndís is an adjunct professor at Iceland Academy of the Arts, in the department of design and architecture.

PALERMO DEATHTRIP

Iain Sinclair

Dead already and dead again.
— Jack Kerouac

The shadows of war planes printing across bare, bone-dry fields. Another invasion fleet in a cloudless sky-ocean. Sandcastles and defensive mounds floating free like barrage balloons. From Africa and the scattered islands, they find their justification in the aerial devastation that travelled the other way, south, with iron crosses on the wings. A golden gerfalcon on a Norman battle standard. Flickering newsreels swamped by martial music and the choke of strident propagandist voices. In the year of my birth. In the safety of windowless studios. Fire-storms against Templars and populace in their cool burrows. In round-bellied grain cellars. And catacombs. Sleeping on platforms of sleepers, the folded dead hidden from sunlight. A harvest of Superfortress bombs for the port, the occupied city. Icarus reflexes in a leather helmet. From this lung-pinching height the landscape is a map of mortality. Gold pillars and tributes to a water clock in the interior dazzle of the Palatine Chapel.

1985. Mid-channel on his 54-mile odyssey, Nicky Farrugia, shaven head butting in phallic frenzy, swims from Sicily to the island of Gozo; to be hauled ashore, an acclaimed hero, by the grid of the saltpans. Water polo for the Sirens. A man disguised in sexual orientation. Fireworks, hard pink cakes. Thirty hours and twenty minutes in a metal cage. Arriving, as light fades, on a Mediterranean Sunday. Calypso in a cave. That mazy passage out of time and into myth. Some of them in cliff crannies are scratching at parchment. Electing books worthy of drowning. Nicky's salt-stiff tongue fills his mouth with crystals. The sea around him is on fire. The naked woman in the painting crests the ruffled surface, showing him how it should be managed. Like crawling out of a swan's nest, slippery with remembered pleasures. The reek of doused candlefat, guano in red-tile gutters. Ancient sea things fixed, still breathing, in limestone. Nicky rises and falls between the fingerprint contours of a painted ocean with its gemstone islands. The double page map from *Book of Roger* by al-Idrisi. Heavenly blue on reed paper. Muslim theology made tender by the stern benevolence of Christian kings. Extinguished stars in the infinity of space. There are fish that flare unseen in fathomless depths.

She picks her way, with graceful discrimination, down steps cut into the rock below the hollow shell of a Roman temple. A fake.

A folly. A strong woman of the north in snowy wrap. Acolytes in white suits and dark glasses. Made darker with aircraft paint. Blinding them from the forbidden sight as a Homeric sun rises, in cloud-piercing searchlight beams, over the blue mountains. Across the harbour. As the fishing boats putputput out to sea. Hefty handmaidens attend, catching the towelling wrap as the presence honours the gentle wash of petrol-slicked water against the privileged steps. A shivering palm tree perched on its ledge is the X-ray of a straw bear about to dive. Crumpled waiters are laying freshly ironed white cloths on breakfast tables, set at a discrete distance one from another, on the terrace. It is Greta Garbo. While she was still Garbo. While the hotel sustained its aura as the private villa of a very rich man and his celebrated wife. The illegitimate photographer secures his shot. The Maltese waiter secures his pocket-bulging bribe, his Sicilian beak. The framing is austere. The naked swimmer emerging, arms raised to receive the spread of the upheld garment. Management asserts the right. A voyeur's heavy album on the polished desk in a locked office. Superstar gods and goddesses bent to the collector's whim. Fornicating across Second Empire furniture. Bored actors trapped in those terrible times of self-impersonation – hollow, hollow, hollow – at the bar, stepping from the limousine, in the bedroom. A photographer is a disposable asset. His Cyclops stare. His darkroom alchemy. A body in a bag. Wrapped in newspaper. Centrifugal displacement. Bombed car burning in quarry. Suspended investigation. Found floating. Sleeping with the fishes. Eyeless in Gozo.

This is the place, but not the story. So many lines of flight. The journalist. The poet. The tenured academic who says that he interprets and also performs, as he follows the steps of the dance. A winter package. Low season. Change at Rome. Drop off the two American priests in designer black, texting ahead, securing Vatican transport. Follow the market. The writer is coming to Palermo to unpick the threads. Lucky Luciano and Joe Bananas, 1957, securing a conference room in the Grand Hotel et des Palmes, to set out a business plan: assassination, people trafficking, narco architecture, meatballs, movie deals. Sigmund Freud, on sabbatical, in a lesser establishment, haunting the gilt and alabaster of antique shops, thefts from archaeological sites, construction sites – and seeing Oedipus, with bleeding eyes, in the dust of a white road. The journalist is here for "an associational tracking of some layers and patterns of vertiginous jostle-spin through history". Or he will respect the oracle of place and kill himself. This story is about death, cameras, crosses and confessions. It is about the dead preying upon us. And the reflex gestures we make to keep them mute. To burn the milk of their eyes. The scribbler blows out his match. He puts his pistol on the table and starts to type.

Palermo. 10.30am. Friday, December 11, 2015. I'm not easy with this commission, he says. I have a sense of what it might cost, that old familiar business of staring into the abyss and having the abyss stare right back. Most of my travels, over the years, have been pedestrian, tramping the neural pathways and motorway fringes of London.

If the poet Raymond Roussel voyaged far and wide – Europe, Egypt, India, China, Japan, America, anywhere to drain the curse of inherited wealth – he was fastidious in his avoidance of mere detail. Local particulars remained local. And as welcome on the ivory page as a blood-inflated malarial swamp fly. Or a handprint in liquid dung. Touring in his *roulotte*, a vehicle like a customised hearse or land yacht, the great solipsist kept the blinds drawn while he stitched an occulted poetry into defence-less notebooks. He imagined machines as fantastic as anything in Jules Verne, but avoided the vulgarity of documentary report-age. Evidence was anathema. He was much photographed, but those images are performances. Roussel could and did invent camera-pens and other cannibalistic devices, but he was wise enough never to use them. (He'd done all that as a 12-year-old child when he received a camera as a gift, and committed a few portraits of family and friends as a way of disposing of them, making them collectable.) The poet understood the necessity for servants. As chauffeurs, procurers and loggers of chemical intake. He knew that Palermo was a good place to close the final parenthesis, without the requirement of inspecting a cellar of monkish husks, overgrown bluebottles in dry sacks, the meat overcoats of former humans who won't be using their cloakroom tickets. A cloister of mummified Capuchin friars.

I need images, the journalist said. Without them, I wouldn't trust my experience of what's required to shape a narrative. *I don't trust my memory.* In writing, we make new memories, improved memories. We cheat the death of time by re-living, repeating, cutting all the clutter. Or not *all* the clutter, because once the first sentence is on the page, the voices start up, the insect chorus clamouring for attention. Every book I have written, he said, is also a book of erased photographs. Snapshots are the only annotations I can usefully draw on. My notebook scribbles are unintelligible, more about making a mark, like the rubbing of a notable brick wall, than retrieving information. I might assemble hundreds of pages of journal entries, quotations, cuttings, diagrams and story-boards. And never consult them. But I do return, taking a breather between sections, to the leatherette photo albums. *What is the attraction?* Without pictures, it is just noise.

A diary of sixty images covers Palermo. I'm well aware that photography is collaboration. A neurosis flattered by recent technology. The madness now is a compulsion to catch everything, to foreground the *me*, or the absence of a valid self outside the captured version, the spectral transfer instantly broadcast to other electronic devices. The internet is essentially vampiric, it fishes for unanchored souls. And its hunger can never be satisfied.

On board the Alitalia flight, in a twilight of shared viruses and safety semaphore signalling the reverse message – *you might all die and there's nothing anybody can do* – we witness evolution in progress: thumbs are growing, becoming prehensile, more like bent cocks than digits, as they stroke and probe across the softly yielding skin of iPads and iPhones. These shrivelled movies, icons of urgency, broadcast acts that were once private: scarlet dresses that scream for attention, amateurs who know just how to pose by thrusting out a leg. The glowing devices illuminate the gloom like an aisle of blue candles. As never satisfied thumbs scroll and enlarge in an orgy of restlessness.

Committing any image is a theft against the integrity of appearance. Like looking at the lines of propped up dead in a catacomb, there is a cost, a service charge: *they look back.* The vision is the vision witnessed by an unacknowledged presence standing *right behind you.* It's relatively harmless to dissolve, as I do, into taxonomies of sunrise, postcard epiphanies across the harbour, as captured through strategically opened wooden shutters. But if I make a portrait of a bulbous armchair, in diamond pattern red-orange, wedged into the corner of the room against the *belle époque* floral tracery of the brocade wall-coverings, or a light bowl like a suspended soup tureen, I am projecting a lie. The objects no longer speak for themselves. They are suborned.

I am thinking, by way of the spidery penumbra around the heavy shoulders of the chair, about Roussel, his suite at the Grande Albergo e delle Palme. I remember the festering wound to his left wrist, inflicted in the bath, the feeble slashes at his throat, and how the heavy ennui of the bedroom was not heavy enough. Those mirrors! We are told that Roussel tried to bribe his companion Charlotte Dufrène – and Orlando, the hotel valet – to put him out of his misery. That's what servants are for: to measure out the barbiturates, the nightly ration of euphoria. Before a hallucinated drive around the back streets of Palermo with a chauffeur who disappears into the dawn, when his employer's body is discovered, sprawled across a mattress on the floor. An overdose is not an overdose, it's the right amount. It gets the job done. Like a hanged man, hooded and bound, Roussel climaxed in transit.

Hungry spores hibernating in velvet curtains and damask sheets, in body perfumes soaked into fat armchairs, couldn't help themselves now. They spoke of Oscar Wilde and all his sad hotels. A last quip: "My wallpaper and I are fighting a duel to the death. One or the other of us has to go."

NO FOTO NO FILM, it says on the wall of the Palermo catacombs. No film, no photo. No story.

Somnambulists who will never wake again are massed in underworld galleries like workhouse donkeys waiting for a dole of gruel. And the champagne decadents in their claustrophobic suites are waiting too. The ones who, terrified of falling into the bottomless pit, curl up on the marble floor like premature effigies.

"I dreamt I was supping with the dead", Wilde is reported to have told his twin watchers, Reggie Turner and Robbie Ross.

After a mocking rosary had been pressed into the playwright's cold white hand, Ross asked Maurice Gilbert to take a flash portrait of the corpse. This was the final indignity. Light scalding blank eyes. Chemicals fixing death. Dead words are now quotations printed on vellum.

The portrait of Roussel and his hired beard, Dufrène, owned by the poet John Ashbery, has a slash, like one of the suicide's wild razor strokes, separating man and woman. When Ashbery tracked down the elderly Dufrène, living in retirement in Brussels – an episode that concludes *The Vorrh*, a fiercely possessed novel by B. Catling – the last witness to the events in Palermo tears the photograph into two parts. She gave away Roussel, whose books she neither understood nor admired in ignorance. She kept her own portion. Perhaps she liked the hat. It sits like a sheep's head with the ears still attached. Or, as Catling has it, "the neck of a dead, inverted swan".

Mount Etna was throwing out flames, the first spectacular lightshow in twenty years. Roussel's overdose followed a major firework display in Palermo, with drums and crowds; a double celebration, the festival of Santa Rosalia and a decree by Italy's new warrior-lord, Benito Mussolini, for the populace to salute the successful transatlantic hop by General Italo Balbo and his squadron of flying boats. The minatory shadows of Regia Aeronautica aircraft, over Atlantic waves, were a premonition of more sinister engagements alongside the Condor Legion in Spain. And the raining of bombs, unopposed, on Ethiopia.

The giant set of prints by the photographer Ian Wilkinson would not be slipping through any floorboards. This folder of rigorously composed images of the Capuchin catacombs with their strange black fruit disturbed me, even when the prints were hidden away in the clutter of a room beneath the desk where I was writing. That was my commission.

Wilkinson had a studio, presses humming, close to a gallery in an English market town. He was very good at what he did, working with artists of the calibre of Paula Rego, Paolozzi and Elizabeth Frink. When I met him, among the chemicals, machines, proofs and trials of a first-floor atelier, he moved easily, rested comfortably, and looked as if he belonged in his environment. The prints derived from obsessive returns to the Palermo catacombs were his secret. He had the modesty of a maker who recognises no obligation to explain his practice. Wilkinson mastered the technicalities of what he was required to do, but there was this other thing, the mammal's spinal dream.

With the prints laid out on a bench like a mortuary slab, I handle them with some reluctance. Conversation overrides close inspection. This is not the moment for ekphrasis, breaking down the elements of the compositions into art-historic references, seeking sources, mapping the madness. I am wary of letting out pre-fictional connections, muffling the piercing shrieks of the originals. Better to let the artist tell his own stories. The corpses yap in an unknown language that sounds like Latin.

There are two journeys: the underworld of the Capuchin catacombs and the flat fields of Northamptonshire. Wilkinson comes to Palermo. He encounters Fabrizio, the genial doorkeeper, who relieves the questing artist of a bundle of euros and allows him to spend time alone in the catacomb corridors, tempting the mummified tenants to stain the purity of his digital screen. The printmaker is an entomologist of fluttering shadows: moth-lace and straw breath in subtle darkness. Images are grounded in velvety black, a perpetual night. Priests howl. Bone is pumice. Hands are empty gloves. A child's flesh is cruelly preserved in waxy curd. There is a danger that the watching dead will become mere décor, flattered, arranged, made into theatre; a last supper at which nobody gets to taste a crumb. They have already eaten their own flesh. The rags of their clothes are more comfortable in their pantomime narrative.

The catholic pilgrimage, the cellar with its respite from a merciless sun, plays against a miracle of crows and hedgehoppers, starlings, thrushes, delicate bones in delicate cages. That was the other walk. Wilkinson came across a deserted farmhouse and a crumbling chimneybreast stuffed with birds. The creatures of the air will enter a dialogue with the mummies in their alcoves. It seemed as if the gaping mouths of the preserved monks, toothless or wrecked, were releasing flocks.

"The project came about primarily because of two dreams and two coincidences," Wilkinson said. "I suffered a lot with nightmares as a child. I was walking down a corridor and at the end were more corridors with people talking to each other, talking about me. I was lying in bed and a black bird flew on to a window ledge. I thought it was checking me out, as to whether I was ready to cross over."

The Capuchin catacombs, accessed with no prior knowledge or expectation, brought back the corridor of that childhood dream. The strangers were still talking – with the voices of birds. Roberto Bolaño writes about the late Joan Vollmer, shot by William Burroughs in Mexico City: "She chain-smokes invisible cigarettes. She tells me that her cigarettes are a strange brand: some make her speak in the first person and others in the third person, in that choked and spasmodically seismic language that is the International Language of the Dead... a language of tremor-like cadences."

The catacomb prints have that tremor. You can *hear* them and feel them touching you. But you have to speak 'bird' to understand what they are saying. Birds are immortal souls. The mummies are empty envelopes, stuffed with straw, stitched from cured bacon.

"It wasn't terror I experienced," Wilkinson reported. "It was a revelation and comforting."

Lucia Impelluso in *Nature and Its Symbols* (2004) tells us that "birds, like butterflies, more generally represented the human soul as it abandons the body at the moment of death." But they can also be interpreted as bringers of bad luck, harpies, creatures that tear and devour human flesh.

When I gave myself up to the index of these necrophile prints, I began to see them as a book of secular saints, existing outside theology, outside time. The mummy shells had not been sanctified for miracles performed during their earthly lives, they were conduits for future miracles. Oracular and blasphemous. Mute but talking in bird code.

"The crow," Robert Graves tells us in *The White Goddess*, "was a bird much consulted by augurs." Graves associates the crow with Bran the Crow-god: "but crow, raven, scald-crow and other large black carrion birds are not always differentiated in early times." Crows have picked out the eyes of the witnessing dead, making battlefield corpses into leather. Into the kind of cloaks studio photographers used to mask their cameras. The Capuchin mummies are not there to be inspected by congeries of awed and shuffling tourists, they are recording instruments, sucking up breath, glistening with borrowed sweat, avid for language. The hung mummies are meat cameras. *And they are looking right back at the thing that is looking at them.*

With the discovery of a labyrinth of underground burials in Rome in 1578, mountains of early Christian bones were disinterred; bones that could be an insanitary nuisance or a resource. The mercantile wing of the Catholic church, with its well-honed predatory instincts, its relic franchise, its travel bureau for guaranteed safe passage to the next world, business class to heaven, recognised a golden opportunity. German churches and religious houses needed a USP, a cash magnet attraction for pilgrims. They needed miracle-working arrangements of bones. And there were plenty on offer in Italy. Decorated in gold thread and pearls, nun-worked lace and fine cambric, spattered with emeralds and rubies, these manufactured replacements for the idolatrous effigies destroyed during the Protestant Reformation were known as *Katakombenheiligen*. Or 'catacomb saints'. Certificates of fraudulent authenticity were purchased. Protestant carriers had no qualms – for a price – about transporting the ossuary bags across the Alps.

New beings emerged from the slumber of sandstone shelves into the light of display in cathedrals and restored churches. Veiled, with lips rouged, wigged in silvery strands, the skeletal saints 'rescued' from the dignity of death were paraded in travesty. Their invented biographies were surrealist hypotheses for a theme park theology. Paul Koudounaris in *Heavenly Bodies: Cult Treasures & Spectacular Saints from the Catacombs* (2013) points out that German saints frequently became books. Engravings were printed as 'souvenirs of translation'. Images "would have been touched to the relic in order to transfer some of its power". Then texts were commissioned "to reinforce the role the newly arrived relic would play in the lives of the faithful." The book of the catacomb saint carried the potency of new myth back out into the world.

Now I understood something of my part in this dubious enterprise. "The skeleton could settle into its new role of patron and protector of the community." And, sprawled in a rattan chair on my balcony overlooking the harbour, I could freeze the trajectory of the silver bullet aimed at my temple until the words ran out.

I met the photographer Mimi Mollica in Hackney Wick. In the lull of the last years before the great Olympic enclosures. Mimi had the habit of hanging huge prints in the window of his first-floor studio: challenging faces of West Africa, Romania, Brazil, Pakistan. And Palermo. Born in the Sicilian city-port, Mimi was a world traveller. Living so intimately with death, he had no need to record the catacombs. The scenes he confronted in the narrow streets of Palermo referenced that intimacy.

When I left him, Mimi presented me with a book of photographs called *Untoccodikalsa*. On the endpaper he drew a serpentine map of his life: Palermo to Brixton, Tunisia to Hackney, and Palermo again. Stick figures in the tarantella of death's festival. The husks of the catacombs were given balance by the men Mimi photographed, eating and drinking at their tables on the streets above them.

The writer Robin Cook, rebranded as 'Derek Raymond' after a stint in the French vineyards, took mortality as his abiding theme. "The General Contract", he called it. Interviewed at the City Airport in Silvertown in 1992, he said: "You can't keep the dead out... They come anyway. They rest on your shoulder, whatever you're doing, they weigh *nothing*... Death lasts much longer than life...The living say, 'It's bad news to be wanted by the dead.' But I don't think so. No, I don't think so."

Cook's favourite quote was from the Brian De Palma remake of *Scarface*. He watched the VHS thirteen times. Al Pacino saying "Every day above ground is a good day."

Mimi's drinkers, substantial males in sleeveless shirts, white vests, religious medallions, joshing around the café table, are materially above ground, but they are also the ferrymen, the facilitators. They are dipped in death and it shows in their cold eyes. They are Palermo Mafiosi, foot soldiers of the Kalsa district. They are gregarious and competitive boozers of small beer. They carve pig cheeks with big knives. Mimi is an implicated witness, a master of the choreography of risk: the drunk man singing or threatening with upraised ham-hock arms, the silver-haired onlooker clutching his balls. Made men suck and swallow the fruits of the sea in a belch of entitlement. They mime contract killings with outstretched fingers. They kill time with greasy playing cards: between markets, between collections. The *pizzo*, the beak. Between assignments. On an exposed thigh, the tattoo of a gun is shown to the photographer. A boast. A warning. Recreational Mafiosi smoke like prisoners. They have bracelets like manacles, watches as heavy as police tags. They are garrotted in thick gold necklaces.

Coming to Palermo, I wanted to pay my respects to B. Catling's novel, *The Vorrh*. And to investigate the role that Raymond Roussel and *Impressions of Africa* paid in the composition of a fabulation that seemed to arrive fully formed out of nowhere. Out of the insect-heavy darkness of a reimagined equatorial night. Out of smeared train windows.

Roussel's craft – shipwrecked on an alien shore – begins with a pun, the first sentence that finds resolution in its mirror image. It is called his *procédé poétique*. "I was led," he wrote, "to take a random phrase from which I would derive images by distorting it, a little as one might develop images while devising a rebus." A shipwreck is always a good beginning, a good point of departure – though now undone, horribly, by the weight of migrants risking everything on that voyage into Italy, the Greek islands, Malta. Out of Africa, Syria, Afghanistan. The unanswered outpouring of the collateral damage of oil wars. The photograph is a dead infant washed ashore. Shakespeare's *The Tempest* is about the magic of renouncing magic, not drawing down lightning strokes to animate gibbet pickings, a midden of broken phrases. It's about flight and song and the kind of otherworldy monsters we ordinary folk, compressing them into respectable dullness, fail to notice. Or to mate with. To our advantage.

Catling notices. Roussel's Egyptian travel journals give nothing away. *Impressions of Africa* is a series of photographs not taken and line drawings found rather than made: the impressions are inky transfers, hints, suggestions. Roussel's fastidiously conceived vanity chapbooks are available for years beyond his death in Palermo.

The poet travels with his mother and with Charlotte Dufrène, the *maîtresse de convenance* paid by his mother: a monthly salary and a flat in the 8th *arrondissement*. He leaves, in cavernous hotel suites, first-class railway carriages, cabins, the sickly perfume of an *impression*: that he would like to absorb. The intangible essence of these women. He dresses Charlotte but does not touch her; fresh white gloves for every appearance, every operation, every ride. Dufrène reports that when she had been written into a new outfit of Roussel's devising, the poet shrunk back into the corner of the car, with the horror of brushing against her person, ruining the *impression* he had created.

I've no idea when Roussel became a significant figure for Catling. Alan Moore, in his generous introduction to *The Vorrh*,

positioning it as "easily the current century's first landmark
work of fantasy", makes no mention of the French poet. But he
does, consciously or unconsciously, use the phrase "corseted and
hidebound" to describe the genre he sees Catling invading and
reviving. *Corseted.* We jump at once to the opening of *Impressions of Africa*, to the sculpture of a slave constructed by Norbert
Montalescot and his sister Louise, at the order of the African
king, Talou VII. Mark Ford in *Raymond Roussel and the Republic
of Dreams* tells us that "the statue is fashioned out of black corset
whalebones and is fixed to a trolley – also of corset whalebones
– whose wheels rest on two red, gelatinous rails moulded out of
prepared calves' lights." Roussel's excruciatingly laboured texts
have been said, by several commentators, to have an addictive
bite. They are coded – with the codes leading nowhere but into
further, more complex equations. Leaving manuscripts on the
shelf, or locked away in a trunk buried in a warehouse depository,
only increases the power of the thing that is unread. Swallowing the light, rather than dissipating it in universal acclaim and
unwonted commentary.

Like Roussel, Catling visited North Africa, without reaching
the equatorial sump, his Edenic forest or heart of darkness. He was
in company with the painter David Russell (a Rousselian near-homonym): friend, patron, mentor. It is easy to image Russell suggesting
or confirming an interest, as they travelled, in *Impressions of Africa*.
But whatever the original infection, Catling produced a typescript
in 1973, forty years before the publication of his novel, a sheaf of
poems. He gave it a handwritten title: *The Vorrh*. When Robert
de Montesquiou (the supposed inspiration for Proust's Baron
de Charlus and Huysmans's Des Esseintes) composed his own
roman à clef, *La Trépidation*, he called the caricature of Roussel:
"Russell". Catling makes his Russell the co-dedicatee of *The Vorrh*.

David, old Etonian alchemist-painter, publisher of private editions, pornographic pop-up fantasies, is thanked for providing "compass, map, and machete". And insisting on the expedition that became, after decades in slumbering suspension, the dangerous book.

Voyaging once more, now in collaboration with the filmmaker Tony Grisoni, Catling arrived in Palermo. The two men had the intention of visiting the Capuchin catacombs, looking into the eye sockets of the dead, and coming out with material for an art installation. Grisoni, covertly or otherwise, would capture the faces, while Catling mediated the script, the voices of the unknown others. A task for which he had demonstrated a particular skill: giving himself up to channelled possession. Beyond the pinch of cured flesh and the overlapping narratives of dust tongues, there was the unspoken ambition to enjoy some good Sicilian cooking, wine, cigars. The aboveground sensory pleasures of sunlight and kitchens. There might be time for a cocktail in the Grand Hotel and a sclerotic lift attendant to show them to Room 224, Roussel's fatal suite. His exit cubicle.

The mummies, in their distinctions of caste and profession, staring out, propped against the walls like prisoners of the Inquisition waiting to be summoned, stayed resolutely silent. Catling was good at knowing when it was better to hold his tongue. The Grisoni carousel of images played on two monitor screens: severed heads in goldfish bowls. The pocket camera, an eavesdropper of no discrimination, had picked up the chatter of the other catacomb visitors: whispers, jokes, asides. Voices of the city filtered from the street above. And that is what they ran when a new audience, an art audience, came to witness the spectacle in Oxford.

Palermo was an opportunity for Catling to inspect the Grand Hotel et des Palmes, as it now calls itself, in Via Roma;

Roussel's Grande Albergo e delle Palme. The Via Wagner, at the
back of the hotel, was named in honour of the composer, after he
had taken a suite while he worked on *Parsifal*. Wagner has a role
to play in Roussel's *Locus Solus*. It was rumoured that a tunnel
ran from the basement of the hotel to the Anglican church on
the other side of the street. The original building was called the
Palazzo Ingham, the residence of a prominent English family.

The Grand Hotel provided the setting for the Prologue to
The Vorrh. As I discovered, when I came to Palermo to set the
experience of being exposed to Ian Wilkinson's prints against the
evidence of the actual catacombs, the hotel had declined from
its status as private Palazzo, wintering retreat for the wealthy,
suitable theatre for voluntary euthanasia, to a high-ceilinged
reception area for coach parties and business groups with
laminated badges searching out the right salon with the hard
chairs and whiteboard.

I tried a few of the corridors, but the ghosts had decamped.
A sunken bar that suggested the waiting room in a crematorium
did its best to invoke the atmosphere of happier days with offers
of 'Cocktail Hemingway' and the reproduction of a painting of
the grizzled author propped in a brown armchair while crushing a
small white dog in the circle of his locked hands. The background
is a psychedelic swirl like the cross section of a heavy drinker's wet
brain. Perhaps the cocktails in this padded chamber are dedicated to celebrity suicides: hemlock Manhattans for sucklers of
shotguns. Cushions are indented with absent bodies.

Why did Roussel choose Palermo? He arranged his affairs
in Paris with his man of business, Eugéne Leiris, father of Michel
(the friend and champion of Francis Bacon). It can't have been
for the catacombs. Roussel had a morbid dislike of tunnels.
Mark Ford says that they "caused him extreme anguish" and

that he avoided travelling by night "for fear of entering one unawares". How he even noticed such things is unclear, with the curtains drawn in his *roulotte*. Roussel's drugged attention was fixed on his work, the endless sifting and revising, or the re-reading of Jules Verne and Pierre Loti. His travels were their travels, composed and completed before he left Paris. All that was required was a set of portrait photographs in immaculate costumes with Basque beret, fez or sailor suit.

Charlotte Dufrène took charge of the medicine cabinet. When supplies of barbiturates ran low, she was sent back to Paris to replenish the Soneryl, Roussel's euphoric of choice. Hopped but corpselike, the neurasthenic dandy who was readying himself for Switzerland (the cure), took his final drive with the chauffeur who would disappear before police enquiries into the suicide were completed. The Grande Albergo was conveniently located for the port, the cruise ships, sailor boys in tight white trousers and dockside hustlers. And if they motored through the four quarters of the city, out to the mountains, the coast road to Mondello, there is no record of a halt at the Capuchin monastery. It would have been tautologous.

Before he left Paris for the last time, Roussel made a significant purchase: a burial site in Père Lachaise. He avoided the family plot in Neuilly and bought an entire catacomb with thirty-two divisions. Returned from Sicily, he was the only occupant.

They refused to become his paid assassins. Or did they? The attendants, courtiers, procurers, connections. Catling has Roussel, naked and shrivelled, thin as a photographic negative, posing in front of a long mirror in a room of "vicious light". Everything that occurred was at his instigation. Now there is a comic other, a phantom double, confronting him on the far side of the ice pond of the mirror. "There were no facts to grip and the fictions were worn out." What happens next is a posthumous dream, a dream that is not his own. *The Vorrh* is the posthumous dream of Raymond Roussel. A somatic topography on the far side of an overdose. But it is much more than that, Roussel is a closed system. Catling's trick was to let his machines write their own stories, like the needle scratching away on the revolving disk of the lighthouse at Trinity Buoy Wharf all those years ago. Roussel is a puppet within the fractal museum of *The Vorrh*, one of his own manikins or reanimated human shells; a mouth-stitched master of ceremonies for Catling's Cabaret Melancholique.

Other figures emerge from the limbo of their post-historic slumbers. Among them the damaged photographer Eadweard Muybridge. Death and the camera join the dance. In retirement, the old man arranges the slaughter of a white horse in a specially constructed barn. He wants to witness the world-tearing flash of the instant of extinguished electro-chemical existence. "Muybridge... busied himself with the cameras, collecting their precious thoughts and taking them away, to be unlocked next door in his night-black chapel of chemicals... He had been at the pinnacle of his life's achievement when he decided to chase another quality in his work: an elusive ghost that permeated everything he photographed. It had led him into deep speculation and personal violation, but still he could not put it aside."

The journalist booked in to the wrong Grand Hotel. Palermo didn't do minor key, all the hotels were grand. Grand Hotel et des Palmes trades on 'faded elegance' and phantoms detached from their shadows leaving no mark on the pre-auction furniture. Roussel's suicide is a specialist attraction for poets and thesis compilers. Grand Hotel Wagner is a "faux-classical monolith, suffocating under heavy wood and gold" in homage to the *Parisifal* composer. Grand Hotel Piazza Borsa, constructed in a former monastery, is "an efficient yet anodyne palazzo restoration".

There are so many decaying palaces. The writer found himself, by the most fortunate of mistakes, in the Grand Hotel Villa Igiea at Acquasanta, an art nouveau mausoleum of considerable charm in a setting so perfect that it was difficult to make any movement beyond the balcony. All this, with upgrade to top floor, perched under blue heaven, harbour view, wooden shutters and original tapestry wall coverings, came, with flights to and from London, for the price of a one-night stopover in a Premier Inn off the Peterborough ring road.

The hotel was the former residence of the Florio family, who made their fortune from wine and tuna. From the balcony, before dawn, the torpid journalist watched searchlight beams break cloud cover like a biblical sign. Open fishing boats were picking their way around the moored yachts and cruisers. If he had stayed at the Villa Igiea to attempt a connection with Roussel and his bitter conclusion, seeing the reflection in the long mirror with its heavy gilded frame (like a late Bacon), he made the right decision.

Villa Igiea was gussied into an operatic *belle époque* set by the architect and designer Ernesto Basile, who was commissioned by Ignazio Florio to convert the cod-gothic heap with its Walter Scott towers and crenellation into a rival to Grand Hotel et des Palmes. Roussel's terminus had been transformed by Ernesto Ragusa in 1874, its luxurious reputation attracting Wagner, Liszt and Renoir. After his 1904 success at Villa Igiea, Basile was invited, in 1907, to work the same magic on Grand Hotel et des Palmes. And so, instead of the tunnel linking hotel and Anglican church, the corridors along which Roussel was supported after yet another smacked ride through the twilight labyrinth seemed to extend to this other Basile makeover, the Marienbad spaces of Villa Igiea. Corridors were endstopped by gigantic mirrors. Every crawl between art nouveau screens, lamp-holders, polished chessboard marble, was an advance on the spectre, the awful double waiting in the frame of the glass. The portrait of death in a dickey bow.

Roussel didn't need to inspect the detritus of the Capuchin catacombs, in his fiction he had already invented methods for bringing the dead back, for reanimating shells of former humans in a simulacrum of life. All those monks on hooks in the subterranean cloakroom are waiting to be scripted by a poet with Roussel's bizarre gifts – and available fortune. The Frenchman tested the language formulae to tap what Grevel Lindrop called "the sleepless memory of the new dead". The shared memory of plants, insects, stones, ancestors, stars. Snow. Sand. Cold semen drying on slate. Death was advancing fast. It was waiting in the suite of a grand hotel. It was waiting in Palermo.

"The hand of death modelled him speedily, soon made his head a skull," Iris Murdoch wrote in *The Black Prince*. "He did not try to write." Death was a release from the obligation to write. Release from the hideous conviction of his own genius, his fate, when the young poet, at the age of seventeen, was possessed "by a fever of work". He saw rays of light streaming from pages he had defaced with images of crowds and factories, fire and smoke. "These terrible compositional tasks," Mark Ford wrote, "seem to prefigure the unstoppable logorrhoea... Equally prescient is the complaint that no one will understand his writings."

In *Locus Solus*, published in 1914, Roussel presents a scholar of private means, Martial Canterel, who conducts a group of acquaintances around the park of "his beautiful villa at Montmorency". The park is gallery, museum, laboratory, philosophical conceit. At the start of the First War, Roussel is bringing back the dead: twitched meat, soulless as cakewalking zombies. Hypnotised sleepwalkers in bone masks. "When Canterel saw what excellent reflexes he obtained with Danton's facial nerves, immobilized by death for over a century, he conceived the hope of producing a complete illusion of life by working with recent corpses protected by intense cold from the slightest corruption."

He succeeded in his blasphemy. "The illusion of life was absolute: mobility of expression, the continual working of the lungs, speech, various actions, walking – nothing was missing." But it remained *an illusion*. Negatives printed into mechanistic performance by doses of the chemical *resurrectine*. Roussel's iced stiffs are nudged towards a temporary status as freakish exhibits. The catacomb larvae of Palermo, generations of Capuchin friars, wrapped in sheets and lowered into a pit, a large cistern under the altar of St Anne, are dried out, drained, stuffed with straw. From the mound of bones, when excavations began in 1599, forty-five corpses are found to be intact, heaped on top of one another in a ghastly Abu Ghraib pyramid. The miracle demands some form of display, and so the cloister of dim corridors is created.

Roussel insisted that a glass panel, a kind of portrait frame, be set in his mother's coffin, to maintain contact until the last possible moment. In the instructions he left with Eugène Leiris, before he departed for Palermo, the neurasthenic author authorised a long incision being made in the vein of his wrist, so that there could be no risk of a Poe-influenced premature burial. The crude excavations of his own flesh, undertaken in the bathroom of his suite at the Grand Hotel, are like a rehearsal for the ritual he has already laid down. You can never trust the servants when they are not properly supervised. The dead poet was embalmed, a technique in which the Capuchins had become masters. Before he was shipped back to Paris and the solitude of his private catacomb.

On the reception desk, when the journalist makes his tour of the deserted hotel, is a lush volume celebrating visitors to the dream hotel, the new royalty of movie stars, actors on location, spillage from the Palermo Film Festival. Sophia Loren with De Sica. Greta Garbo going into the sea from the rocks below the fake temple. Gloria Swanson, the revenant's revenant, former mistress to Joe Kennedy, now accompanied by Paul Newman and Gore Vidal. This way, ladies, for the ballroom of the dead. Burt Lancaster, unlikely Sicilian aristocrat, slips away from Visconti, to drink at the hotel bar with Alain Delon. Kirk Douglas (the last old-Hollywood Russian cowboy standing) escorts Irene Papas. Onassis, in trademark bat-clamp shades, affronted by daylight. Hilary Clinton and her hairdresser. The Blairs, between villas, with their pirate patron, Berlusconi. Actors all in the great game. Take your places, ladies and gentlemen. *Faites vos jeux*.

The car is ready. The journalist's first excursion is to the Capuchin catacombs. The taxi, powered by the spirit of Roussel, cruises the docks and the back streets. It turns right off Via Cappuccini, towards the site of the convent that must once have been on the outskirts of town. Towards the entrance to the underworld. The road is busy, the car is penned against an overflowing stall of fruit and vegetables. The man Fabrizio is waiting in his office.

The entrance fee is so reasonable that the writer suspects there must be a catch. Two euros to set off down the tunnel. Two hundred euros if you elect to take a photograph. He doesn't. The act would be a gross trespass, on what is here, and on the portfolio already achieved by Ian Wilkinson. The sooty, *edible* darkness of his prints. The chimney of birds he has dropped into this bone pit like a funnel for colonic irrigation. The writer hears their brittle chatter as he passes down the steps and along the lugubrious passage to the catacombs.

No other living creature in the place. No *visible* creature. We have trained ourselves not to see. They are with us always, the *others*, as Robin Cook knew. As we drop our guard, tire of the grind, they touch our shoulders. There must have been spiders, dust-excreting insects. But, mercifully, no tour guides, no camera flashes to activate the silent screams of blackened gumless mouths. The rictal chorus of still hungry incisors.

The promenade around the rectangle of the catacomb is slow and steady, shockingly calm. The vertical dead are so many oversized crows. Voices from the street above ventriloquise the gaping mouths. The husks are not separate from the old world, from the city. The writer hears a woman call out "Carmela". And he thinks he hears the leathery creak of the vulture necks of the mummified friars as they turn to locate the source of the sound. The interruption of their special silence. Their *nested* contemplation of mortality.

The Capuchin friars came to this part of Palermo in 1534, establishing themselves in the church of Santa Maria della Pace. It was part of the belief of the time that burial within a sacred building was the smoothest transit lounge for heaven, a ticket of privilege avoiding mobs of the unwashed and plague-ridden. But lay burial was discouraged – up to the point where the economic advantage of selling limited real estate in the afterlife became obvious.

Dead friars were sheet-wrapped and lowered into a communal cistern, a dry well of dark body liquors. The excavations begun in 1599, to construct an underground cemetery, revealed an interlocked stack of corpses: "whole bodies with flexible and fresh flesh, as though the men of faith had been dead for merely a few hours". To make the miracle into a marketable installation, a provocation for pilgrims, the shells of the persevered friars, three-dimensional prints of themselves, were arranged in rows. Some of the monks wear their names on cards like ambushed Mexican bandits or early settlers of the American West who posed for postmortem portraits in strategically tipped coffins.

Before 1670 there were few lay burials. But the pressure of demand – financial, political – began to be felt. The rich and important citizens of Palermo wanted to be preserved like game, dressed for celestial transfer as they had been in life. In 1783 the right to catacomb internment, as part of the Capuchin exhibition, was conceded. There was a candle tax, an obligation to perform certain rites for the souls of the dead. Families made regular visits, to dress and undress their ancestors, to maintain respectability. Natural mummification gave way to the processes of science: draining rooms, removal of brain and entrails, curing, vinegar rubs, stuffing with straw.

No fresh bodies were accepted after 1880. Two exceptions were made: Giovanni Paterniti, the vice-consul of the United States of America, in 1911, and Rosalia Lombardo, a two-year-old child who was embalmed in 1920. Rosalia now rests as the final exhibit and the most disturbing. She is bedded in a display case, waxy, suspended, red gold hair damp with the sweat of fever and tied with a yellow silk bow. On the crumpled cerements over her chest a devotional image has been laid, a sentimental cameo in a snowstorm of spores. The nostrils have been plugged with some white substance, but the sticky eyelids seem to be open, lifeless, but staring out.

There is a glass floor over a beach of memorial stones. The morbidly inclined writer cannot hear his own footfall. The husks, pressed so closely together, a mute jury from the past, absorb sound. There is a division between the bone armatures shrink-wrapped in tanned leather and the clothes that cover them. Clothes age. Clothes have a date and a time. The husks are timeless. They are anaesthetised, waiting on judgement, hands roped. The challenge for the writer is to capture the sense of being suspended between these drained representations, mummified Xeroxes of departed souls, and the reservoir of prints that Wilkinson has made for his catacomb theatre. His animating device is the introduction of English birds. Birds as the missing voices. Birds plucking at straw as the mummies come apart, abdicating their grisly parody of life. The photographer's eye focuses on texture: fraying rope, embroidered silk, rusting key. The roughness of bone as it turns to coral. Any hope of light takes the form of a white feather floating on an unsourced current of warm air. Cobwebs. Stitches. A wine stain of dead hair. Beaks. Wings like the exposed ribs of cat umbrellas.

The writer begins to understand the courage it demands to make an image. Photography is a mortal risk. Beyond the spoiled ghost of Roussel, mesmerised by his Grand Hotel mirror, Catling summons Eadweard Muybridge, the man who tried to break the stream of time into a legible sequence of single frames. Imprisoned within the complex currents of *The Vorrh*, Muybridge is "a hollow man". He is both photographer and photograph. The perfect model for any attempt to register the catacomb prisoners. We, the pilgrims, are the light the dead drink. The sound that troubles their stopped memory.

Death and the camera. Death *is* a camera. Catling presents Muybridge (whose paint-smeared books of naked acrobats and blind animals lay on the floor of Francis Bacon's Kensington studio) as a bladder: "a camera without an aperture". Passing alone down the avenue of grinning Capuchin skulls, stuffed friars, uniformed corpses, mummies in mourning rags, the journalist convinces himself that these *things* are cameras, hungry for whatever wafers of light he transports from the upper world. They suck. They absorb. The slender images of passing visitors feed the synapses, creating false or borrowed memory cards. When the intruders depart, skulls croak like stretched birds.

The friars, the lawyers, the catacomb saints of Palermo are so many wet prints drying on hooks. Huge hands have atrophied. Straw bursts from the sliced sternum. The mummies are Eliot's "Hollow Men". Wilkinson recognised them as scarecrows. The sacks of avian skeletons, sculpted by natural process, rescued from their English chimneypiece, voice the tiled avenues of Sicilian dead. Those who are ambitious to scare crows must first attract them. "Sightless," Eliot said, "unless the eyes reappear as the perpetual star."

The garden of remembrance is immaculately kept. White angels guard white tombs in which the dead are laid out, facing the glittering belt of stars. Naked saints on their plinths, near the cathedral, closer to the centre of Palermo, were not so fortunate. Shocked nuns struck off their noses, in lieu of exposed dangly parts they were ashamed to touch. Processing down the cypress avenues, breathing deep to expel the dust, it was hard for the writer to shake off the imprint of the shelves of skulls and half-skulls, the disarticulated jawbones. They invoked contemporary atrocity photographs, massacre reports from Rwanda, Cambodia, Second War Poland and Russia: the universal concentration camp. Multiplying horrors of a digital world feeding on an eschatology of woodcuts from the dark ages.

The bereaved tended small gardens within the grave plots, memory allotments. Among the grey and white blocks, beds of pink and red flowers, uncloying scents. Some of the sepulchres were as large as temples, an unoccupied suburb waiting for the next volcanic eruption. There were memorials to victims of the Mafia. PIO LA TORRE COMMUNISTA. ASSASSINATO DALLA MAFIA. But the detail that pricked the journalist's attention was the way that so many of the headstones were implanted with photographic portraits of the deceased. The chosen badge of a living moment imposed on the plurality of death. Oval portraits glinted in the sunlight like proud brooches. Like snails fed on light.

At the sharp angle between two walls of family photographs, a woman in a red wig is making a call on her mobile phone. She has arrived at the optimum position for contacting her lost ones. The *L* of the wall is one of the missing letters dividing *Roussel* from Russell. Oh yes, they talk back: the departed husbands, sisters, children. The fire-wigged woman gestures in exasperation. Death has done nothing to smooth away old faults. Stripped of her hair-hat, this widow in her smart black coat would call up the naked skull of the wife in the tableau of the married couple, down below in the catacombs. The ones leaning together, with empty sockets and two teeth between them, arguing for eternity. And becoming a popular postcard on the carousel beside Fabrizio's office. *Marito e Moglie. Mann und Frau.*

A circuit of the tombs, inspecting every stone, resting on a stone bench in the cypress avenue, does not reveal the journalist's name on any of the memorials. No oval portrait. Not yet. He puts a small cigar in his mouth, but does not light it. To hold the hour, he takes out a slim book. "My work took me to Sicily... I've been there. There is nothing more to see, there's nothing more to investigate, nothing. There's nothing in Sicily to investigate." *Silence.* "I had a great crew in Sicily. A marvellous cameraman. We took a pretty austere look at the women in black. The little old women in black." *Silence.*

Two postcards, then, and no photographs. The double page map. The ceramic dish or shield with *triskeles*, three legs on a pin running their mad circuit. Freud incubating his cancerous jaw. Roussel nursing his last dose. Luciano offering a Judas kiss. A city spoiled by history. A monkish walker returned from the mainland to found a refuge for the dispossessed. It is time for the writer to align himself at the quadrivium where they bury suicides, skulls lopped off as trophies, stakes through the heart. *Il Teatro del Sorte*, the Theatre of the Sun. The four quarters of the city. It is time to walk.

Iain Sinclair has lived in Hackney since 1968.

He is working on *The Last London*, the endgame of a long sequence that includes *Lud Heat* (1975), *Downriver* (1991), *Lights out for the Territory* (1997), *London Orbital* (2002) and *Hackney, That Rose-Red Empire* (2009).

CITY OF PALACES, CITY OF GHOSTS

Silvia Moreno-Garcia

In the 1905 novel *Santa*, Federico Gamboa charts the path of a small-town *ingénue* turned wealthy, big-city prostitute, and her inevitable decline and death. It's a novel that has been called Mexico's answer to *Nana* and which reproduces, with detail, what Mexico City was like at the turn of the 20th century.

This is a world where areas are filled with "the infectious social rot, the lice only the police dare to scratch", but also a city where rich young men dine in private rooms at the Cafe de Paris. During the daytime, Santa's neighborhood is a place with "a modern and neatly painted butcher shop... with three open doors, smooth artificial flooring, and a counter of marble and iron", a school, restaurants, three electric streetlights, signifying middle class respect and morality. At night, however, it becomes the territory of prostitutes and their clients.

Santa takes place at the crossroads of Mexico City, in the waning years of the Porfirian era. By 1910, the country will have exploded in a Revolution which will take a decade to unwind. In 1905, it is flush with life, having recently become cutting edge. Just like Haussmann's renovation of Paris forever altered the face of that city, Porfirio Diaz's plans of modernization changed Mexico City. The desire of the elites was to become 'modern', and that meant more Parisian. After the Revolution, this changed. It became a desire for the American experience, France having been eclipsed by the Charleston and Art Deco, and this is felt throughout popular culture. In his 1920s short novel *El joven*, author Salvador Novo sprinkles phrases in English throughout the pages. "There the boys and the girls all say dese, dose and dem," he writes, as his teenage protagonist looks at transit ads.

The Mexico City you experience today has much more in common with the Porfirian city than the pre-Porfirian. The project of modernity which began in the 20th century was thoroughly embraced during subsequent decades. The desire, now in the 21st century, is for Mexico to become even more 'modern', to ape more foreign conventions, creating a never-ceasing frenzy of activity and improvement. American-style malls, gyms and condos have multiplied to help this dream come true.

I grew up in a working-class *colonia* dotted with factories and tenements. I, in fact, grew up in one of these tenements, the traditional *vecindad*. This type of housing became popular in the 19th century as a spot for the lower classes. As the city grew and expanded, it constructed *vecindades*. The *vecindad* is made up small dwellings which share a hallway or interior patio, complete with the ubiqituious *lavaderos*, the public washing area made up of stone sinks. The individual dwellings were small, often a single-room which housed a whole family with several kids.

The *lavaderos* were not only a space for the completion of an important household task – the washing – but a social center, where women would gather to talk and even fight. My great-grandmother, a country girl who like Santa made the journey from a rural town to the big city, but became a maid instead of a prostitute, also lived in a *vecindad,* though of a lower rung than mine. She frequently got into scuffles with the other women and, having developed a knack for fist-fighting, would cause many bloody noses.

The *lavaderos* also provided a play area for children who had no other place to go in a city which seldom took any pains to design public spaces for the lower classes, although it did design pretty green gardens for the people in the well-off *colonias.* The playground of any urban child, then, was a cement one. As the women did the washing and hung their clothes to dry, the kids played around them and ran up and down the hallway of the *vecindad.*

The *vecindad* was the object of study of several anthropologists, including Oscar Lewis, who looked at this living arrangement in the 1950s. He studied two *vecindades* in Mexico City and found that the city, rather than becoming a place of alienation and impersonality, allowed for the retention of social bonds through *vecindades,* since people were constantly in touch with each other.

By the time I was a child, the *vecindad* was already in decline. Nowadays, many of them have evaporated. One around the corner from my home has become a fancy new condo development, filled with the kind of affluent hipsters I could never have imagined walking down our street.

When I was growing up, since I had the privilege of going to a private school, I lied about the *colonia* where I lived, pretending that I either inhabited a neighbouring one which was of a better social class, or that I lived at the edge of mine, in the nicer outer sphere. This meant I seldom had friends over, although, being anti-social, strange and having no sense of fashion, I was often left to my own devices anyway.

There are, however, a few *vecindades* left, including the one where I grew up. Looking for them nowadays is like digging for ancient bones. And that is the neat trick Mexico City plays. Despite the desire to knock every old building down and institute a Starbucks in its place, big chunks of Mexico City remain intact.

The downtown core, of course, persists. Avenida Plateros, which became Madero in honor of that president slain in 1913, sports some of the same fancy establishments which were patronized by people a century before. There are many plaques downtown which attest to the previous names of all the streets, when the city still had a colonial air and Diaz had not risen to power. And, of course, the streets come with legends attached to them.

The legend which made the most impact on me as a child, was the one about La Calle de la Quemada (The Street of the Burnt Woman) because it was considered a love story. Love story? It's a ghoulish tale about a man who can't take no for an answer.

La Calle de la Quemada, now the 5a. Calle de Jesús María, is the street where there once lived a beautiful young woman sometime during the 16th century. The girl wasn't only pretty, but sweet and well-mannered, like a Disney character. She had a large number of suitors, but none more persistent than a certain marquis, who was so infatuated with the woman he stood outside her house every night, and whenever he encountered a rival suitor, he killed him in a sword fight. The woman decided to put a stop to this. So she did the only rational thing a young lady with a psychotic stalker could do: she burnt her face. Yes. The legend says she grabbed a brazier filled with hot coals and pressed her face against it, hoping to be rid of the terrible burden of her beauty which was causing a man to kill for her.

The man, upon discovering that the woman he loved had disfigured herself, explained he loved her for her kind, modest and thoughtful soul, and married her. And they lived happily ever after.

The book of Mexico City legends where I first read this story came complete with an engraving of a dramatically fainting woman next to the brazier, and assured me the woman in question wore a black veil from that day forward. Oh, and it was a story of true love.

True love! You can imagine the saucer eyes of a child of eight.

There were many other streets with amusing old names and stories. Devil's Alley, Alley of the Toad, Alley of the Dead Man. My father said that if you ever run into an old man downtown and he asks to know what time it is, you should refuse to answer. If you do, the old man will gleefully take out an old pocket watch and say "it is the time of your death", and you'll perish at his feet.

This story seems to be a bastardization of the legend of Don Juan Manuel. And while my father insisted that the mysterious gentleman was dressed in Porfirian clothing, with a pocket watch and a top hat, and thus a product of the turn of the century Mexico City, the legend seems to be older. It is set sometime in the colonial period, on a street behind the convent of San Bernardo.

The story goes that a wealthy, honorable man is married to a beautiful woman. He fears his wife is unfaithful, and asks the Devil for assistance. Why this upstanding citizen is on speaking terms with the Devil, I do not know. Anyway, the Devil tells the man to go out of his home at eleven that night. The first man he sees walking outside his house is the one who has been sleeping with his wife.

The man goes out, encounters a random pedestrian and asks him what time it is. The pedestrian answers and the man replies "Lucky the man who knows the hour of his death", and stabs him.

However, the next night the Devil returns and tells him he killed the wrong pedestrian, but assures him his rival will walk by his home at eleven that night. As you can imagine, the jealous husband goes out and kills a man each and every night, until one morning he discovers he has just murdered his cousin. Or his son. Or some other family member. The story then is muddled, somehow the man ends up committing suicide or is killed, but it all ends with a noose.

The legend of Don Juan Manuel, altered and bloated and snipped into pieces, was turned into a short novel published in 1835 by Justo Gómez, Conde de la Cortina. Or it might never have been a legend at all. The book *Poliantea*, published in 1944, states Cortina made it all up. If that is true, the legend came after the book. And it might have been this book which in turn inspired my great-grandfather, who, my father says, was the one who told him the story.

It is pertinent to note that in my father's telling the elements of the colonial era, of New Spain, have been removed. Don Juan Manuel, now called Don Puntual, looks like an early 20th century dandy and he carries no sword. Instead, he kills his victim through some magic act. If the story is still told or if I were to tell it to my children, perhaps it would be adapted to feature a man in jeans carrying a cellphone, who knows.

Oral history. The beauty (and also the problem) of it is that it changes constantly. Since my great-grandmother could not read or write, her stories were all spoken. They reside only in my memories, they are the source of my own stories, transformed just like my father, my great-grandfather, must have transformed that book.

At any rate, the Church of San Bernardo, still stands just south of the Zócalo, the main plaza of the city. The convent was demolished to make way for the avenue 20 de Noviembre, back when it was called Ocampo Street.

San Bernardo came to be thanks to a rich merchant by the name of Don Juan Márquez Orozco, who died, leaving his house and goods to the Church. A nunnery was established with the money. The cornerstone of the church was laid in June of 1685 and the church was dedicated in 1690. When the Reform swept Mexico in the 19th century and all monasteries and churches were closed by national decree, its nuns vacated the building, which was then used as a storehouse.

A nun, Sor Maria Getrudris de San Lorenzo, spent more than 30 years enclosed in a cell there because she was "demented". The church also housed the Niño de las Suertes, a "miraculous" child figurine which the devoted visited during the month of his festivity in January. He now seems associated with the brand-spanking new cult of the Santa Muerte.

There are other holy children throughout Mexican churches; most of their adoration strikes one as quite pagan and sometimes disturbing, but Mexico seems to excel at blending its Catholicism with all manner of un-Christian endeavours. There is a Niño Limosnerito (Beggar Boy) and a Santo Niño Mueve Corazones (Holy Child Who Moves Hearts).

Women in search of a sweetheart, however, always pin their hopes on San Antonio de Padua. Any single woman has heard how she should put a statue of the saint on its head, until he grants her a new man. There are generally a number of prayers involved with this ritual, one must light a candle, and others say you have to tie a red ribbon around him.

If this sounds like magic, it is. Magic, of all stripes, is practiced in Mexico. Saints and virgins are obviously not exempt from these rituals, and Mexicans have no problem mixing other religions in their spells. A quick journey to the faded shopping mall Plaza Galerias reveals an Esoteric Passage (this was literally the name of a section of the mall) where New Age mysticism combines with cheap trinkets from China.

But the *chilango quedado* – a *quedado* is someone who has been left behind, generally a woman, unwanted and growing a bit too old – is probably better served by going to the grand center of all magical things: the Mercado de Sonora.

This urban market, full of tiny stalls, has existed for more than half a century, first opening in 1957. It was established, along with other similar markets, to try and regulate the informal commerce which plagues Mexico City. Wherever there is a street, there is a vendor willing to occupy it and sell food or merchandise, never mind proper permits.

Sonora is the place for buying traditional plants and herbs for healing purposes, but it is also where people buy charms against the evil eye. Dried rattlesnake, bits of starfish, candles of all colors, special soaps and lotions, can be used to obtain love or money. The lotions and "waters" have amusing names: *atrapahombres* (mancatcher), *ven a mi* (come to me), *levanta negocios* (business raiser), *llama cliente* (client caller). There's always a verb in there, and often an interesting illustration on the packaging.

One popular service provided by the witches is an *amarre*, literally a "tie". There are different types of *amarre*, but a popular one consists of tying a piece of underwear from the man you wish to get back – yes, a man; odd seems to be the occasion when a love spell to ensnare a woman is needed – or who you wish to ensnare.

My dabblings in magic as a child were haphazard and disorganized. My mother attempted it more seriously and I remember at least one occasion during which we went to the Mercado de Sonora to purchase items. I still have a bracelet against the evil eye which she procured from this market, with its wide-open, blue eye.

The spell I used most frequently as a teenager was one to find lost things. This consisted of a type of *amarre* where you'd tie a piece of green cloth and ask the gnomes in the house to return your lost property, or else you wouldn't undo the knot.

On one occasion, my friend and I attempted to cast a love spell on a boy. My friend was interested in a particularly handsome high school specimen, and desired him as a boyfriend. We obtained everything we needed, including his hair. At fourteen most teenagers don't have much common sense and I actually ended up cutting a lock of his hair when he sat in front of me in class. Then we got together, performed the spell, and waited.

It seemed to work. To an extent. The boy did meet with my friend and made out with her, but he did not become her boyfriend. After the incident, she developed a reputation as a 'slut', and having grown accustomed to her scarlet letter or figuring a reputation cannot be washed once it is stained, she proceeded to make out with many other boys. Sadly, this did not make her happy and the boys were crueler to her the more she gave them her sexual favors.

Mexico is prudish, it must be admitted, and it was even more prudish when I was growing up. My novel *Signal to Noise* is not just speculation,[1] but a massaging of, sometimes, nasty truths. The spell cast on a boy, then gone wrong, was one of the bones that make the skeleton of my narrative.

Witchcraft was at the Market of Sonora, in my mother's interest in New Age practices, which included natal charts, manuals for meditation and numerology. But it was also in my great-grandmother's stories of her rural home, of the sierra where men turn into coyotes or witches chase men off cliffs.

Her witches were always malicious. At Sonora, there might be some blabbering about white and black magic, some division between spellcasters willing to sell you hexes and others who would pray to angels, but in the sierra witchcraft was never divided. It was dark, it was meant to bend the will of others, each of the stories of witches was a warning.

The most famous witch of all of Mexico spent time in the island fortress of San Juan de Ulúa, off the coast of Veracruz. She supposedly escaped her cell by drawing a boat on the walls of her cell and jumping on to it, sailing away.

The possibility of escape, of drawing, or in my case, writing, your own escape, was one which attracted me at an early age. When you consider escape, you also consider prisons.

The most fabulous prison in Mexico City was The Palace of Lecumberri, popularly known as the Black Palace of Lecumberri. The story goes that when it was being constructed, people walking by thought a palace was being built instead of a prison. The name stuck.

Lecumberri opened its doors on September 29, 1900 and operated until 1976. The building was a result of the Reform to the Penal Code of 1871, which established the need to construct a penitentiary.

The design of Lecumberri is famous because it was supposedly 'panoptic', with a central tower in view of all 896 cells. The guard can watch the prisoners without them being able to tell whether someone is looking; they feel as though they are always being observed.

Lecumberri developed a reputation that matched its nickname, as a dark, vile prison. Several famous figures spent time in there, including author José Revueltas, who was jailed for his political activism and his participation in the student movement of 1968. When he was released, he wrote the famous novel *El Apando*, which was turned into a movie. Lecumberri is supposedly haunted: strange noises and the like, even a man in black and the ghost of a prisoner.

Only two people ever escaped from Lecumberri, which now houses the General National Archive. One of them was Pancho Villa, the revolutionary immortalized in pictures wearing a big floppy hat. He even starred in *Life of Villa*, a silent film about himself. He was assassinated in 1923.

If you head downtown, you can supposedly go into the Bar La Ópera and gaze at a bullet Pancho Villa fired into the ceiling. It's not there, just a legend. The Bar itself was inaugurated in 1876, a business by two Frenchmen who wanted to recreate a Parisian cafe and entertain the crowds headed to the National Theater.

Near the bar, on the corner of what was San Juan de Letrán (and now is the Eje Central Lázaro Cárdenas) and Avenida Juárez rises what was once the ultimate symbol of modernity, the Latin American Tower. It is a hideous construction, hailed as the first skyscraper in the city. It has 44 floors and opened in 1956. There's no ghosts here. Although the massive earthquake of 1985 turned many old buildings into rubble, the tower was able to withstand the destruction.

The Latino served as a sort of landmark for anyone swanning around downtown in the 50s and 60s. "See you by the Torre Latino", you'd say. Coded message which meant "we are going to go to a Chinese cafe".

The "cafe the chinos" was never that Chinese, nor was there a real Chinatown in Mexico City by that point, since the country had expelled most of its Chinese population *en masse* during the 40s. Nowadays, the government of the city has manufactured a strip of a street to pass it off as the real thing. Two blocks on the street of Dolores, that is where people say lays Chinatown.

But even if there was no true Chinatown like in the movies, there were Chinese people who did not get caught by the Mexican government's furious expulsion efforts, and they opened cafes. The dishes they served were coffee with milk and sweet breads. When a city didn't have a Chinese cafe, it was considered a very small, provincial place indeed. "Not even a Chinese cafe!" people cried.

My grandmother did not attend high school, instead enrolling in a secretarial course and graduating at 15. She was a teenager in high-heels and stockings, walking through this downtown, which in the late 40s and early 50s, offered, aside from cafes where she could meet her beaus, an assortment of ice cream parlors and entertainment venues.[2]

There were also movie theatres in Mexico City, to keep the young crowds busy. The beautiful Chinese Palace opened in 1940. It had 4000 seats, two levels, orchestra and balcony. It was, of course, decorated in a 'Chinese,' style, with fake pagodas, dragons and lions. By the time I first visited it in the 1980s it had already been subdivided into four screens and it was in decline, its lacquered interiors coming apart, the bathrooms filthy, the floors covered in bubble gum.

Another beautiful movie theatre of the era was the Cine Teresa, which began operating in 1942. It was known as the "movie theatre for the metropolitan ladies". It was constructed in an Art Deco style, the work of Francisco J. Serrano, whose other modernist buildings adorn the Colonia Condesa.

When my grandmother was young, the Cine Teresa was a fine movie theatre, the place to hold premieres. The entrance to the movies was 2 pesos, and the chance to be seduced by the looks of a hot movie star like Pedro Infante awaited inside.

By the time the 80s dragged around, though, the Teresa had come down from its heights. It showed pornographic movies. The

Golden Era of Mexican cinema was also over and instead of gritty noirs, festive musicals or lavish dramas, the movie industry was churning out cheap titty pictures. When, as a child I walked by the Teresa, my mother rushed me and tried to place horse blinders on my head. Still, I caught a glimpse of the lobby cards which advertised *Emanuelle 5*, brief glimpses of naked flesh.

I never went in, not even when as teenagers we goaded each other to enter the premises.

There were, last time I checked, still five movie theatres in Mexico City which show pornographic movies. The Savoy is probably the most famous one, operating since 1970. But the Teresa has turned good and saintly again. It now shows art films and contributes to the "cultural amusement" of the city.

Frankly, I miss the old Teresa. The grit and squalor of Mexico City is what made it fun. Chain stores and fancy gyms bore me and fill me with dread every time I visit again. Mexico City cannot be the city, I think, unless it somehow retains the pool halls where as a girl of 13 I could buy a beer. And yet, what pool halls? What beer? Even the arcades are disappearing, that place where I spent all my coins in the evenings. And it's not only the downtown core which changes, the outskirts, too, although, I never cared much for the outskirts and places like Coyoacán.

Some folks have a great affection for Coyoacán. It is mainly because of Frida Kahlo. They point and say "Look, we have the Kahlo House!" at which I roll my eyes. The Kahlo myth has been mainly constructed for foreigners, but it sells, and so it sticks. Not that Kahlo did not make interesting paintings but nowadays her face is on every crummy bag you find in Coyoacán.

Coyoacán started off as a small village, separate from Mexico City, until the city devoured and annexed it. You can still see some of its old colonial self in the cobblestone streets and the facades of what were once country homes, but it has long lost its sleepy quality. There is a large plaza with arches, the Plaza Hidalgo, which serves as the town square. There you can find a kiosk with a stained glass cupola, a present donated by Porfirio Diaz to commemorate the Centennial of the War of Independence in 1910.

If it seems like everything in Mexico City circles back to Porfirio Diaz it is because, as I said, he seems to divide the city. The Porfiriato is like a meridian for the time traveler.

Coyoacán has its legends, too. It also has its alleys with funny names. The most notorious alley is the Avocado one. It has so many ghosts, it is difficult to quantify them. The stone-cobbled street is supposedly haunted by a hanged man who appears on the nights of the full moon, a ghost child, and other apparitions. There is an altar to the Virgin in the alley, which is said to weep tears of blood. More modern urban legends say a group of teenagers played with a ouija board and summoned the devil in this alley. Bad news, this place.

There are also tunnels in Coyoacán, or at least, that's the way the story goes. Supposedly these were built during the time of the Guerra Cristera, when Catholicism was abolished in Mexico, so that the faithful could meet and worship.

The oldest house in Coyoacán is a colonial abode called the Casa Colorada, named for its bright red color. It is also called the House of the Malinche, named after the Mexican interpreter and lover of the conquistador Hernan Cortés. The story goes it was the home of Cortés, where he strangled his wife.

The story seems to be a bastardization of the legend of the Llorona, which is sometimes associated with the Malinche. La Llorona, the woman in white, the weeping woman, is likely the most famous legend to come out of Mexico. There are Lloronas everywhere, in Mexico City and in the countryside, and they all behave a little differently and have slightly different origins.

The story my great-grandmother told went like this: There once was a beautiful woman who married a Spanish man. They had children and lived happily together until the day he decided to separate from her and marry a Spanish woman. Because, you see, she was an indigenous lady, therefore less desirable than a European woman. The Spaniard was determined not only to abandon his wife, but to take their children with him. Instead, the woman drowned the children in the river, then killed herself. Since then, she haunts the roads, crying out "Oh, my children!" This version of Medea can also be seen as a metaphor for the Mexican nation, the indigenous nation crying for its lost children, now under Spanish yoke.

In reality, the red house likely never housed Cortés nor the Malinche. As for the strangled woman, Cortés said his wife died of an asthma attack, but her death three months after landing in Mexico set tongues wagging for centuries.

There is another ghost that is said to haunt a hospital. Her name is "La Planchada" (the Ironed One), because she wears a prim and properly ironed uniform.

She is found at Hospital Juárez. Like the story of "La Llorona", this is a tale of a man betraying his lover. A nurse, the legend goes, falls in love with a physician, who promises to wed her. Instead, he seduces her and marries another woman. She poisons herself. After her death, however, she is seen roaming the hallways of the hospital and even administering medicine to the sick. Other versions, however, say the woman is very old and her uniform is ancient, moth-eaten. There is also the problem that, like "The Llorona", this ghost seems to travel the whole country. Other cities and towns have their own "Planchada".

There are, as you may have guessed by now, many dead women and angry men in the legends of Mexico City. Mexico City is, in short, haunted. I am haunted too. Having left the metropolis in my twenties I now live in calm, pretty, glass-towered Vancouver. Everything is new here, clean and shiny. Streets don't have old names and they are traced efficiently. Nor are there many convoluted legends. It is a carefree city.

Mexico City is more malicious, chaotic, organic, bedevilled. I miss it, sometimes, warts and all. I also carry the weight of its stories, of my family's stories. It is haunted and it haunts.

I realize one day I will make the journey there to bury my father. In this sense, I am awaiting a new ghost. I realize, too, I've left my old ghosts there. My great-grandfather and my grandfather share a plot of land in the cemetery of Dolores. My father's family, once moneyed and now not at all, still owns a mausoleum at what was once a fashionable cemetery. Once I've seen the doors of that mausoleum open to receive my paternal grandmother.

On that occasion, when we dressed in black and watched them carry the coffin, my father reassuringly told me my great-grandfather had taken great pains to ensure his children and grandchildren and great-grandchildren would all fit in there.

"There's a lot of space", he told me.

However, I will not be buried with my father's family.

"I know how men in exile feed on dreams of hope", said Aeschylus. It doesn't quite apply to me. I dream of ghosts. Once a year I bake the bread for the Day of the Dead, gather my flowers and light my candles, hoping the dead can make the long walk to my abode.

I have not shared most of the legends of Mexico with my children, nor my great-grandmother's stories. I guard them like jewels, they were the only inheritance she left behind. I'm also afraid the children will not take to them, so I'm quiet. Instead, I have inserted the ghosts into my short stories and novels. Unseen by anyone, they will rest there.

My resistance to speak the stories probably stems from my belief that the written page will make them more permanent. Death, after all, erases all spoken words. Even if I tell the stories to my children, there is no guarantee they will have children and recite them. Therefore, I write.

More than that, though, my reluctance to repeat the tales likely comes from a place of superstition. The belief that we are filled with a finite number of tales and if we speak them all, we will grow empty. We will become walking ghosts.

Silvia Moreno-Garcia is the award-nominated (British Fantasy, Locus, Aurora and Sunburst) author of the novels *Signal to Noise* and *Certain Dark Things*. She has also edited several anthologies, including *She Walks in Shadows*, for which she was nominated for a World Fantasy Award, and *Dead North*, among others. She serves as co-editor of the magazine *The Dark* and *The Jewish Mexican Literary Review*, and edited a special issue of *Nightmare* magazine dedicated to writers of colour. Her short fiction has been collected as *This Strange Way of Dying*. Mexican by birth, she has lived in Canada for more than a decade and English is her second language. She has an MA in Science and Technology Studies, but does not live the scholarly life, instead working in corporate communications.

She can be found online at silviamoreno-garcia.com and on Twitter at @silviamg.

The Real Estate Book

FREE

STEALING THE LIGHT TO WRITE BY

Damien Patrick Williams

I've always charted my history in direct relation to where I've lived. Every time someone asks me, "hey, do you remember when...?" I reflexively put the event in question with my place of residence, at that time. I moved a lot as a kid, so the words I can use to describe the memories of what things happened when have always been equally weighted and bound to remembering which of them happened *where*. For much the same reason, my history with magic and the concepts, entities, or spirits therein, is intimately tied to all the places I've called home. Tricksters and cycles of death have marked out the gifts I've received and the lessons I've learned. One of the most important of those lessons is that the gifts of tricksters are never unequivocal.

The first time I ever experienced the death of a loved one, I was six, going on seven.

My grandmother – my mother's mother – died of glioblastoma. I didn't attend the funeral, and in fact didn't visit her grave until many years later. But the memorial wake at our house sits clear as a bell in my mind. Not the individual people, but the feeling of the thing. The combinations of memories and emotions and the sense of everyone there, pouring themselves into an emptiness, wrapping each other in their grief and love. My family has always been blessedly close, mother side especially, but everything I think about death as it relates to family was influenced by this moment.

I grew up in Washington D.C., a place that is emblematic of secrets, lies, power, and intimations of occult power. There's always been this apocryphal tale that the very streets of D.C. were created with particular Masonic symbolism in mind, and among the so-called founding fathers, Ben Franklin's persona is the one that best occupies the Trickster archetype. He was the virile, winking student of everything, even that in which he didn't believe; he even stole light from the heavens and handed it to mortal man. That being said, as tricksters frame my life, starting in Chesapeake Bay, they're best embodied there by young Raven and baby Hermes: tentative and awkward, but precocious. Simultaneously at home and *unheimlich*. There is a thread of the banal and the uncanny in their appearance, both connected to death, the creations of language, and the conveyance of messages from one world to the next.

I don't remember the first time I met Raven. I do know that when I was nine years old my fourth grade class put on a performance of *The Quest for the Golden Fleece*, in which I played Hermes, whom I have resonated with ever since. As for Raven, I know that I must have met him very young, because I was already familiar with his and Mr Poe's collaboration, by the time *The Simpsons* Did It, in 1990. By some combination of English classes, Boy

Scout trips through the woods of D.C., Maryland, and Virginia, and basic proximity to Baltimore, I became acquainted with the presence of *Corvus corax*. Ravens being a sleek, cool-looking, clever species of bird was more than enough for a grade school boy to make them the sought-after center of my attention on car rides and hikes. Finding out even the barest hints of their symbiotic relationships with wolves was just icing on the cake. But it wasn't until I read Poe's invocation that I started to feel we had more in common than our good looks.

At this point in my life, living in D.C., I wasn't actively practicing or studying magick; I was a prepubescent kid. I was deeply interested in the fantastic, and had dreams that I considered to be prophetic (and which I would much later learn that my grandmother had shared), but at this age, my encounters with trickster figures weren't (to me) obviously synchronous. It wasn't until I moved to the American Southeast – to one of the furthest edges of the Raven's habitat range – that I began to see synchronicities at play, both at the crux of my adolescence and reverberating earlier in my life. This transition wasn't easy for me, as I felt I was being made to leave my home against my will. It wasn't until much later that I would understand my mother's reasoning for this move, and while adult ravens may be charismatic, stately creatures, juveniles are awkward, prickly things, wobbly, uncertain in the world, and much more likely to want to remain close to the nest. Their transition into adolescence is marked by their playing of games with and teasing of young wolves – a dynamic which may at first seem both malicious and foolhardy, but which is in fact representative of a deeply symbiotic relationship between the two species.

There's a long-observed connection between adolescent development and perceived occult activity; poltergeists, for instance, have been interpreted as manifestations of teenage psychic turmoil. But as Carl Jung outlines in his case studies in *Psychology and the Occult*, violent outbursts aren't the only way in which pubescent development and seemingly supernatural phenomena intersect. In my case, the move from my hometown felt both sudden and traumatic, forcing a removal from friends and loved ones which seemed all the more unjust when paired with the sense of nebulous, cosmic injustice to which one tends to feel subjected throughout puberty. I began to dig deeper into the more occult aspects of the music and art I loved, and to act out against those around me. What started as traditional teenage fare culminated in an outburst that changed my life. I found a new high school, and slowly (but, in retrospect, inevitably) began the development of my dedicated study of magick.

New Horizons

At my second school, I learned about philosophy, psychology, sociology, collective action, and magick. The work of my instructors and cohorts in these areas seemed far more devoted and official than my previous pop cultural introductions to the topics. Through various pathways and vectors, I became further acquainted with the Irish and Norse mythologies that had captured my attention in my youth, as well as Inuit, Navajo, and Tlingit stories of Raven and Coyote. My new friends made sure that I found Neil Gaiman's *Sandman* series, where the Raven Matthew and Lucien the Librarian struck multiple chords. The first book of *The Sandman* I ever read was "The Kindly Ones", which contains a subplot about thousands of ravens gathering in a battlefield. During the gathering, a story gets told by and about Noah's raven ("One of seven, actually"), about how the world was recreated after the Flood, and why we shouldn't entrust ravens with those kinds of tasks. Doves come back with signs of dry land; ravens just crap out the land, piss out fresh water, and fly off wherever the hell they want.

When we collect creation myths from around the world, we're often confronted with a trickster who gives us the sun, the moon, the stars, and the language to call their names – but only after the object of their affection didn't want to wear any of them as jewelry. Or who gives us fresh water and arable land, after the flood – but only if they get to snicker about how we got it, every time they see us. These tricksters create the world – but only by accident and incident. I didn't learn the term for it until much later, but what I was doing could be considered weaving together a pop cultural Chaos Magickal mythos, and this mode of viewing the world was becoming a part of everything I did; synchronicities were building fast. The more work I did in this framework, and the more I learned, the more echoes of my steps would resonate throughout my world. Obvious caveats about confirmation bias, the Baader-Meinhof phenomenon, and apophenia aside, my general school of thought, at the time, was "synchronicity breeds synchronicity". Unconsciously, I knew that following one thread would lead to more, and so that's what I continued to do, and the results were not always pleasant.

Many new students undertake to learn about stupid, dangerous magick. Looking to impress instructors, peers, lovers, they engage in projects which are potentially harmful to themselves and others. I was no exception. At this point, there was far more of Loki's fire and spite to the course of my investigations – a "because I can" maliciousness, rather than Raven's playful and (generally) benevolently amused curiosity – and that sentiment led to choices that greatly endangered my options for continued

education. My mentors, then, were tied to the school I attended, and one of them in particular had so much of awe and myth
about her that I was decidedly loath to lose her influence in my
life. Lorraine was fluent in Latin, Greek, Italian, Spanish, French,
Esperanto, and Navajo; held a doctorate in psychology; walked
as quietly as a ninja; and believed deeply in second chances – but
only in those cases where the party being afforded said could
not only accept but clearly articulate the consequences of their
actions. She was a huge believer in the principle of integrity, and
she had a wicked sense of humour.

As principal and director of this very small school, one of her
favourite things to do upon meeting new students was to tell them
about themselves, based on where they sat in the room, their body
language, and how they presented themselves to her and other
new people. She took great delight in how this tended to unnerve
people, especially since one of the first things people would
"somehow" find out about her was that she was legally blind. But
subverting expectations while randomly displaying ridiculous
feats of skill and intellect weren't just opportunities for her to
preen; as the person who *literally* built the school from the ground
up (the halls are hung with photos of her, the faculty, and the first
graduating class hammering and welding the place together), it
was meant to create in each new student a sense of wonder and
possibility. Every activity and tradition in that institution became
infused with her ethos, and everyone who lived, worked, and
studied there – if they, too, would engage and embrace that ethos
– found themselves transformed by the experience.

Lorraine died in 2002, but her work, embodied in the creation
of such a space, was designed to instill those perspectives in students
who would then, ideally, take them out into the world and suffuse
each new thing they created – each project, relationship, family, life

– with their essence. The nature of that place fostered and cultivated an atmosphere in which questions about the nature of perception, what it meant to truly believe *in* anything, and what was required of a person to frame and sustain a world out of that belief could all be investigated. It's unknown whether she thought of this process as magick, but it was, by any definition, a Great Work of Refinement. And had I not been given a second chance to stay there, I would not only have lost my other mentors and peers in magickal practice, but I would never have been given my first opportunity to teach a class of my own. And it was those two things together that changed the course of my life, from that point forward.

Up to this point, my projected career path was to become a comics illustrator for a major publisher and to then become friends with comics creators whose work I admired. When I started college, my passion for drawing was still intact, but a new drive was developing: to think more about perception, thought, magic, religion, and the nature of reality, as well as my desire to help younger generations discover the same. I began taking more classes in philosophy and comparative religious studies, and learning in the process the academically accepted names of things I'd been muddling through for years. This new language formed the concept structures that allowed me to communicate with others about these ideas, with names like "epistemology", "ontology", "eschatology", and "ritual liminality". Fields of study like Ritual Theory and New Religious Movements further showed that there were untold combinations of perspectives in the world through which I could come to think about any number of things. Simultaneously, the Internet opened wide and the paths I took online expanded further into magical spaces. Internet Relay Chat (IRC) chatrooms became covens and circles, and vectors for experimentation and exploration.

Several Other Worlds

A lot of time's been spent turning over the idea of the Internet-As-Place and asking, if it *is* a place, then what kind of place is it? Since shortly after William Gibson's groundbreaking *Sprawl Trilogy*, the notion of cyberspace has been a component of the public imagination. A world made of binary code and other-worldly light, made of collective unconsciousness and mutual hallucinatory states. The vision of this world and the promises it held shaped the next several decades of our conception about what it meant to be online, and to be, online. I was one among the first generation to make friends and fall in love, *because* of the Internet. My partner and I met online, and our friendship developed and changed over a great many years. Many people were having this experience and, for a very long time, many others held that those relationships were to be considered hollow or unreal. But those who could navigate and even shape this realm to their will were increasingly portrayed as modern day wizards, holding arcane knowledge and ever more often battling each other for primacy. As a culture, we might have been better off if more journalists at the tail end of the 20th century had been familiar with the archetype of the Tungus shaman or the Native American medicine men and women.

As I note in my papers "Fairytales Of Slavery: Societal Distinctions, Technoshamanism, and Nonhuman Personhood" and "Presentations of Non-Human Consciousness in Specula-tive Fiction Media", the role of the shaman in the context of their community is to guide those in need through the nebulous, ill-defined, and almost-certainly *hazardous* Otherworld. The shaman is there to help us navigate our passages between this world and that one and to help us know which rituals to perform in order to realign our workings with the workings of the Spirits. Shamans walk between multiple worlds and do the work of keeping safe those who walk with them. Had more people in the 80s, 90s, and early 00s had a working knowledge of these traditions, then that early sense of camaraderie and mutual exploration could have truly blossomed.

Regardless, as time went on, there was a corresponding increase in the use of message boards, IRC channels, ICQ instant messaging groups, and more being used as meeting halls and ritual spaces. Religious scholars like Catherine Bell and Jonathan Z. Smith discuss the idea of marking out ritual space – something innately familiar to anyone who's ever entered a house of worship. But the concept structure of ritual space can be applied to any time or place which, for reasons of mentality and mood, must be set apart. In sociological and trauma studies, we discuss this idea in terms of "safe spaces"; in martial arts, we have the dojo; in magic, the drawing of the circle. In all of these instances, we use words, or a knife, or chalk, or a song, and we carve out something sacred from within the profane, and the 1990s Internet was pretty much a perfect expression of this. The complex protocols to log-in, the aforementioned terminology and conceptual framing, all of it conjured an intentional *Otherness* of place and mind. The people I met in this era opened up opportunities for new synchronicities of language, anthropology, philosophy, religion, and technology, all of which combined with those perspectives on science and the occult which were already colliding in my sphere.

In the same two years that I learned about all of these concepts, I also found several new cohorts on IRC and read Gibson's *Sprawl Trilogy* and Neal Stephenson's *Snow Crash* for the first time, both within months of each other. The idea of language as technology as magic and gods *of* communication as personifications or superdense concentrations of that conceptual perspective made the kind of perfect sense that starts to worry one's friends, once the notebooks need their own wing of the house. It was at this point that I started to work with the archetype of not just the Trickster Scribe, but of the Crossroads Deal-maker. Legba, being the Vodun *loa* of communication and crossroads and thresholds – of messages between one world and the next – took almost immediate root in my psyche. And at precisely this moment in my life, I moved into one of the most haunted houses I have ever known.

HOUSE OF MY DREAMS

This house was a three-storey antebellum-style mansion in the American Deep South. Not to put too fine a point on it, but the land where it stood had once been a slave plantation. When I moved into this place, with the eight other roommates who lived there, I was told three separate ghost stories which, at first, I assumed to be a mild, run of the mill hazing. I was told about the Little Girl who liked to try to push people down the stairs; the Old Man who could be heard wandering around, talking quietly to himself at night, a Presence on the second floor that just seemed to emanate malice; and the basement. The basement held no storage as it was supremely unfinished. All it contained was a pile of dirt which could be seen in the far right corner from the door, and a set of French doors, just inside said main entrance. These doors had no glass and weren't connected to a full wall; you could just walk around them. I was told (and shown) that when you looked through the panes where glass should have been, the light on the other side would seem somehow 'wrong', and if someone was to walk around them and stand opposite you, the timing of their voice and motions wouldn't line up. There was also a disused sump hole, down there, in a pitch dark corner, out of which was growing lush green ivy, and it was very cold.

These are obviously fairly standard haunting tropes, and I took them as such, until the second or third week I lived there. That's when friends who'd never heard the stories started corroborating the previously-supposed effects of these hauntings. Multiple people reported the feeling like a hand in the small of their back when no one was behind them, or a stair they were stepping on twisting away from under them; the step in question was checked multiple times, by different people, and all found it sound. Many newcomers to the house reported hearing the voice of a man who definitely did not live there, and a couple even said they saw him. One of my friends even decided to walk through the basement's French doors, on a lark. He immediately stopped, turned around looking ill, walked back through, and from then on refused to either talk about what had happened, or to ever enter the basement again. He also warned any new person in the house not to go down there.

Now, we can of course put all of this down to confirmation bias and collective hallucinations, if we're so inclined. But even if we do that, then the effect of this place and the people in it on each other was staggering. We all communicated elements of this mythic narrative to ourselves and to people who'd never been there before, to the point that when I held my nineteenth birthday in that house, two different people had the same detailed dream about the Little Girl, and the Old Man, and the horrible thing she did to her half-sister and the unthinking revenge he took on her for killing his biological daughter. The resonance of this house, at this moment in time, was such that it quite literally made an impression on everyone within it.

The less said about the circumstances under which we were forced to leave that house, the better, but I've always promised myself that if I ever come into just an utterly ridiculous amount of money, the first thing I would do is buy that house. It was a nexus – a literal crossroads – at and out of which several groups of friends met, re-met, coalesced, and grew; a trend that would continue in my life for another decade. After that house, I made a habit of turning every place I lived into a crossroads, fulfilling the function of transactional hub, crux of decision-making, and bawdy community tavern. Parties became events where disparate groups could intersect and something new could be made in the process. Regardless whether it was in a house or apartment, the homes where my friends and I lived for the next several years were invested with a sense of centrality and camaraderie. A kind of placeness that made people willing to take the kind of life-altering steps toward new relationships and chances that they might otherwise never have seen. It wasn't until the end of graduate school that this began to slow down. Because graduate school devours time.

THE HALLS OF THE ACADEMY

Grad school, for me, was invested with several senses and meanings. Accepted and acceptable scholarship, of course, it being my center of educational refinement in philosophy and the comparative study of religion; but also a kind of competitive companionship. There was a sense that, in graduate school, we were all there to learn and to create new things and then to test those things against what our cohort had learned and created. The process was friendly, on the whole, but certainly not without its sharper edges, in the form of one-upmanship and intense debate. But even for that, it at least seemed like a place where you could find a group of people who spoke a common conceptual language, or perhaps were simply deeply dedicated to becoming fluent in as many different ones as possible. The process of learning to speak to and understand one another was fundamental, and every new conversation within and without the halls of my departments was infused with a sense of revelation.

This was the point at which I began to seriously work on the process of mainstreaming my perspectives on magic. At the intersection of continental philosophy and the theory and method of the comparative study of religion, I saw a place where the permutation of the will and the perceptions of self and others could be investigated by placing names like Frazer and Faivre and Schopenhauer and Hegel and Baudrillard and Foucault in context with ones like Jung and Crowley and Adler and Moore and Carroll. There is nothing that is not magick, if apprehended correctly, and there is nothing that is not technology for the same reasons. The roots for both technology and magick are in the concept of "craft". The Greek root for this is *techne,* and you can look to Athena, Hekate, Hermes, and Hephaestus and see deities of both art and artifice; skill and cunning and language and creation and weaving and theft and all of these things are bound (woven) together. This is part of what I mean when I talk about magic and technology, and what "artificial intelligence" really means when we break it down.

But the Western world's Greek ancestors aren't the only ones who bound their technology and their magic together. Egypt saw Thoth creating language and magic, being a god of technology and the repository of all memory and knowledge. Odin is the master speller and the great artificer (and thief and cunning man). Legba and Ellegua are spiritually tied to crossroads, thresholds, beginnings, endings, and communications, making the *loa* the obvious choice for Gibson to map onto the Internet. And in all of this we have the root technology of language: the manipulation of words and memories and "spelling" and, again, "craft".

Graduate school was, indeed, where I learned that it was through the process of seeking legitimation that the tension between assimilation and subversion became most apparent. This was yet another way they made sure that, at every step of the way, the framing and presentation of our research and discourse could be moulded to fit each new conversational partner. Though I still don't know what the exact ratio was of intentional refinement and nudging to entrenched orthodoxy, in retrospect their effects are patently obvious. At the time it was maddening. It took three different combinations of committee before I found a group willing to work with the concepts I wanted to explore, but once I did, it was a matter of me showing them – and them me – how my work fit into the existing discourse. Once I learned how to do that and my thesis was ready to present to the world, I graduated, and came almost immediately to another crossroads.

French Press, Turkish, Espresso, or Drip

When I left graduate school, I managed to fulfill a dream I'd had since I was very little: I started working at a coffee shop. That sounds like a dark joke, right up there with, "What's the most important phrase for a philosopher to learn?", but the fact of it is, my grandmother and I used to sit together on Sunday mornings and she would let me have sips of her coffee while she read me the Sunday comics pages. She and my parents taught me how to cook and how to appreciate both comics and coffee, and all throughout my childhood I had the dream of opening a combination coffee and comics shop. At my second high school, every year the student body had to perform two theatrical productions, one of which was also student written and produced. One of the two years I was there, I co-wrote an ensemble piece, my segment of which was called "I Am The Coffee-Maker; I Make The Coffee". This was also the title of my first website. Working with coffee was something I named and marked out for myself early in my life.

While working at this coffee shop, there was a large community chalkboard wall, and the staff controlled the music with near impunity, save for two rules: nothing "too harsh" and nothing profane. And so of course these rules got stretched and tested daily. We used the blackboard for quotes and drawings and sigils and physics equations, and we used the music to set a mood and atmosphere; to spark conversation and to make people comfortable, but interested in their environment. This meant that, more often than not, customers would ask what was playing, and this ideally led to many different paths of discussion. Living and working in a college town, all of my regulars were students and academics, and so it was almost a guarantee that, in the course of our talks, we would discuss teaching and the various disciplines we'd all studied, and the question of why I wasn't getting a PhD or teaching courses myself would come up again and again.

After my MA, I had applied and gotten accepted to a PhD in Western Esotericism at the University of Exeter in England, but the funding simply wasn't there to foot the bill for moving across the Atlantic. At this point in time, the academic market for teachers without a PhD was drying up, and the thought of going back to get a PhD was still a bit too much for me after what had at times felt like the knife fight of writing and defending my master's degree thesis. But the thought stayed with me throughout the three years I worked at the coffee shop. While I was using shared spaces, music, and art to craft a particular kind of intention and sense of place, I was being pulled back to something I felt in high school and grad school, both, and I started to feel, again, like the work I needed to be doing needed to be done in the classroom. At the end of my time in that shop, almost the moment I left, I was hired for two different teaching positions.

JORMUNGANDR AS BRASS RING

For many academics, teaching – even adjunct teaching – feels like finally making it. Being able to stand in front of a room full of students at a university and teach them about what it was you spent so long coming to understand, it feels like looking everyone who ever asked you "what are you going to do with that degree" square in the eye and saying, "this, dammit; it was always this". It's a vindication and an affirmation of talent and skill, and it's a high you ride for a while. As we've seen, the intersections of the stations of my life seemed to keep resonating and iterating on what had gone before, and this moment was no different. I came to find out that I was now colleagues in one of my teaching positions with one of my former coffee shop regulars (we usually discussed the history of jazz, and the progression of experimental music in the 20th and 21st century). I continued to work retail, at this point, selling cheeses in an artisanal shop in one of the rich parts of town, even as I got more opportunities to travel for my academic work. When I thought about the massive hustle it was taking to gather the funds to live this life, it just felt every bit like being truly alive and living the dream of the globetrotting academic, but it was slowly distancing me from my enjoyment of the work, while it was happening. Over the next three years, I continued to focus on writing, teaching, and discussing the connections between technology and magick, and as I did so, I noticed more and more what seemed to be a stark dichotomy between the personal and professional aspects of my life.

The first international trip I ever took to present my work was to go to England for a joint meeting of The British Society for the Study of Artificial Intelligence and the Simulation of Behaviour (AISB) and the International Association of Computing And Philosophy (IACAP) to talk about Alan Turing's work on the centenary of his birth. I was a part of the Machine Question Symposium, organized by Joanna Bryson and David Gunkel. My partner and I had a layover in Amsterdam's Schiphol Airport at some ridiculous time in the morning, and the jetlag was strong, so we should have known it was going to be a surreal trip when the first thing we saw as we stepped off the gangway was a giant raven sitting right on top of one of the windows. It was during this trip that I started seriously thinking about how to teach artificial intelligences to understand non-Western ethical and epistemological systems like Zen and Taoism. It was also where I had the best shawarma I've ever tasted. At the end of that conference I learned that the next year's AISB and IACAP meetings would again be split. AISB was going to be hosted by the University of Exeter. IACAP was to be in Washington, D.C.

In 2013, we travelled to France, for the 13th annual Virtual Reality International Conference in Laval. The entire program was about the nature of virtual and augmented reality, and its intersection with and role in the physical world. An entire conference about investigating what makes a place real, and what kind of beings we have to be to engage with it. I presented my paper "The Metaphysical Cyborg", in which I outlined the idea of what kinds of minds humans will have to have, in order to think the kinds of thoughts necessary to deal with the fundamentally new kinds of reality we've been building for the past few decades. On our lunch break, we took a brief walk around the absolutely gorgeous town of Laval, and there, in the middle of it, was an actual castle, with a well-kept green yard, and in the middle of that, stood a single huge black raven. On the next day, my partner and I took a trip to the Louvre, our first ever time in Paris, and the first things we were confronted with on entering that huge complex were statues of Mercury and Hermes. If you're unfamiliar, as I was at the time, the Louvre is home to no less than fifty pieces of iconography devoted to Hermes, and contains an entire wing devoted to Egyptology, including a room solely for icons made expressly for use in Kemetic magic.

In fall of 2014, I lost a good friend to a sudden heart attack, and in December I attended Magick.Codes. This was a kind of un-conference specifically focused on the overlap of these ideas. Magick.Codes was put together by Ingrid Burrington, whose work focuses on showing people the hidden infrastructure that makes their daily lives possible. Her work on finding the largest data centers in the U.S. and on mapping the telecommunications nodes and networks of New York City is undergirded by a sense of the secrets hidden within the everyday; she deals literally in occult knowledge. Everyone brought together for and by Magick. Codes does work on the perception of the unseen, in magick, art, sociology, psychology, data, coding, philosophy, or some combination of the above. My trip there started with a contemplation on a traditional chant of invocation to Legba, while standing in the center of the world's busiest airport. In addition to being a lord of the crossroads, in the traditions where he is revered Legba is meant to be invoked at the start of any magical working or large undertaking. This is because Legba, like Hermes, is the linguist and messenger of the spirit world; he is in charge of language, and making sure that your prayers and intentions are properly relayed. As I was meant to be speaking, that weekend, language deities were on my mind.

The day before the presentations, I stayed up until 2 a.m. checking and rechecking my notes, arranging my slides, making everything as perfect as possible. The next day, when I got there, I found out both that there were a number of people in the room whose work I'd long admired, *and* that I was going to be presenting first. I started to get nervous until I saw that someone in attendance was very pointedly wearing red, white, and black, which are the colours of Eleggua in the Yoruba Tradition, and Legba in the Vodun tradition. She was, in fact, wearing the *vévé*, or sigil, *of Eleggua*. We struck up a conversation, and I was immediately at ease. The talk was well-received, and the tone of the rest of the weekend was one of strangers finishing each other's thoughts, and new ideas spiraling up and out into the world.

March 2015 was a roller coaster of death and triumph. In addition to the continuing increase in both number and visibility of instances of police killings of unarmed non-police in the U.S. – a situation that has the potential to imbue a siege-like mentality on a population – I also lost two of the most important family members in my life, in the course of two weeks. My great aunt – my mother's mother's sister – died a week and a day after her 88th birthday. Our family has always been close, and she was like a third grandmother to me, another parent to my mom, aunt, uncle, and cousins. The night before she died, I had a dream that took place in her house. In the dream, I was finally able to connect the components of the Internet and my computers and my phone to the old stereo there. Later, I had to use the same system I'd just built to burn the house down. The technological connections were a major accomplishment – something no one else had ever been able to do. Burning down the house was a necessity – a means of unnamed freedom and escape. It came with a sense of pain and loss but also a certainty that it needed to be done.

In the waking world, that week, I had a series of conversations about artificial intelligence and the occult, and got a number of people to see the world in a way they'd never conceived of, before. I wrote my article "Fairytales of Slavery...;" words that bound up concepts from my family's history and lineage together with the modern world in a way that had never been done before, and it resonated with people who've never met me. In the waking world, that day, my great aunt died in her sleep, after a long battle with a degenerative illness. Though her death was still a blow, to the family, it wasn't a surprise. Two and a half weeks later, though, when my uncle died in a car wreck, no one saw that coming.

THE KINDEST UNKINDNESS

My mother's brother was born nine years, ten months, and twenty-one days before me. So every year I turned an age, one month and 9 days later he'd be ten years older than that. He was more like an older brother to me than an uncle. And, so, on my birthday, he'd find me and say, "Happy Birthday Buddy! How old are you, this year? [His Upcoming Age]?" And I'd say, "Yep! And you're gonna be [My Age]!" And he'd say, "Man! You're gettin' old!" Every year since I was old enough to think it was funny. He taught me about a great many of the pop cultural touchstones that animated my life, from comics, to movies, to music, and TV shows. His influence on my life was synonymous to the house in which we grew up, like memories and dreams of the stairs and basement rec room we ran around like mad. At his funeral, his childhood friends – men and women I'd tagged along behind, back when we were all boys and girls – came in from around the world to pay their respects, and we shared memories of VHS movies and car trips into the nearest town. Being back in Maryland for all of this, I couldn't help but count the ravens out the car windows, again.

This is when it started to hit me. Interwoven through these major personal deaths, my professional life was undergoing massive beneficial upheavals. I was being requested for interviews, and people in my fields knew my name and my work, and my writing and speaking were garnering acclaim, and I felt nothing but a weird sense of guilty ambivalence about it all. I was strongly torn between my grief and my elation, and unable to compartmentalize it all, until, in April of 2015, during the Theorizing the Web Conference, in NYC, Klint Finley offered me the opportunity to take over Technoccult.net. Back at the beginning of March, Klint had interviewed me for the Mindful Cyborgs podcast, to talk about both Artificial Intelligence and the interplay of technology and the occult. Technoccult had been his creation and charge for fifteen years, but he was finding less and less time to devote to the work of exploring the topics the audience there wanted to see, and after our conversation, he felt I would be a fitting successor. I was blown away, and deeply honoured, but the guilt at feeling any joy whatsoever when I'd just lost two of the most important people in my life was keeping me from accepting this. It was only when I talked to several people and thought for a while about all of these ups and downs in the context of the kinds of gifts tricksters give (remember: they're never unequivocal) that the clichéd sentiment finally made any sense to me: they'd be happier if I was happy. I might never have taken Technoccult if I hadn't realised this. I had to work through being shredded and raw, first, and then turn that into a need and a drive to live a life that those I'd lost would be happy to see me living.

In the fall of 2015, I very suddenly got offered a full time position at my university. All at once the amount of hustling I'd been doing between an adjunct teaching load and a part time job to stay afloat came into stark relief, and I knew that I needed to take it. With the advent of my own office, cards, phone line, and a much higher likelihood that the university would fully reimburse my travel expenses for conferences, I was able to quit retail and start focusing on my own work. Or so I thought. In my first semester as a full time instructor, I had a teaching load of five classes, which was shocking to every other full time instructor I met. Their mouths would gape, and I would say, "eh, it's okay. I've done four per semester, before; it'll be fine." It was not fine. One more class is not merely an additive increase, it's exponential. The amount of time it takes to address that many concerns and meet the needs of that many students, in a lecture and response framework quickly becomes dizzying. I started to look forward to my breaks more than my classes, my office becoming a place of refuge and imposed solitude. I felt increasingly disconnected from this job which had once been everything to me, the source of my sense of self and power, and I began to question my place within it.

In February 2016, my partner and I travelled to Albuquerque, New Mexico, for a conference on the study of pop culture in academia, so I could give my talk, "Presentations of Non-Human Consciousness in Speculative Fiction Media". The whole of New Mexico had a very Trickster-friendly vibe to it. In downtown Albuquerque we saw Raven symbolism on literally every corner, from city-funded murals to hand-drawn graffiti stickers. But Raven didn't so much appear in that place as it was embodied within it. Every day was filled with a sense of laid-back playfulness and a teasing jostling. But at one point, while I was in the middle of thinking about the racial politics of Albuquerque – such as how most of the black people I saw were homeless, and a lot of people seemed to get tense and terse when they saw me, even when I was in a suit – a homeless black man walked up to us and asked to borrow a few pennies. When I gave him all the pennies I had, he told us about how his sister had made the smart choice and escaped, and how he wasn't racist, himself; he even had quite a lot of African ancestry. I've been thinking about ABQ's history with slavery, since then.

New Mexico is also defined for me by its food. Weird fact: Albuquerque has a *lot* of Italian food, and specifically New York-style Italian food. The first place we ate when we got to town was called the New York Pizza Department. We thought it was a quirk until we walked down Central Avenue (also known as Route 66, one of the most famous roads in America), and saw three more NY-style pizza joints and restaurants. Other than this, Albuquerque is green chili everything. We ate at a really great place called Lindy's Diner, on Central and 5th, right next to the KiMo Theater. They do a variant on the traditional town dish, "The Albuquerque Turkey". The original is a turkey club with green chilies, but Lindy's adds avocado. Friday night, we met up with someone I've known for over twelve years, but had never met in meatspace. We went with her and her husband to the Marble Brewery, which is literally *just* a brewery that serves their own beer, which was a weird concept to me, as every brewery I've known has had food. But this is actually a brilliant strategy, as set up outside the brewery was a Taco Truck, serving really simple, truly Mexican tacos, at around eight U.S. dollars for four of any kind you want. Asada, carnitas, pescado, pollo, and all freaking amazing. They also did quesadillas, which were more cheese than anything. Like, so much cheese that the structural integrity

started to give way. If you're in Albuquerque and see the Chich-
arroneria Don Choche truck, do go to it.

The next day, we travelled to Roswell, N.M. – because it was
going to be at least another year before we were back in the state,
and I figured, if you were an adolescent in the 1990s and are less
than three hours' drive from Roswell, you gotta go; you just *gotta*.
Before going to the UFO Museum, we'd had some of the best
Northern Mexican-style grilled chicken we'd ever had. But on
the way out of Roswell, driving through the desert in the perfect
dark, with no sodium lights and no city pollution, we listened
to David Bowie's *Blackstar* and at one point we pulled off the
road to watch the stars in the deep dark desert. We were joined,
in that moment, at a distance of maybe 100 ft (~30 meters), by a
coyote, rooting through the underbrush, and tentatively sniffing
in our direction.

On the whole, we loved New Mexico, and Albuquerque in
particular, and we were somewhat reluctant to leave it. It apparently felt the same way about us. The day we were set to leave, we
woke up early, got dressed, took the car back to the rental office,
and took the shuttle to the airport. In transit, I realised that I'd
somehow lost my phone between the car and the shuttle, so we
took the shuttle *back* to the rental place, retrieved my phone,
shuttled back, again, to the airport, where we promptly missed
boarding for our flight. Then we found out that, right after we got
back from finding my phone at the rental car facility, the police
had disabled a car bomb that was attached to a rental car. Which
was terrifying. We were trapped in ABQ airport until 4:45 p.m. A
full work day after we were supposed to have left. If you ever find
that you have to spend twenty-three hours and forty-five minutes
in cars, shuttles, airports, planes, between leaving your hotel and
getting home, it may help to remember that interstitial condi-

tions are all that airports are: a giant set of crossroads between everywhere in the world.

In May 2016 we travelled to Vancouver, British Columbia, for the IEEE Ethics Conference. Two days before flying out, I was having trouble with the messages I needed people in my life to receive being garbled in hilariously frustrating ways, so I made a Twitter post saying, "Trickster gods, man. whaddaya gonna do? [Shrug Emoji]." If you've never flown into the international terminal at Vancouver International Airport (which I had not), the very first thing you're confronted with as you leave your gate to go to the main terminal is a massive walk-through diorama of the Inuit story of Raven bringing Light (and thus Knowledge, and Language) to the World. We soon found out that ravens inhabit Vancouver the way pigeons inhabit most other cities. They are on every corner, and every window ledge. In the course of this conference I made friends and contacts and gave presentations and had conversations with people in the fields of philosophy of artificial intelligence, algorithmic learning systems, design, and technology. People from military and corporate hierarchies got to hear me tell them that their approaches to developing machine intelligences, and the potential biases they were programming into them, were far more frightening to contemplate than any supposed "Terminator" scenario.

The closing keynote was called "Techno-Ethics: Upon Shifting Selves and Translocal Networks Constructing the Metropolis". Six minutes into it, the speaker touched on *Ghost in the Shell*, *Serial Experiments: Lain*, architecture, cybernetics, and Michel Foucault's theories of power and technology. Specifically discussing the ethics of architecture, built environments, and the notion of throughput as they pertain to information systems, communities, and communities as information systems. Then he drew an analogy between Information and Communications Technologies (ICT) and Coyote as Trickster God, at which point I was convinced that that weekend was some kind of very pointed object lesson. He discussed the idea that ICT is beneficial to us, when we regard it correctly, but that its uses and intersections in our lives can take turns that are mysterious and shocking, if we aren't careful. Then he closed out with a quote from David Gunkel, one of the two organizers of 2012's Machine Question Symposium.

While we were in the security line to leave Vancouver, I noted to my partner that I thought certain entities may have taken that initial twitter post as a prayer, and the lack of sleep that weekend as a sacrifice, and my mind wasn't exactly changed on this score when, after I got back to my office on Monday to do some end-of-semester paperwork, I found out that I'd been accepted for a sponsored trip to the Frankenstein's Shadow Symposium in Geneva. Shortly after my initial burst of excitement died down, the person who sent me the acceptance messaged me and one other, hoping to introduce us and get us in each other's orbits. The only problem was, the other party and I had already met and hit it off quite well, the first day of IEEE Ethics. The next day I was quoted in *WIRED* magazine.

Geneva in June was a whirlwind, multiple crossing paths, and diverging options, such as having to choose between seeing the grave of Jorge Luis Borges, and seeing the Villa Diodati, where Mary Shelley had written *Frankenstein*, 200 years earlier. I chose the latter, and in so doing, I had deep conversations with three amazing people, all massive talents in their field. The spirit of Mary Shelley lived in that place on the Shores of Lake Geneva, and the conversations the 25 of us had resonated with her genius and innovation. Discussions ranged over the responsibility we have to the kind of minds we create; the prospects and ethical status of created life; the impact of Shelley's writings on the field of biomedical ethics; the gender politics of Shelley's life; the overlap between Frankenstein, AI, and the Miltonic view of Lucifer; and the idea of monstrousness and inhumanity as a cipher for nonwhiteness in Western society, for good and ill. The week touched on everything I had been working on for the preceding dozen years, and the people there all connected in a sense of understanding.

Through all of this, I met people connected to these places. Some of them are people whose presences had always been a part of my life, and were now reoriented and expanded upon. Others were people we met at conferences and with whom we've kept in touch online, hopefully achieving the same goal, from different directions. In all of these instances, the nature of these linkages became tied to a place and a moment in time, a clear memory of where we were when this particular threshold was crossed. In the building of each of these relationships, there was something of a recognition, an understanding that there was a shared or perhaps complementary perspective between us, when it came to perception, assumptions, and our potential to think beyond or differently through our own points of view. And the more I found this, in my academic life, the more I realised how much I'd been missing it. While I had a couple of close friends in my departments, these conversations weren't often being had, because the language needed to have them was still too niche; but through these conference experiences, we met people who helped me remember how to translate that language into broader application.

FINDING THE WORDS

It wasn't until very recently that I parsed a fundamental disconnect, the existence of which had made it so hard to get my thesis through committee. Some weeks ago, I got an academic call for papers under the special title "Logic As Technology", and as I read it, I realised that the discipline of analytic philosophy somehow hasn't yet understood and internalized that its wholly invented language – symbolic logic – *is a technology*. On the heels of that realisation, I saw that Analytic Philosophy hasn't understood that *language as a whole* is a technology. It clicked right then that while graduate school was where I formalised my methodology for presenting the idea of language as a technology, the people from whom I was learning how to craft and deploy my tools did not think of it in the same way. Because language isn't just any technology – it's the foundational technology. It's the technology on which all others are based. It's the most efficient way we have to cram thoughts into the minds of others, share concept structures, and make the world appear and behave the way we want it to. And that can make its very nature invisible to us.

Through the manipulation of language and other vectors of perception, we can string two or more knowns together in just the right way, and create a third, fourth, fifth known. We can create new things in the world, wholecloth, as a result of new words we make up or old words we deploy in new ways. We can make each other think and feel and believe and do things, with words, tone, stance, knowing looks. And this is because language is, at a fundamental level, the oldest magic we have. I learned this lesson again and again, in the course of my life, through repeated encounters with death and joy and loss and opportunity; through the constant input of people and gods and religions and other beloved concentrated collections of perspective and thought. In each new place I've been, there was an echo, a shadow – sometimes faint, sometimes stark, always present – of everything that had gone before. Memories of moments and words standing like signs at crossroads, reminding me of where I'd come from, and showing me where I might yet go.

Damien Patrick Williams holds a Master's Degree in Philosophy and Religious Studies with a concentration in Occult Systems. Over the past decade, he has worked as an instructor, researcher, and writer to explore the intersections of philosophy, popular culture, technology, and the academic study of the occult. He has written articles, presented at conferences, given interviews for publications such as *WIRED* magazine, and appeared on numerous podcasts, all in the service of discussing the impact that studying media representations of autonomous created intelligences, alchemy, magic, and religious belief can have on the philosophical, social, and legal status of those concepts.

As program organizer for the Comics and Popular Arts Academic Conference in Atlanta, Damien has worked to bring together entertainment industry professionals, academicians, and non-academic audiences to investigate the role and impact of the popular arts in academia and the world. He also works equally hard to address the converse question of what academia can learn to express through its engagement with the popular arts, and seeks to do so in several different fora.

Damien currently operates both afutureworththinkingabout. com and technoccult.net, and also instructs philosophy and religious studies for Kennesaw State University in the US state of Georgia.

He can be found on Twitter at @wolven.

COAL MEMORY

Alan Moore

S pirits of Place. The clue is in the name: better, perhaps, to leave them where they are.

Also in the name, embedded, is the question of what we are naming. Place is easily defined without controversy but Spirit is more slippery, more loaded. By spirit of place, presumably, we mean some entity or essence that emerges from location, a phenomenon first noticed under the shamanic aura of cognitive revolution, roughly seven thousand years ago. With all the attributes of modern consciousness – dreams, memories, imagination – yet no understanding of what these things actually entail, a tree or stone or stream might seem the source of the associations, recollections and unusual atmospheres that it provokes; internal images and voices seen as evidence for some indwelling djinn.

This, then, this apprehension of a personality in place, is hardwired into us from our inception, is the default way we perceive our environments. Landscape is memory, and memory in turn compresses to become the rich black seam that underlies our territory. This usually manifests in an associated ambience, a potentially marketable terrour, and only artists of one stripe or other will feel the necessity to dig, to excavate, to willingly immerse themselves for days on end in that inadequately lit and deep-dug labyrinth of crumbling facts, where struts of theory creak and threaten to give way, to bring the whole thing down on top of you. Famously, it's a dirty job.

Less so, perhaps, during the 18th century when the divining of these local energies was more straightforward and more literal. In the *Grimoire Pour Conjurer L'Esprit D'un Lieu,* a facsimile edition bound in gold and purple taffeta and perfumed with an incense of vervain and frankincense, it recommends the verbal cursing and the ritual mistreatment of "a young white piglet" until such point as the Spirit of the Place in question speaks through the tormented animal and submits to the bidding of the artist, of the conjuror, for a period of thirty to three hundred years, a tenure which appears to be negotiable. The piglet is unfortunately stabbed, though these days vegetarian options are available.

A more modern approach to poking somewhere till it squeals would substitute a pen or pencil for the ritual sword, but may include as many angry and repetitive entreaties to Asmodeus, God, Lucifer and Jesus. In its practice it involves a frantic circling of the target area, on foot or in pencil on a map, in an attempt to give the seething local information some kind of perimeter, enclosing the live histories and the dead bodies in a bored and angry graphite vortex, a grey scribbled cyclone of intent surrounding the selected city, town or neighbourhood, keeping its data ring-fenced and contained. The map, of course, knows nothing of the cyclone while the city, in its turn, knows nothing of the map.

Our sense of whereabouts is always a construction, if we're physically there or if we're not, a quilt of media stereotypes, popular perceptions, reminiscences, personal observations, bleached out history – a geography entirely of the head. The fictions of a place precede it. In the case of Newcastle, specifically, the early echo soundings seemed to have a signature ferocity, from first parental references to Hadrian's Wall and muddled comprehension of the Jarrow March, to gawping from a teenage playground at Tom Pickard's blistering dialect poem "Shag" in Michael Horowitz's Blake-blazoned *Children of Albion*. As far into the cold north as the Roman Empire ever reached, they say.

Then there's the Newcastle of Bulwer Lytton's Nazi-captivating narrative *The Coming Race,* as referenced surprisingly by Peter Noone on "Oh! You Pretty Things", the real town undermined by fictions of winged superhuman giants, the Vril-Ya, our subterranean superiors that heal with kisses and subsist upon the life-giving Vril energy. This last notion proves popular, inspiring the beef extract that abbreviates Bovine Vril to Bovril and, also, lending a name to an occult fraternity enjoined by the elite of the Third Reich. In a location that apparently invites underground fantasies – Coal City, Roman State – there's the suggestion of some buried force, inhuman, fierce, and transformational.

The place-name's first appearance in the current author's work occurs around the middle Eighties as a throwaway, an ominous bass note struck in an urban warlock's backstory, the hint at an occasion and a city where the magic goes disastrously wrong. It could be anywhere, yet the associative fog attached to the word Newcastle makes it incongruously perfect, rivet-hard reality that renders sorcery inevitably poncey; plausibly, a catastrophic venue for a ritual summoning of the uncanny. Getting on a decade later, having somehow personally strayed into the role of urban warlock, all these fictional foreshadowings are more or less forgotten, on the back-burner, irrelevant.

With an initial site-specific magical extravaganza at London's Bridewell Theatre, during which a spirit of the place appears to register on photographic film, a basic methodology presents itself: one-off performances focussed entirely on the place and time of their manifestation, form and content having been derived from some preceding ritual, privately enacted. Given the intensity of these productions, making them an annual event affords a tolerable schedule and so when Newcastle-based arts funding body *Locus+* extends an invitation to appear around the end of 1995, the nature of the presentation and its venue both to be determined, this is construed as divine direction.

Early in that same year an initiating ritual is improvised with musical collaborators Dave J and Tim Perkins, the resultant flood of school and pre-school recollection taken as an indication that the theme, this time, is childhood. Though this is conceptually vague and lacks a central metaphor, our Newcastle associates commence the search for a suitable venue – possibly a disused primary school – and settle on a birthday date of November 18th for the event. Then, over summer, mum sickens and dies in the same hospital/converted workhouse that's the site of this nativity almost forty two years before. Her personal effects include the preserved birth-caul of her older brother, Jack.

The membrane, yellowed wax streaked with improbably bright crimson, clings to night-blue bandage wrap that's dated by a stamp-sized label to 1919, this eldest son no doubt resulting from relieved homecoming copulation at the cease of the Great War. A tattered rectangle, its shape turns out to be that of the hole in our performance, words emerging from the gory creases. Our Newcastle organisers, meanwhile, having failed to find a child-related stage for the endeavour propose a Victorian court building which, while having no apparent relevance to cauls or infancy, feels nonetheless appropriate for what is now a forensic inquiry into womb, grave, and the life between.

Following months of stinking heat the autumn bites down icy. Unexpected snow on the drive north prompts last-minute revisions to the text – sat in the rattling hired van's rear beside Tim and Melinda, Dave J having lately upped stumps for Los Angeles – making it more unerringly about the moment. Newcastle opens a fistful of industrial estates and cheerily waves us into a city that, confusingly, turns out not to be drawn by *Viz's* Simon Ecob. Architecture bulges like grey muscle built up over centuries and indicates a burly soul, a Tyneside golem confident in its sufficiency and keeping its own counsel, wearing flimsy tinsel chains in droll pretence of subjugation.

The Old County Court in Westgate Road is sombre, atmospherically exact, and daughters Leah and Amber have arrived from Liverpool for this nonstandard birthday bash. Fourteen and seventeen, looking like trouble they paint medicine-man spirals on the brow, the cheeks above the beard-line, in fluorescent white to flare against the ultraviolet lighting. In the belly of the court an upturned bicycle is an impromptu instrument, the ragged natal pennant of the caul suspended by a thread above the bench from which the sentences will be pronounced. Tim Perkins, in a black hood, waits to execute the show's non-verbal element. Melinda films. The audience, as ever, are the jury.

The next hour, almost precisely, is conducted in those shimmering and oblivious purlieus of consciousness occasioned by nerve-wracking concentration, by attempting not to be there, trying to erase the reader and leave nothing but the narrative's umbilical progression. The awareness that a live recording is in progress, every syllable pre-polished for the tape-heads, only incubates the eerie tension. Near the start a spectre of historic Newcastle is summoned to this site of the submerged wall (that positions Hadrian as a 1st century Donald Trump) decked out in vanished priory grounds, cholera epidemics and untrammelled industry, this very court once requisitioned for an episode of *Spender*.

Near the end, the caul by now worn as a mask with traceries of human fat fluorescing in the black light, the conclusion is delivered by an uninvited voice. Human experience winds back into placental blackness and the evening ends in a collage of slapped backs, incandescent synapses and after-party, this last walked to through unruly chucking-out time streets where remnants of mascara and a woolly jumper strip away any last vestiges of masculinity. Glimpsed through the celebratory smoke-haze is the sense that while this uterine jazz-voodoo has achieved its aims, engagement with the manacle-hung shade of Newcastle, its walking skeleton, has proven more elusive.

Sometime later there is the discovery that birth cauls, famously acquired by mariners as talismans preventing drowning, were also much prized by the legal profession, worn upon the head to denote wisdom and precursor to barristers' wigs, a retroactive validation of our work's judicial venue. Subsequently, fifteen years sluice through the mill-race of mammalian life and working productivity with a remote awareness of unfinished business, the commenced but uncompleted divination of a place's punch-drunk soul, a working's vital lightning-lines left hanging in the stinging northern air without their closure, with no prophylactic banishing, the no-score draw that begs a rematch.

2010 arrives, making its bumpy landing on the plane-bombed runways of a different century, another planet, a bare-ribbed zombie economy. Paul Smith and Iain Sinclair, on an ongoing safari in pursuit of rare, fugitive energies – a kind of shadowy and metaphysical Pokémon Go – are currently engaged in reinventing J.B. Priestley's *English Journey*, with an earlier invitation to attend a stopover in Aldeburgh gratefully accepted, Shirley Collins and B. Catling rubbing shoulders with Witch-finder General Matthew Hopkins and Rendlesham Forest's otherworldly lights. This time, with J.M.W Turner's *Hannibal* beside John Martin's *Sodom and Gomorrah* at the Laing, the target's Newcastle.

A singular convergence of works by these elemental voices, these contemporaries who never meet and yet whose closest relatives end in the same asylum, whose works hung together are distinct apocalypses with a common composition, these two violent beauties will inevitably set the tone of the engagement. Whether some authentic wraith of place can be cajoled out of the pavement-cracks and brickwork is less certain but the pencilled dates are inked; arrangements made. No longer in the intense aura-state of fifteen years before, this time the journey has a different kind of urgency and seeks a different Newcastle, by tilting train from Peterborough and up Britain's scoliotic spine.

Arriving, unexpectedly exhausted from the effortless contin-uum of travel, at the wiped and gleaming face that cities show to visitors by rail, met by a waiting Paul Smith who extends the offer of an evening with Kenneth Anger to the smoke-deprived and twitching voyager, by this point desperate for a silent, motion-less hotel room. And besides, the Luciferian flicker of that L.A. neon-magic feels like a wrong frequency, an inappropriate wavelength for this territory, this forthcoming evocation. Here, the local Genius seems pre-Christian rather than flamboyantly transgressive anti-Christian. The invite's declined, politely, and night passes in a neutral space that could be anywhere.

Gateshead next day from the room's window is scrubbed clean by sun, opened like a stone daisy with holiday paintwork, a new city seen in decent daylight. There's a meeting with Iain Sinclair who reports that he has found Tom Pickard in a hauntological abandoned service station by a dried-up highway on Newcastle's edge. Apparently the lyric shipyard giant and teen-hood hero has a comic book collected volume he'd like autographed and asks, unnecessarily, if anything of his would be appropriate in exchange. Remembering the wife's forlorn infatuation with a vanished copy of Tom's *Guttersnipe*, a spare signed to Melinda is suggested if the poet has one anywhere around.

First on the day's agenda is an afternoon appearance at the Laing, accompanied by mesmeric Sunn O))) soundscaper Stephen O'Malley with Martin and Turner's paintings both *in situ*. Set together, the resemblance of their twin, obliterating vortices to glaring and disastrous eyes – one orb all ice and wind, the other night and fire – is clear. Although a mortal crowd is present, this is obviously an audience with the artworks and the force behind those oblong, canvas lenses, the performance wholly for and carried out beneath that awful, unforgiving gaze. Iain points out that the thunderbolt in Martin's tableau accidentally reproduces Turner's grotesque profile and his turnip nose.

The reading goes well, timbred vocals creaking in the chain-drag and the undertow of Stephen's tidal drones, but feels as if its tarry conjurings are dissipated, bleeding out into the sunny weekend taking place beyond the institution's cleared-throat hush, a kind of light pollution. An extended reconstruction of the piece at the nearby Sage gallery that's planned for later on will hopefully allow the covering topsoil of containing darkness that the work requires in which to incubate. Projected images will understudy for the two originals, their whirlpool cataclysms understandably confined here at the Laing. Nevertheless, that same stare will survey the second house.

Before that, everybody is convened at this nocturnal venue and Tom Pickard – tough, kind, funny and young in his bones – has, overwhelmingly, inscribed his personal pencil-corrected and dog-eared copy of *Guttersnipe* to the absent Melinda, who will furnish prison tattoo illustrations for the extract from Tom's hair-raising autobiography in underground reanimation *Dodgem Logic* out of teary gratitude. Amidst the pre-gig chatter Iain mentions casually that his impeccable and revelatory text for the event was written during an odd moment earlier that day, inciting a deep envy that's professional and a regret arising from personal inability to hand over control and trust the moment.

Finally it's time to take the stage, Stephen O'Malley's aural fogbank supplemented by the swirling keyboard ectoplasm of the Band of Susans' luminescent Susan Stenger and the shingle-dredging scrap percussion of Einstürzende Neubauten's earth-deity Mufti. Sonic broth, the music stews and rolls, is broken into eddies by the pull of a relentless circling current, an acoustic analogue of the frenetic pencil-lead tornado scoring the insensate map. Thick shadow crowds in to compress the fugitive idea congealing at its centre and our newly-born white pig is led into the circle, prodded and tormented, with the spirit of the place thereby provoked to speech and this is what it says:

"Horns groan, apprehensive, through a cold steam on the river. Periodically it rises. First the bridges topple in and then the houses; solid homes with corners, walls and doorsteps momentarily suspended in an eerie yellow storm-light, upside down, impossible. Extend your colliery shafts past the groundwater level and they flood for want of an effective pumping system. Boy apprentices drift, slumped like starfish, through evacuated tunnels, ride the corpse-flume down into anthracite black. The chokedamp drops you in your tracks and doesn't even have a smell while at a spark the firedamp blossoms to explosion and they haul up their recoverable dead in buckets. City as an anvil. Rain and gas and pit-collapse and flame, these are God's hammers, thundering upon the bitter edge of Empire.

Essaying the dirty ebb-tide of the eighteenth century, prophetic debris lunges jagged out of blinding estuary sands, junk from the future, ideas and idealists cast up in the backwash of a world yet to exist: pistons and cylinders, padlocks unpickable, decapitated kings to flop and flounder in the thin grey surf. 1770 and Jean Paul Marat is in Newcastle decanting the electric fluid, trying to distil the lightning as a crackling and dangerous vocabulary, as a handwriting to copperplate the leaves of his intended book, his *Chains of Slavery*, by means of seething electrolysis. At the Bigg Market, hunched above his coffee while it sours, he lives in morbid expectation of an unjust treatment, smoulders with anticipatory resent and, in the sooty motion of incipient machineries, longs for a bath to make him clean, to soothe the tumbrel itch. Abandon England to industrial revolution as its only means of staving off the other sort; slick the protesting cogs with oil rather than an arterial spurt. Civilisation trembles in the arc-gap. Indistinct new vistas shudder in its glass.

Hawking incendiary phlegm militant keelmen from upstream with Border Reivers in their ancestry burn down the jetties where outlandish mechanisms funnel coal direct from cart to coaster, rendering their ancient boats and their five hundred year-old settlement at Sandgate surplus to requirements. Mob breath clouds the windows, hobnails kick hot glitter from the cobbles. Wooden continuities are broken and recast in metal. Angry muttering of the retort and Byron in the House of Lords conceding that the poor may have a point. Astride the mills and mudflats Riot hikes her blazing skirts and asks if anyone is dancing. Poets, painters, engineers and insurrectionists stampede to mark her card while at the Café de l'Echelle beneath the Palais Royal's colonnade Marc Isambard Brunel gets in a scrap with Maximilien Robespierre. It's raining heads.

Spirits are lifting from the vapours. Heaven shimmers in a bell-jar and hermetic heartthrob Humphry Davy is at the Pneumatic Institute in Bristol eagerly inhaling his oxide of nitrogen to find out if it kills him but instead his handsome skull segments, is opened to the aether, consciousness become a single pin-sharp bubble in the rising effervescence. Outside history and space, he understands. He is made luminous, dilates to fill the universe, with countless stars and periodic table all inside him and the joy, the ecstasy of everything. He's laughing uncontrollably. He drums his feet exhilarated on the floorboards' worn and sombre varnish while the transformation of mankind, a new society, rolls down his cheek in sizzling tears of mirth. The Pentecostal gassing leaves him messianic with his scientific demonstrations soon fronting a nitrous oxide cult, Coleridge and Wordsworth reeling giddy and exalted in the fumes of its periphery when elsewhere William Blake puts his red hat on to watch Newgate Prison burning. Chemistry and curfew simmer in the crucible. In foundry light is raised an iron Jerusalem.

At Redheugh on the Tyne's north side a shot tower is erected in anticipation of the run on musket balls. Tipped through a copper sieve, dropped from a height to equal Nelson's column, beads of molten lead have time to gather surface tension, rounding into perfect spheres before they hit cold water down below, a hissing bullet monsoon. The new century wears thunderbolts for spurs, gunpowder trickling from its heels and now we bore our cannons better. Breughel landscapes over decades kippered into Lowries, dioramas crawling with beetle humanity, with manikins dwarfed by their times. The skies begin their slide on a black gradient where Joseph Wright of Derby catches an alembic under-light that pools beneath the jaw. Machines are built to build machines, machines are built to disassemble men. Guillotine baskets brim like market stalls, Halloween fruiterers.

The godparents of Frankenstein trade pamphlets round the crib. Tom Paine of Thetford lists his *Rights of Man*, establishing that staying in the country after publication isn't one of them. He takes the night boat out of Dover following an alleged prophecy from William Blake, suspiciously direct and unambiguous. In France, 1792, the new Republic dawns. Paine is elected deputy of Pas de Calais, argues against executing Louis the Sixteenth on both political and moral grounds. Jean Paul Marat meanwhile insists the new arrangement is a house of cards without a tyrant's cranium as centrepiece and Paine draws the attentions of the Committee for Public Safety, busy rolling out the Terror unencumbered by a sense of irony. The king's head hits the wickerwork in January the next year and there amidst an awestruck silence following the thud is Blake's other associate, Mary Wollstonecraft, who'd recently replied to Tom

Paine's *Rights of Man* with her own *Vindication of the Rights of Woman*. She's seen Heaven's vengeance lurking in the subtle flame and watches now the weighted blade, its lofty drop to cut the ribbon on Pandora's pent-up mischiefs. Four years later and she's married to another friend of Blake's, the proto-anarchist and writer William Godwin. Everywhere the grind and rumble of epochal gears, the flat stones of Satanic mills as they commence to turn. A creaking at the limits, at the edge of our condition, a raw frontier of our lust and fear and capability. The tarry hawser slips to burn the hand and Bonaparte puts on his boots.

The friction heat around this junction of two worlds is fierce, where people melt into an alloy with their artefacts; become soft moving parts in great indifferent mechanisms they have coaxed to motion. Marat sinks into a celebratory tub and Girondine fanatic Charlotte Corday brings the claret. Tom Paine stoops to rub away the chalk by his cell door that marks him for the guillotine and skips out for America, a troubled land where he can once more bring his calming influence to bear. Within twelve days of giving birth to her and William Godwin's daughter Mary, Mary Wollstonecraft is dead leaving a husband in his forties to bring up their child, a clueless man responsible for nurturing the living being that he and his late wife, his assistant, had created from their stitched-together chromosomes and animated in a lightning storm of rhetoric. The nineteenth century bursts its restraining straps and sits up on the slab. This is the English Journey, the trajectory that landscape will describe through time, the blurring view out through the windscreen of the present as it hurtles past grotesquely morphing scenery at the unvarying and frankly reckless speed of one minute per minute. By 1803 Napoleon is thirty-four, France's dictator and First Consul following his *coup d'état* of four years earlier and warming up for over two decades of a cordite and horsemeat Armageddon. J.M.W. Turner, twenty-eight years old, has been to Paris in the short-lived lull after the Peace of Amiens but now he's safely back in London when hostilities, inevitably, are resumed. In that same year, thirteen-year-old John Martin and his family move to Newcastle where hell-glow from the forges stains skies that are dark and heavy with particulates, an entire firmament collapsing with the weight of its accumulated carbon crust to rain down on the town below in smutty chunks as big as factories.

Within a dozen circumnavigations of the sun the Davy Lamps are winking on across the underworld and fewer dead are being dredged up from the subterranean reaches under Newcastle where Bulwer-Lytton by the century's end will situate the habitat of his Vril-Ya, his Coming Race, transcendent cave-angels who heal with kisses through their mastery of the Life Force. Bovril, concentrating the life force of cows into a bottled paste, is just a faster way of saying Bovine Vril. In 1814 married Percy Shelley is already feeling the Vril energy and at the age of twenty-two runs off abroad with William Godwin's sixteen-year old daughter Mary and, ambitiously, with her half-sister Claire. Harriet Westbrook, Shelley's wife, will soon be floating face down in the Serpentine. In 1815 Mary bears a baby girl who lives only a fortnight, dreams her child was only cold and simply needed rubbing by the fire to bring it back to life. As yet unmarried, the bereaved pair spend a memorable holiday in Switzerland with Byron and the conversation turns to ghosts, to horrors. Glint of an idea, of a stark modernity in the electrodes but by 1822 the faceless body of her husband nuzzles the Italian tide-line and Mary's a widow at the age of twenty-four. This is the chronologic soup, magma of incident our days are born from. Here is the laboratory where a monster hatched that would conclude its narrative on an endangered icecap. Horns groan, apprehensive, through a cold steam on the river. Periodically, it rises.

Fog on the meniscus hovering, a condensate of phantoms and the opaque waters slapping at the hull. Homesick Italian spectres from the Roman forts at Benwell and Pons Aelius flap ragged on a shoreline where the Bridge of Hadrian once stood, frayed ectoplasm flaking at the edges, carried off by river winds. This is as far north as the Romans ever got.

A smog of history above the surface slop, detergent foam of apparitions. Anglo Saxon revenants from Monkchester creep with the evening current in their Ceol boats, design and name near indistinguishable from the vessels of dead keelmen drifting there amongst them in a smoulder of blue jackets, yellow waistcoats and bell-bottom trousers, both their trade and their Sandgate community erased by a rampage of industry that might yet take us all. Bright ribbons on their black silk hats, weel may the keel row on the memory of aggrieved and snarling lips and ever watching for the lantern in St. Nicholas's tower.

The scum of wraiths floats in a quivering lattice, delicate and phosphorescent. Levitating cavaliers borne from Carpenter's Tower and shambling mummies in a flurry of papyrus dust from the Hancock museum, crying children, biting children, coffin strippers and a shapeless blackness oozing through a wall up at Newcastle Keep, a flotsam of the afterlife that clots about the banks in séance suds. Astral suspensions in the atmosphere, the marinade that young John Martin steeped in. A precipitate of dream cobwebs the brick walls with black curds of factory breath, a layered papering of voices peeling in forgotten floods.

A coloured slick upon the rising swell, a scumbled spectrum, oils for canvasses, oils for machines. Faith in mankind's mechanically assisted progress, born to the Tchaikovsky roar of a transition from eighteenth to nineteenth century is exhausted by the time the First World War concludes but by then it's too late to stop, and here we are with the Cormac McCarthy limits of our tarmac road in sight, at the extremities of our electrical utopia. Our New Prometheus blunders bellowing from room to smoke-filled room around the burning castle as we near the ragged edges of the only diagram we had. Beyond that, decimations: earthquake and tsunami, hurricanes that skittle oaks and fire as an emergent property of vegetation. Naked to the pulverising elements we writhe below a toppling sky, always amazed and terrified to find our visions have their draughty boundaries when the planet shrugs, as if civilisations never stopped before, as if ambition never previously ran out of track.

This is where England and the English journey end, here at the ghost sluice of the Tyne, our past's breath on our neck and threatening to catch up with us. Our science fictions and our promised lands go down in flame and wind and water, alpine snowflakes melted on the yellowed skulls of elephants. Unable to see forward we look back and in our useless and nostalgic retrospection turn to salt, become our own memorials, have our Ozymandias moment. In the drip and grotto echo of a haunted waterway our glories gradually reduce to a dull textbook sediment until only our scattered words and memorable images are left undamaged: Marat's *Chains of Slavery* in the library of Newcastle's Literary and Philosophical Society, John Martin's paintings at the Laing and in the Museum of Antiquities the severed granite head of a Romano-British god, our fossil master-plans, and after that only the noises of a swollen tide.

This is as far north as the Romans ever got with their Mediterranean tans, thin tunics and short skirts, freezing their arses off at Wallsend, Segedunum, thus commencing a tradition. The precarious margin of their territories scares them, alien and elemental, liminal and filled with unknown hazard, too close to the Arctic for their skimpily-dressed gods to follow and watch over them. They need a local hand to mediate between them and a savage landscape and, at the wall's other end in Benwell, Conderecum, they erect their temple to a borrowed native deity, Antenociticus, god of the antler-fringed brow and therefore a Horned One, a Caernunnos.

Called the greatest and the best, Antenociticus is clearly on a par with Jupiter, the wielder of the lightning whose dominion extends to all things, to the squall and avalanche and hunted boar, god of a hostile universe that lies beyond their world's Hyperborean rim, upon whose whim survival rests. Beautifully fashioned in the Celtic style his psychopathic pinprick eyes are merciless, omnipotent, mad with divinity, a pagan gaze that promises the end of cities, a condition that seems far away back in the tumult of the late eighteenth and early nineteenth centuries when modern industry still gurgles in its infancy, in its gunmetal cot, or at least further than it seems today.

Neither Newcastle lad John Martin nor his Covent Garden colleague Joseph Turner, artists tempered by that era's locomotive steam, are strangers to insanity. Both Turner's mother and John Martin's brother Jonathan will end their lives at Bedlam in the orbit of contemporary apocalyptic visionary William Blake. Both men are photo-sensitive to their new age, reacting to its light, its shocks and promises exposed in their emulsions. Martin ends the world in cataclysmic *Great Day of His Wrath*, Titan upheavals and the heavens falling. Turner ends the world by boiling all its form away into a fearful and obliterating immanence. Towards the end, in his Great Western Railway conjuring *Rain, Steam and Speed* only the dark stroke of a smokestack tells us what we're peering at.

Though painted forty years apart by men of widely different temperament and age and style, both Turner's *Hannibal* and Martin's *Sodom and Gomorrah* possess many similarities and have the stamp of catastrophic times upon them. Turner's piece is executed during 1812 while John Martin is hanging his first painting, *Sadak in Search of the Waters of Oblivion*, in the Royal Academy. Just a year previously, Napoleon has tried to invade Italy across the Alps, Hannibal style, defeated by the stark realities of weather and terrain. Turner conceives a warning, a reminder of the shattering and gigantic forces of the earth that wait to wipe away our kingdoms, our Republics, our delirious ambitions, a tribunal that brooks no appeal. He steals a murderous Yorkshire sky from over Farnley Hall in Otley, revels in the drama of a northern light.

John Martin's levelling of the Cities of the Plain, painted in 1852 with Martin in his early sixties has the same
regional atmospherics, has the furnace glow of his Newcastle youth deployed to similar ends. It shares with Turner's
painting an enormity of scale and moment, tiny Breughel
figures only there to illustrate the vastness of destruction
that surrounds them, the futility and insignificance of
human grandeurs faced with natural disaster, faced with
carpet bombing from the angels. Both works have the same
intention, a critique of overreaching national arrogance
couched in a language that is classical or biblical.

Most strikingly, they share a composition: rocky terrain
in the lower foreground rising on the right where miniatur-
ist figures cower, Lot and his daughters, Hannibal's doomed
soldiers. Over all this, in the upper background's whirl and
spectacle, Martin and Turner both depict the same annihi-
lating vortex, one with flame and one with snow. Some say
the world will end in fire, some in ice, but both factions in
the debate agree that it will end: Rome's rule, Napoleon's,
Gomorrah, the industrially warmed world that we inhabit
straining at the end of their respective tethers, facing the
same whirlpools of demise. This is a terror of the world's
edge, is the vertigo of an accelerated culture. Out beyond
the lights of every city, every town and every century, this
is the abyss that abides.

These lethal vortices are each ellipses, one that sears and
one that freezes. At the Roman garrisons hunching against
the rain in Westgate Road beside Hadrian's Wall these are
the terminal configurations of civilisation's margins, are
the forces outside that must be appeased. In 2010 at this
unique convergence, hanging side by side together the twin

maelstroms of extinction can't help but suggest an optical arrangement, these storm sockets pooled with hail and magma and eradication.

We stand at the precipice of ourselves and look down into a gaze that has not blinked or wavered since before we were and would not notice if we were no longer. At these snowblind precincts of our empire, at this limit of our possibilities we stare into the cold eyes of Antenociticus. **"**

Antenociticus. So, not a spirit but a god of place, which sounds like a considerably higher pay-grade. One conceives of Genius Loci as accumulating from associations, memories and dreams in the Palaeolithic mind, a consciousness that is not conscious of itself entangling its unwitting processes into a certain atmosphere that it assumes must emanate from that specific tree, that stream, that rock, having no concept of where else these eerie apprehensions might originate. Hence dryads, naiads, gnomes, facilitating some form of communication with the unpredictable and often violent landscape, although come the plague, the wildfire, the eclipse, a bigger concept is made necessary.

Gods, then, can be seen as local spirits re-imagined to include the entire visible environment, the perceived world, the tribal universe, and from the ice and smoke and hunters' moons of prehistoric Newcastle there comes Antenociticus, encompassing the all of its precarious condition; its scar-faced experience. Figment of a tradition that is almost wholly oral, the god of the horn-fringed brow would seem unlikely to survive the churn of aeons were it not for his adoption by the weather-pummelled legionnaires of Conderecum who, with customary syncretism, make Antenociticus equivalent to Jupiter, a planet-shaker, and next render him in stone lending the immaterial a dangerous corporeality.

Following Rome's collapse, the wind and history inter its occupation's rubble with no thought to resurrection: Time ends with the empire and a dark millennium is commenced. Consider, then, the unexploded god, donner and blitzen underneath a steadily accreting Benwell, ticking ominously, subterranean, a life force in its fashion, a Vril energy but not about the healing or the kissing. Nearly fifteen hundred years and no one knows he's there until Victoria's empire exceeds Rome's and scratches the compacted Geordie dirt in search of antecedents, histories to own and to incorporate with no disposal expert anywhere at hand, no one who knows if it's the blue wire or the red.

Unearthed, Antenociticus returns to a changed world where printing presses now exist and can extend his reach; his aura; his stern, staring image far beyond the place that he begins his myth-life as a spirit of. The carefully delineated features of the excavated deity are unforgettable, the antlers two-dimensional and slicked down to the scalp, this flattened bone fringe swept dramatically to one side and, scored on the upper lip, the grooves of a toothbrush moustache. This is the merciless visage of an authentic ancient god envisioned by his worshippers. The era's Symbolists, of course, continually hungry for reverberant iconography, can't get enough of this still-volatile material.

Franz Von Stuck, uniquely skilled at capturing an archetype's Romantic essence – his impassive and industrial *Lucifer* is after Blake, its darkness and its Satanism pointedly embodied in its factories and mills – is almost certainly attracted to Antenociticus, the horned god, the Caernunnos thundering at the head of the Celtic Wild Hunt, the horde of wrathful spirits led up annually out of the underworld, the buried national dream. Von Stuck borrows the features of Newcastle's stygian Zeus for a depiction of the hunt's Teutonic counterpart, the throng fronted by Odin, in his *Wilde Jagd*, painted in 1889. To a Wagner-obsessive born that year, this might well come to seem significant.

Is this where the two-thousand year-long fuse first lit at Conderecum leads: a shattered Europe with that face, the emblematic 'tache, the fringe biased to the right, presiding over gas-chambers and ruins from the flickering newsreels and front pages, from the editorial cartoons and *Radio Fun* caricatures? A sense of presence whispering in Julian Jaynes' bicameral mind, become a mood that haunts the field and barrow, made an All-Father of stars and tempests, raised at Benwell and unwisely relocated, through the medium of Von Stuck's self-fulfilling prophecy, to Nuremberg. Winged supermen ascend the mineshaft. Black dogs lift their ears to a sepulchral horn. The hunt is on.

Spirits of Place. The clue is in the name: better, perhaps, to leave them where they are.

Born Northampton, 1953, **Alan Moore** is a writer, performer, recording artist, activist and magician. His comic-book work includes *Lost Girls* with Melinda Gebbie, *From Hell* with Eddie Campbell and *The League of Extraordinary Gentlemen* with Kevin O'Neill. He has worked with director Mitch Jenkins on the *Showpieces* cycle of short films and on forthcoming feature film *The Show*, while his novels include *Voice of the Fire* (1996) and his current epic *Jerusalem* (2016). Only about half as frightening as he looks, he lives in Northampton with his wife and collaborator Melinda Gebbie.

NOTES AND SOURCES

I HAVE TROD SUCH HAUNTED LAND
Gazelle Amber Valentine (p. 15)

Title image:

Photo of Gazelle Amber Valentine in Norway, by Edgar Livengood. © Edgar Livengood, used with permission.

THE PALACE BUILT OVER A HELLMOUTH
Maria J. Pérez Cuervo (p. 41)

Title image:

Cropped from *The Garden of Earthly Delights (Hell)*, by Hieronymus Bosch (1490-1510). Public domain image.

Notes:

1. Lucas de Heere's painting in the Cathedral of Gante (1559) depicts Philip II as King Solomon. The Window of the King, in Saint Janskerk of Gouda (1557) contains a representation of Philip II next to his wife Mary I, with the inscription "ECCE PLVS QVAM SALOMON HEIC" (Here is that who is more than Solomon)

2. In The Judgement of Solomon (1 Kings 3: 16-28), when two women claimed to be the mother of the same baby, the king resolved he should be cut in two halves. His verdict was a trick to reveal who the real mother was, as she chose to surrender the baby to the other woman.

3. Philip II's obsession with Hieronymus Bosch is the reason why El Prado holds so many of his paintings. As well as *The Garden of the Earthly Delights*, it owns *The Table of the Seven Deadly Sins, The Extraction of the Stone of Madness* and *The Haywain Triptych*, among others.

Bibliography:

Calvo Poyato, José. (1996) *La vida y la época de Carlos II el Hechizado*. Planeta, Barcelona.

Gómez Roán, M. Concepción. "La causa inquisitorial contra el confesor de Carlos II, fray Froilán Díaz". Revista de la Inquisición ISSN: 1131-5571 2006, 12: 323-389

Lezcano Tosca, Hugo. (2013) "Lecturas espirituales prohibidas en la Real Biblioteca de El Escorial". Libros de la Corte, no. 6.

Lisón Tolosana, Carmelo. (1990) *La España mental 1: el problema del mal*. Ediciones Akal.

O'Malley, Charles Donald. *Andreas Vesalius of Brussels, 1514-1564*. Accessed through Google Books.

Parker, Geoffrey. (2014) *Imprudent King: A New Life of Philip II*. Yale University Press. Kindle edition.

Rey Bueno, Mar. "La Mayson pour Distiller des Eaües at El Escorial: Alchemy and Medicine at the Court of Philip II, *1556–1598*."

Sepúlveda, Ricardo. (1898) *Antiguallas: crónicas, descripciones y costumbres españolas en los siglos pasados*. Open Library, digitised by University of Michigan.

Sigüenza, Fray José de. (1907) *Historia de la orden de San Jerónimo*. Bailly-Baillière, Madrid. Open Library, digitised by University of Toronto.

A COMPENDIUM OF TIDES
Warren Ellis (p. 61)

Title image:

Edited version of a photo of the Maunsell Sea Forts, by 'Flaxton'. Creative Commons licence (Attribution 3.0 Generic).

AGONIES AND ENCHANTMENTS
Kristine Ong Muslim (p. 79)

Title image:

Photo of North Upi Arch. No attribution requested.

THE GREAT MONGOOSE
Vajra Chandrasekera (p. 99)

Title image:

Edited version of "Sri Lanka Devil Mask (Vesmuhunu)", photo by Russell Trow. Creative Commons licence (Attribution 2.0 Generic).

Death Imitating Art at Castle an Dinas
Joanne Parker (p. 119)

Title image:

Edited version of "Bronze age barrow, Castle an Dinas", a photo by Alex Valavanis. Creative Commons licence (Attribution 2.0 Generic).

Notes:

1. This is suggested by Historic Cornwall. See www.historic-cornwall.org. uk. The same claim is made by Cornwall Heritage Trust, the current owners and managers of the site. See Cornwall Heritage Trust, "Scheme of Work, Classroom and Visit-Based Activities for Key Stages 1-3", p. 8 (pdf available at www.cornwallheritagetrust.org. Accessed 14/09/16).

2. William Worcester, *Itineraries*, trans. by J.H. Harvey (Oxford: Clarendon, 1969), p. 237.

3. Geoffrey of Monmouth, *History of the Kings of Britain*, trans. by Aaron Thompson (Cambridge, Ontario: In Parentheses, 1999), p. 142.

4. Geoffrey of Monmouth, *History of the Kings of Britain*, p. 142.

5. See Geoffrey Ashe, *Arthurian Britain*, p. 109.

6. See Frank Barlow, *The Feudal Kingdom of England*, 1042-1216 (Abingdon: Routledge, 2014), pp. 220-222.

7. Quoted in Thomas Green, *Arthuriana: Early Arthurian Tradition and the Origins of the Legend*, p. 80.

8. *Beunans Meriasek: The Life of St Meriasek, Bishop and Confessor. A Cornish Drama*, trans. by Whitley Stokes (London: Trubner, 1872), p. 61.

9. John Leland, *Itinerary*, vol. III (1538), p. 184.

10. *The Western Antiquary*, vol. I, p. 35. The term 'scapegrace' here is an archaic term for "a mischievous or wayward person, especially a young

person or child; a rascal" (*Oxford English Dictionary*).

11. On these stories see Albert Hartshorne, *Hanging in Chains* (London: T. Unwin, 1891), pp. 93-96. See also https://thewildpeak.wordpress.com/2013/01/21/hanged-in-chains.

12. Rider Haggard, *A Farmer's Year: Being his Commonplace Book for 1898* (London: Longman's, 1899), p. 355.

13. William Harrison, *The Description of England*, ed. by Georges Edelen (New York: Dover, 1994), p. 188.

14. Henry Chettle, *England's Mourning Garment* (London: Thomas Millington, 1603), p. 20.

15. See Laura Ashe, "Holinshed and Mythical History", in *The Oxford Handbook of Holinshed's Chronicles* (Oxford University Press, 2013), pp. 153-170.

16. I am indebted to Prof. Ronald Hutton for this information.

17. These seem to have been the established sites for executions in Cornwall in the 1670s. I am grateful for this information to Dr Jo Esra.

18. Sarah Tarlow, "The Technology of the Gibbet", *International Journal of Historical Archaeology*, 18:4 (2014), pp. 668–69.

19. Sarah Tarlow, "The Technology of the Gibbet", *International Journal of Historical Archaeology*, 18:4 (2014), pp. 668–69.

20. On this see Owen Davies, *The Haunted: A Social History of Ghosts*, (Basingstoke: Palgrave Macmillan, 2007), p. 53.

21. Sarah Tarlow whose research on gibbeting will inform her forthcoming publication, *Hanging in Chains: Gibbeting and the Murder Act* (Basingstoke: Palgrave, forthcoming)

22. A.E. Housman, *A Shropshire Lad* (London: Kegan Paul, 1896), p. 7.

23. "The Western Antiquary", *The Weekly Mercury*, 30th April 1881.

24. The *Illustrated Police News*, September 20 1884, p. 3.

25. The *Western Times*, 15 June 1904, p. 6.

26. "The Inquest on Miss Jessie", The *Times*, 21 June, 1904, p. 10. The *Cornishman*, 16 June, 1904.

27. The *Penny Illustrated Paper*, 25 June 1904, p. 404.

28. *West Briton and Cornwall Advertiser*, 16 June 1904.

29. "The Cornwall Tragedy", *Western Argus*, 9 August 1904, p. 41.

30. *Cornish Magazine*, September 1961, vol. 4:5, pp. 149-151.

31. Ivan Rabey, p. 94.

32. Ivan Rabey, "The Legends of a Famous Hill Fortress", *West Briton and Royal Cornwall Gazette*, 10 April 1986, p. 12.

33. "Castle an Dinas Iron Age Hillfort, St Columb", in *Cornwall Heritage Trust Newsletter*, 49 (Winter 2012-13), p. 7.

34. Curtis, letter to the *Western Morning News*, 6 May 2015, www.westernmorningnews.co.uk

MALLEUS SPECULIS
Mark Pesce (p. 143)

Title image:

Edited version of "Cloud Gate Touch", a photo by Tony Webster. Creative Commons licence (Attribution 2.0 Generic).

BECOMING ELF – BECOMING WITCH

Bryndís Björgvinsdóttir (p. 165)

Title image:

Photo of 'elf-stone' at Jofridarstadir, by Svala Ragnars (svalaragnars.com). ©
Svala Ragnars, used with permission.

Bibliography:

Árbók Hins íslenzka fornleifafélags. 1923. 37. issue. Timarit.is.

Ármann Jakobsson. 2006. "The Extreme Emotional Life of Völundr the
Elf". *Scandinavian Studies* 78: 1-28.

Ármann Jakobsson. 2015. "Flokkunarkerfi hins yfirnáttúrulega". *Mæna
2015*, Listaháskóli Íslands: 85-90.

Ármann Jakobsson. 2003. *Tolkien og hringurinn*, Reykjavík: Forlagið.

Árni Óla. 1968. *Álög og bannhelgi*, Reykjavík: Setberg.

Ásgeir Guðmundsson. 1983-4. *Saga Hafnarfjarðar 1908-1983.*
Hafnarfjörður: Skuggsjá.

Íslenzkar þjóðsögur og ævintýri I. 1961. Jón Árnason collected. Reykjavík:
Bókaúgáfan Þjóðsaga.

Marteinn Sindri Jónsson. 2016. *Öðrun og örðun: Um hugtakið að-verða-dýr
í verki Gilles Deleuze og Félix Guattari, Þúsund flekar: Kapítalismi og
skitsófrenía.* MA-thesis in Philosophy. University of Iceland.

Matthías Viðar Sæmundsson. 1990. "Íslands er þjóð, öll sökkt í blóð:
Tyrkjarán og Spánverjavíg". *Skírnir* 164. year, autumn 1990: 327-362.

Reimleikar, episode 5. 2016. Bryndís Björgvinsdóttir og Rakel
Garðarsdóttir. Reyjavík: RÚV og Vesturport. A TV-show that will be
broadcasted at the National Television Station in December 2016.

Tolkien, J. R. R. 1993-95. *Hringadróttinssaga I (The Lord of the Rings I).* Þorsteinn
Thorarensen þýddi. Reykjavík: Fjölvi. (English version: J. R. R. Tolkien: *The
Fellowship of the Ring, Lord of the Rings I,* Grafton, London, 1991).

"Tónn sleginn fyrir náttúruvernd". 28 May 2015. *mbl.is.* Accessed 25 August 2016, www.mbl.is/frettir/innlent/2015/05/28/tonn_sleginn_fyrir_natturuvernd/

Valdimar Tr. Hafstein. 2003. "Hjólaskóflur og huldufólk: Íslensk sjálfsmynd og álfahefð samtímans". *Þjóðerni í þúsund ár?* Háskólaútgáfan: 197-213.

Valdimar Tr. Hafsein. 2006. "Menningararfur: Sagan í neytendaumbúðum". *Frá endurskoðun til upplausnar: Tvær prófritgerðir, einn formáli, þrjú viðtöl, sjö fræðigreinar, fimm ljósmyndir, einn eftirmáli og nokkrar minningargreinar af vettvangi hugvísinda.* Miðstöð einsögurannsókna og ReykjavíkurAkademían: 313-328.

"Vöktuðu Gálgahraun í nótt". 24. September 2013. *mbl.is.* Accessed 25. August 2016, www.mbl.is/frettir/innlent/2013/09/24/voktudu_galgahraun_i_nott/

Films:

Lars von Trier: *Antichrist,* 2009
Robert Eggers: *The Witch: A New-England Folktale,* 2015.

Oral Source:

Svala Ragnarsdóttir, inhabitant of Álftanes, 2014.

Endnotes:

1. Matthías Viðar Sæmundsson: "Íslands er þjóð, öll sökkt í blóð: Tyrkjarán og Spánverjavíg", *Skírnir* 164. ár, autumn 1990, pp. 327-362. p. 329.

2. Ármann Jakobsson: "Flokkunarkerfi hins yfirnáttúrulega", *Mæna 2015,* Listaháskóli Íslands, 2015, pp. 85-90. p. 88.

3. Ibid.

4. Ármann Jakobsson: "The Extreme Emotional Life of Völundr the Elf", *Scandinavian Studies* 78 (2006), pp. 1-28. p. 5.

5. Ásgeir Guðmundsson, *Saga Hafnarfjarðar 1908-1983.* Skuggsjá, Hafnarfjörður, 1983-4, pp. 9-25.

6.   *Árbók Hins íslenzka fornleifafélags*, 37. issue. 1923. p. 31.

7.   Árni Óla, *Álög og bannhelgi*, Setberg, Reykjavík, 1968. p. 240.

8.   Valdimar Tr. Hafstein: "Hjólaskóflur og huldufólk: Íslensk sjálfsmynd og álfahefð samtímans", *Þjóðerni í þúsund ár?* Háskólaútgáfan, 2003, pp. 197-213.

9.   *Íslenzkar þjóðsögur og ævintýri I*, Jón Árnason collected, Bókaúgáfan Þjóðsaga, Reykjavík, 1961. p. 41.

10. Valdimar Tr. Hafstein: " Hjólaskóflur og huldufólk", p. 199.

11. Ármann Jakobsson: *Tolkien og hringurinn*, Forlagið, Reykjavík, 2003, bls. 109-110.

12. *Íslenzkar þjóðsögur og ævintýri I*, p. 4.

13. J. R. R. Tolkien: *The Fellowship of the Ring, Lord of the Rings I*, Grafton, London, 1991, p. 505.

14. Ármann Jakobsson: *Tolkien og hringurinn*, p. 109.

15. Ibid.

16. Ármann Jakobsson: *Tolkien og hringurinn*, p. 110.

17. Ármann Jakobsson: *Tolkien og hringurinn*, p. 108.

18. *Íslenzkar þjóðsögur og ævintýri I*, pp. 5-6.

19. Valdimar Tr. Hafstein: "Hjólaskóflur og huldufólk", p. 210.

20. Valdimar Tr. Hafstein: "Hjólaskóflur og huldufólk". pp. 197-213.

21. Ibid. p. 205.

22. Ibid. p. 200.

23. Ibid. p. 200.

24. Mark 5:9.

25. Valdimar Tr. Hafstein: "Hjólaskóflur og huldufólk". p. 199.

26. "Vöktuðu Gálgahraun í nótt", *mbl.is*, 24 September 2013, accessed 25 August 2016, http://www.mbl.is/frettir/innlent/2013/09/24/voktudu_galgahraun_i_nott/

27. Valdimar Tr. Hafstein: "Hjólaskóflur og huldufólk". p. 200.

28. "Tónn sleginn fyrir náttúruvernd", *mbl.is*, 28. May 2015, Accessed 25 August 2016, http://www.mbl.is/frettir/innlent/2015/05/28/tonn_

sleginn_fyrir_natturuvernd/
29. Genesis, 1:28.
30. Lars von Trier: *Antichrist*, 2009.
31. Robert Eggers: *The Witch: A New-England Folktale*, 2015.
32. *Reimleikar*, Bryndís Björgvinsdóttir og Rakel Garðarsdóttir, RÚV og Vesturport, episode 5.
33. Valdimar Tr. Hafsein, "Menningararfur: Sagan í neytendaumbúðum", *Frá endurskoðun til upplausnar: Tvær prófritgerðir, einn formáli, þrjú viðtöl, sjö fræðigreinar, fimm ljósmyndir, einn efitrmáli og nokkrar minningargreinar af vettvangi hugvísinda*, Reykjavík: Miðstöð einsögurannsókna og Reykjavíkur Akademían, 2006, pp. 313-328. p. 315.
34. Valdimar Tr. Hafstein: "Hjólaskóflur og huldufólk". p. 200.

PALERMO DEATHTRIP
Iain Sinclair (p. 189)

Title image:

Edited version of "Monks' Corridor in Capuchins' Catacombs", a photo by 'Sibeaster'. Public domain image.

CITY OF PALACES, CITY OF GHOSTS
Silvia Moreno-Garcia (p. 221)

Title image:

Photo of *Dream of a Sunday Afternoon in the Alameda Central*, a mural by Diego Rivera, taken by 'Momo'. Creative Commons licence (Attribution 2.0 Generic).

Notes:

1. *Signal to Noise*, published in 2015, went on to be nominated for the British Fantasy, Locus, Sunburst and Aurora Awards. It takes place in Mexico City in the 1980s and revolves around a trio of teenagers who cast magic using records. Like most of my fiction, it steals from my life, in this case drawing upon the hazy memory of a high school classmate of mine who ended haunting me years after we ceased speaking to each other. He lives in Paris now, where he is a designer, and appears in different guises in my stories. There are other stolen bits, including my parents, who were both radio announcers. My mother had a fit when she read my debut novel as well as the story "The Doppelgangers" (which appeared in my first collection, *This Strange Way of Dying*) because she thought I had written about her and depicted her unkindly. All I can say is it is all absolutely real and an absolute lie. The things we remember are seldom accurate, just the most pertinent version we choose to remember.

2. For a short while I worked in the downtown area where she once worked. I was also very young and making a living in a grown-up world. It did not occur to me at the time, but I probably rested my elbows against the same sandwich counters she visited.

STEALING THE LIGHT TO WRITE BY
Damien Patrick Williams (p. 239)

Title image:

Photo of "The Real Estate Book", by Damien Williams. © Damien Williams, used with permission.

Coal Memory
Alan Moore (p. 269)

Title image:

Cropped from *The Destruction of Sodom and Gomorrah*, by John Martin (1852). Public domain image.